Understanding Attitudes About War

Pitt Series in Policy and Institutional Studies

Bert A. Rockman, Editor

Understanding Attitudes About War

Modeling Moral Judgments

GREGORY G. BRUNK

DONALD SECREST

HOWARD TAMASHIRO

University of Pittsburgh Press

Published by the University of Pittsburgh Press, Pittsburgh, Pa., 15260
Copyright © 1996, University of Pittsburgh Press
All rights reserved
Manufactured in the United States of America
Printed on acid-free paper

Library of Congress Cataloging-in-Publication Data
Brunk, Gregory G.
    Understanding attitudes about war : modeling moral judgments /
Gregory G. Brunk, Donald Secrest, Howard Tamashiro.
        p.   cm. — (Pitt series in policy and institutional studies)
    Includes bibliographical references and index.
    ISBN 0-8229-3926-6 (cloth : alk. paper). — ISBN 0-8229-5585-7
(pbk. : alk. paper)
    1. United States — Foreign relations — 1989–   — Moral and ethical
aspects.   2. War — Moral and ethical aspects.   3. Politicians — United
States — Attitudes.   4. Soldiers — United States — Attitudes.
5. Journalists — United States — Attitudes.   6. Catholic Church —
United States. — Clergy — Attitudes.   I. Secrest, Donald.
II. Tamashiro, Howard.   III. Title.   IV. Series.
E881.B78   1996
172'42'0973 — dc20   95-53043
                                                                       CIP

A CIP catalog record for this book is available from the British Library.
Eurospan, London

In memory of my parents, who taught me that matters of right and wrong cannot be decided by elections.
— *Gregory G. Brunk*

For Camilla, Glenn, Anne-Marie, and Matthew.
— *Don Secrest*

For Yeiichi and Betty Tamashiro, and Aiko and Jean Miyahira.
— *Howard Tamashiro*

CONTENTS

FIGURES AND TABLES

PREFACE

In the short time since the end of the cold war, the American debate over the use of military force has changed in a dramatic fashion. On the one hand, numerous cold war hawks have proclaimed themselves opposed to the use of U.S. troops in Kuwait, Somalia, Haiti, Bosnia, and elsewhere. A few of them even have adopted an isolationist "fortress America" view. On the other hand, President Bill Clinton and some of his fellow doves from the 1960s initially supported military intervention in overseas ethnic disputes. Such humanitarian intervention is advocated as well by a number of religious leaders who were vocal opponents of American military force policy during the cold war when they advocated a position not far from unilateral nuclear disarmament.

Such extreme policy shifts would seem to defy any simple explanation, and certainly no standard model of attitude formation can be drawn from the public opinion literature and applied successfully to the recent debates. Indeed, behavioral social science has been quite myopic regarding the moral bases of public policy attitudes. There is surprisingly little empirically based theorizing on the normative influences that mold people's attitudes, and there is even less quantitative evidence available for testing theories about moral reasoning in public policy matters.

In marked contrast to this scholarly neglect, many policy practitioners have included moral considerations in their deliberations. Moreover, their discussions have not been polarized between the amoral and the moral but usually have involved choices among various moral positions. A striking illustration of this pattern was the debate over the use of force during the 1990–1991 Persian Gulf crisis. Shortly after launching the air war, George Bush devoted an entire speech to describing traditional just war principles and claiming that the United States was adhering to them. Likewise, many members of Congress drew upon the principles of just war theory in their arguments. In recent memory, moral concerns also were important in the policy debates over Vietnam, nuclear deterrence, and the use of American troops in Bosnia.

Many powerful reasons account for the failure of social science to satisfactorily investigate policy makers' moral concerns. The dominance of the realist tradition in international relations, the power and appeal of rationality and self-interest as explanations among social theorists, and the desire to construct a value-free political science all made the study of applied ethics seem irrelevant. However, interest in the moral features of foreign policy has increased in recent years, but this new literature focuses mostly on critiques of the realist paradigm or specific policy issues, such as the morality of nuclear deterrence, rather than on the attitudinal sources of policy positions. Regrettably, the study of the ethical aspects of decision making has remained on the periphery of research in empirical social science.

Theoretical efforts to model these important policy attitudes also have been impeded by the large number of contending views about the proper use of force that exist in moral philosophy, the highly complex and contingent nature of applied ethics, and the difficulty of gaining access to appropriate elite opinion data. A final detrimental influence has spilled over from economics, where there is widespread confusion regarding the separate simplifying assumptions of rationality and self-interest. These are not the same, and rational people may pursue goals that depart from their narrowly defined short-run self-interest. Until recently, any serious investigation of morality was anathema to most formal modelers, who embraced the longstanding tendency in economics to equate rationality with individual self-interest.

OVERVIEW

This study seeks to bridge the gap between the normative and empirical enterprises of social science by exploring the attitudes of U.S. decision makers and opinion leaders toward war. Based on our empirical evidence, we offer a theoretical framework that suggests the ways people reach their positions on such public policy issues. In the broadest sense, our study is a mapping of contemporary thinking about international conflict and a description of some important factors that influence attitudes.

Our work rests firmly on statistical procedures, which allow a more reliable basis for generalization than do the case studies and narratives that have predominated in past research. However, this book is not intended to be a definitive mapping of every intricacy found in contemporary American thinking about foreign affairs. Instead, we hope that our efforts will motivate others to use empirical methods to further investigate the moral aspects of public policy attitudes and government decision making.

Chapter 1 provides an overview of the ongoing debate regarding the proper role of morality in social science theorizing. Here we also describe some of the forces that have worked to devalue morally based explanations of public policy decision making in past research efforts. Chapter 2 summarizes the various nonethical and ethical perspectives on war in the traditional literature on religion, philosophy, and politics. The treatment of these outlooks will be useful in our later modeling of attitudes. Chapter 3 sets the stage for the analysis to come. Here we introduce such basic concepts as moral sensibilities, which will be used to organize the attitudinal data we have collected. Chapters 4 and 5 introduce the research design and present a general, descriptive profile of our initial results. We also describe some salient characteristics of the elites and opinion leaders who participated in our research. They include over two thousand diplomats, military officers, journalists, members of Congress, and members of the Catholic clergy and hierarchy serving in the United States.

Chapters 6 and 7 offer a deeper statistical and conceptual analysis of the attitudinal data, which suggests that three basic concerns underlie most real-world beliefs about the proper use of military force. These are risk sensitivity, views about the legitimacy of the use of military force, and acceptance of moral constraints governing war entry and war conduct. Using these three concerns as fundamental organizing principles, we can reconfigure the traditional schools of thought toward warfare and can identify and characterize more accurately real-world belief systems. Chapter 8 briefly investigates some implications of these belief systems with respect to the longstanding debate over the morality of nuclear deterrence.

Chapter 9 offers a general model of attitude formation that accounts for the patterns uncovered in our empirical enquiry. The purpose here is theory building. Our model suggests that people in positions of authority recognize the importance of moral conduct in war but have misgivings about the risks connected with accepting moral constraints on military action. The appeal of our model rests in its simplicity. Using only two criteria, we are able to explain why people adopt most of the traditional normative positions on the use of military force, the circumstances under which people will change their opinions on the appropriateness of warfare, and why attitudes toward the use of force only appear to have changed since the end of the cold war.

The same set of decision-making criteria can explain attitudes during both the cold war and the post–cold war period equally well. Our model explains the puzzling transformation of some cold war hawks into doves and vice versa. The model further identifies the types of people who are the most likely to switch policy positions and the circumstances that will cause them to switch. Elaborating on this theme, we suggest, as well, that a parallel model might be useful in explaining many domestic policy attitudes.

Chapter 10 examines the relative importance of the fundamental moral sensibilities that shape beliefs about conflict. Finally, chapter 11 relates our findings to other recent results in the social and psychological literatures; here we also examine some conjectures hinted at by our findings and interesting enough to be made explicit. We hope that this speculative discussion will serve as a stimulus for new research agendas.

ACKNOWLEDGEMENTS

The authors owe debts to many people. In particular, we would like to thank the American elites who participated in our study. Many of them not only responded to our standardized inquiries but also took the time to write or talk with us about the issues we raised concerning public policy. Our efforts would not have been nearly as fruitful without their real-world insights into the dilemmas faced by practitioners and opinion leaders. Camilla and Glenn Secrest helped with phases of mailing the survey, while Sheilah Watson, Lani Malysa, and Laura Wilson helped with data entry. Our friends and colleagues offered support and suggestions as we labored on the project. In this regard, we would like to thank Kristi Andersen, Edwin Bock, Michael Cartwright, Irwin Gertzog, Ralph Hummel, Doug Kinnard, C. Ken Meyer, Steve Sloan, Timothy Tatum, Stuart Thorson, and Malham Wakin. Finally, our thanks to Kathy McLaughlin and Jane Flanders of the University of Pittsburgh Press for their contributions to this volume.

Understanding Attitudes About War

ONE

Ethical Values and Public Policy

For as long as men and women have talked about war,
they have talked about it in terms of right and wrong.
— Michael Walzer

When one considers the importance that always has been attached to the ethical aspects of military conflict, it is surprising how little empirical research has focused on the rules of war and the moral justifications for war. A major purpose of our work is to examine the attitudes of American elites on such matters. It may be possible to discover a coherent underlying structure to their beliefs by using empirical methods. We have two further goals. We would like to help bring the discussion of normative decision making back into the mainstream of social science research. We also hope that our work will provide a blueprint for how to use statistical methods to study the normative belief systems associated with public policy. In pursuit of these goals, we will show how behavioral techniques can be used to model people's reasoning paths on normative problems involving issues usually described as matters of right and wrong.

As a problem in model building, attitudes about the use of military force are particularly interesting. The issues of modern warfare are complex, but not so complex as to render an empirically based theory of conflict impossible. Nevertheless, while thousands of volumes have been written about foreign policy and military strategy, these works shed little light on the decision paths elites use when, and if, they incorporate moral values into national policies. In fact, reason of state theory, which is one of the most important schools of thought in international relations, contends that morality should play no role in these decisions at all. Most economists also assume that normative matters can be ignored as peripheral influences when one explains public policy. Accordingly, it would also be valuable if we could demonstrate the truth of such contentions by showing that morality is inconsequential in structuring the foreign policy attitudes of contemporary American leaders.

THE NEGLECT OF ETHICS

The empirical lapse in studying the ethics of conflict is acute. There are at least five important reasons for the general failure of quantitative social scientists to gather evidence about the role played by morality in attitude formation and real-world decision making.

Realpolitik

First, a realpolitik perspective dominates the contemporary study of international relations. Since the seminal advocates of this viewpoint all denigrated morality as they interpreted it, this led to a general neglect of explicit normative reasoning in foreign policy decision making by their successors. Instead, moral reasoning has been viewed principally as a Machiavellian way for leaders to justify their actions to a politically naive public with a short attention span.

In this paradigm, morality is an opiate for the masses, an influence to which a nation's political elite prudentially ought not to succumb. Furthermore, moral reasoning is viewed as a process that few sophisticated people actually use, and the elites who profess to do so have been offered as textbook examples of what should not be done by government officials. All correctly formulated actions are supposed to be taken only for reasons of state. The real sources of foreign policy in the modern world, according to this view, have nothing to do with moral principles, only with power politics. Consequently, morality is a scholarly topic fruitless for quantitative social scientists to pursue. Worse still, it is actually a normatively bad pursuit because if behavioralists were seriously to study morality their actions might mislead government officials into assigning morality a greater importance than it deserves, thus causing them to repeat the naive errors of the past.

Marginalization of Ethics in Building a Value-Free Science

Even those contemporary writers who support inclusion of a moral component in statecraft often question whether ethical principles have an effect on real-world decision making (see Yoder 1984; Kreml and Kegley

1990). Leftist scholars see the publicized ideals of American society as insincere utterances designed to justify or disguise economic exploitation. They dismiss all the professed ethical positions of capitalists as irrelevant to the practice of public policy. From the opposite ideological perspective, most social choice scholars see everything in terms of individual self-interest and refuse to admit the possibility of the altruistic motives that are necessary before many types of morality can flourish. Finally, in international relations, proponents of realpolitik have written numerous books ridiculing moral principles and those who seek to apply them in foreign policy.

The net impact of these influences has been to structure scholarly research agendas so that anything involving ethical issues has been perceived by behavioralists as the bailiwick of traditional normative scholars and of little practical consequence. While nothing prevents behavioralists from discussing the potential influence of normative matters on public policy, relatively few have done so. The sources of this reticence are found in the intellectual history of political studies. A major goal of the behavioral revolution was to establish a value-free social science, while the intellectual tradition of social choice borrows heavily from economics and its emphasis on formal models and axioms based on self-interest. These intellectual developments tended to move the focus of political research from its more traditional collective goals to individual behavior.

Until recently, most behavioralists were reluctant to accept any alternative approaches as valid, since doing so might reopen the intellectual battles of the 1950s and 1960s. On those rare occasions when moral issues were discussed by behavioral political scientists, they were addressed in a traditional, normative, or prescriptive manner, and such discussions bypassed the mainstream research paradigm of the discipline. As a consequence of the inability of traditionalists to make the study of ethical values relevant to the majority of social scientists, and the behavioralists' deprecation of moral explanations of real-world politics, the study of ethical values in decision making has languished among quantitative scholars.

Ethical Complexity

Anyone who attempts to conduct empirical research into the ethical bases of policy making or attitude formation faces the daunting task of organizing and operationalizing the large number of contending views that exist in moral philosophy. This morass of philosophical complexity deterred many behavioralists, often untrained in moral reasoning, from attempting to formulate morally based explanations of behavior. The landscape that faced national decision makers seemed a hopelessly tangled thicket of competing ad hoc viewpoints with little underlying structure.

The apparent complexity of philosophical issues was thought to increase significantly as decision makers examined real-world ethics rather than ivory-tower issues. When one attempts to move past theoretical moral philosophy into the realm of applied ethics, each new problem at first seems contingent upon unique situational factors. These situational factors, in turn, are often assumed to overwhelm any systematic components to reasoning about ethical contingencies in public policy. Reflecting this viewpoint, a senior diplomat in our study commented on the situational messiness of politics in noting, "We make foreign policy decisions on the basis of specific current circumstances, not general principles. Furthermore, we do so tentatively since information may be inaccurate or obsolete, development occurs, and the foreign policy actors change."

If situational complexity and uncertainty indeed overwhelm people's general moral principles, the prospect of successfully integrating ethical values into models of attitude formation and decision making is highly unpromising. Hence, it is not surprising that many scholars choose to denigrate or ignore the role of practical morality in foreign policy.

Self-Interest

Another reason for the contemporary neglect of ethical values is found in the writings of those who borrow their methodology from economics and use deductive models in attempting to understand political behavior. In this literature one finds almost universal confusion regarding the separate, simplifying assumptions of rationality and individual self-interest. Instead of being seen as two separate axioms of convenience that could be discarded if they proved inadequate for theory building, they are viewed in tandem as a single, inflexible law of behavior.

Mathematical modeling came into political science through the back door from economics, and social choice theorists are as hesitant as behavioralists to discuss the merits of their assumptions, since their approach has not yet been fully integrated into political science. Many contemporary political scientists still are not receptive to social choice analyses. Although a few deductive theorists allowed for the incorporation of factors besides self-interest into models of human behavior, such broadminded scholars were a small minority viewed as mavericks until recently. Traditional ethical theories challenge the fundamental precepts of standard social choice theory and behavioralism by arguing that individuals do not always directly maximize their own utility and sometimes try to maximize the utility of a larger reference group.

By the 1970s, under the influence of such scholars as George Stigler most students of administration had reached the similar conclusion that bureaucrats usually maximize their own goals rather than the general good. As organizations grow larger, it becomes increasingly difficult for anyone to have a measurable impact on overall performance, and while the general good cannot be increased by one's own actions, it usually cannot be reduced either. Bureaucrats recognize this, and it follows from the self-interest assumption of economics that it makes no rational sense to strive for your organization's goals apart from your own. Eventually, it became almost a normative prescription that bureaucrats should be concerned principally with their own self-interest and not the general good. A steady stream of research implied that bureaucrats should feel free to use the government as a means to achieve their own personal ends rather than striving for the betterment of society. Having discredited the public-minded goals of the past, by the 1980s Americans had become the "me generation," and a realpolitik viewpoint had achieved dominance in public administration as well as international relations theory.

A separate intellectual tradition reinforced the self-interest paradigm of "economic man." Early sociological studies labeled those who disagreed with a group's attitudes as deviants and mavericks. By the 1970s, such observations had become another justification for maximizing self-interest. The sociological literature on norms gave administrators a justification for silencing those who did not act in a way consistent with a superior's personal plans for advancement. In the military, this was reflected in the management of the Vietnam War, where commanders' self-interest often dominated. Field officers were shifted so rapidly from assignment to assignment that they developed little loyalty toward their troops, and their troops felt even less loyalty toward them. Administratively, the war became a means by which officers got their tickets punched for promotion. Indeed, many battlefield generals had little idea of the war's policy goals (Kinnard 1985). Eventually, it seemed that the war's managers no longer had any specific goals other than avoiding defeat and damage to their careers.

Among Americans, ethical decision making in government and morality defined as taking actions for the public good were out of fashion in the 1970s and 1980s. Indeed, what flourished was an organizational spirit that legitimized the goal of individual self-promotion in a system in which managerial appointments were used as a means to achieve one's own career ends. The Vietnam debacle, the Challenger disaster, and the savings-and-loan crisis were some of the prominent consequences of this egoistic trend. Strong and repeated warnings were issued about these problems, but in each case the suppression of information (such as the Pentagon papers case) and distortion of fact (as in space shuttle efficiency estimates) seemed to prevail until disaster was unavoidable.

While some continued to hold professional norms that decried such behavior, there was no easy way to counteract this trend toward amorality. Why? In part, perhaps, because there was no intellectual tradition in contemporary social science that provided an empirically justifiable means for resistance. The only readily available rejoinder for dissenters was to appeal to traditional religious prescriptions, but in a secular society increasingly dominated by large, compartmentalized, and competing bureaucracies, religious appeals had little effect. Some professionals, frustrated by corrupting pressures and practices but fearful of retribution, embraced individual forms of resistance, such as private, voluntary withdrawal or a more activist whistle-blowing path. The persistence and salience of such ethically compelled behavior has attracted increasing scholarly interest (see, e.g., Elliston et al. 1985; Jos, Tonkins, and Hays 1989).

Despite strong forces working against morality in contemporary public policy, certain moral and ethical values have apparently remained important for some decision makers. Accordingly, following a period of almost total dominance by the self-interest paradigm, many researchers are starting to conclude that ethical values cannot be dismissed as a fad or written off as only self-serving justifications used by the governing elite to buttress policy positions.

Lack of Systematic Data

There also is the matter of access to appropriate data about American foreign policy attitudes. During the cold war it was difficult to obtain physical access to elite actors, but there is an even more fundamental problem when investigating sensitive ethical issues. Questions about deeply held moral beliefs can produce intense hostility toward the investigator. Since moral values often are taught to children as the rules of God, many people see their views as the only correct moral views. Such people are highly ethnocentric in their viewpoint and are hostile to all opposing moral positions.

It appears that many people are incapable of comprehending ethical beliefs that differ much from their own. While such people, if they are well educated, may be able to describe the theoretical outlines of alternative normative belief systems, they lack an empathic understanding of their contours. As a result, they are unable to predict the actions of an opponent who follows a radically different set of beliefs unless it is assumed those beliefs are equivalent to the opponent's self-interest. In international relations, this myopia manifests itself in the commonly held opinion that all countries straightforwardly strive to maximize self-interest. Consequently, failure to predict the policies of an adversary is assumed to have only two possible sources. Either we misperceived the adversary's national interest as they viewed it, or they were unsuccessful in implementing a reasonable maximization strategy.

The tendency of some people to see their own beliefs as the only possible moral outlook was recognized in a broader context by a military officer who participated in our study. As he put it, "War is a military reaction to political stupidity. Unfortunately, so long as there are people of different cultures and the overwhelming attitude is that our system, theirs or ours, is best, then a likelihood of armed conflict is high. Understanding and accepting differences in the real world is the answer, but we have yet to reach that plateau."

Early in the study of public opinion, pollsters noted that respondents resisted questions dealing with fundamental moral issues. Only rarely do major polling organizations include any items that might enable researchers to construct sophisticated, ethically based theories of attitude formation.[1] Such inquiries are often too controversial for commercial firms, since they may reduce response rates, displeasing clients and threatening profits. Because of the aversion to dealing explicitly with such controversial questions as the morality of military force, particularly during the cold war, public opinion scholars have been unable to use their standard database of national poll items to construct detailed moral theories in this area. Instead, most public opinion researchers who deal with these issues are forced to use survey items that are far from ideally suited to the task.[2] It is not surprising that inquiry into the moral aspects of international relations has languished in the behavioral literature without this usual source of data.

VIEWS OF FOREIGN POLICY ATTITUDES

Many American decision makers have long held the public's opinion on foreign policy matters in low regard. In the *Federalist Papers* Alexander Hamilton, James Madison, and John Jay referred to public opinion using such derogatory terms as "unreasoned passions," "violent movements," "fluctuations," and "temporary errors or delusions." The continual debate throughout American history over the role that citizens should play in the formation of foreign policy nicely points out the distinction made by most contemporary public opinion scholars between the structure of elite and mass attitudes. Elite actors are viewed as relatively sophisticated and knowledgeable, while the public is viewed as having little specialized knowledge, little sophistication, and, consequently, little potential for holding coherent foreign policy positions.

Among contemporary commentators, Gabriel Almond's mood theory represents an early example of this common view: "Foreign policy attitudes among most Americans lack intellectual structure and factual content. Such superficial psychic states are bound to be unstable since they are not anchored in a set of explicit values and means calculations or traditional compulsions" (1950, 69). This interpretation holds that citizens are generally indifferent to international politics and become interested in foreign affairs only when a crisis arises. As soon as the threat has passed, popular opinion returns to being just moods about international affairs.

Since most early researchers concluded that the public lacked a coherent structure for integrating their thoughts about foreign affairs, the collective public mood was believed to be capable of violent swings. Because of the unstable nature of the electorate's attitudes, many realist scholars and diplomatic practitioners decided that U.S. policy makers should be shielded from the destabilizing influence of public opinion. In particular, the evil influences of public morality should be avoided.

Such an elitist interpretation of the potentially damaging effect of public opinion on foreign policy can be contrasted with the government's close attention to public reaction concerning the state of the domestic economy. Politicians recognize that voters reward those who successfully manage the economy, while those who preside over poor times are punished at the polls. Unlike this easy way of discerning patterns of political popularity based on individual preferences, most of the international relations literature argues that public attitudes on foreign policy matters are unstable, if not simply incoherent. So while U.S. leaders must pay close attention to the public's perception of economic conditions, politicians are offered little guidance in formulating foreign policy in accord with citizens' preferences, as most Americans do not have strong preferences on such matters.

At the heart of this common assessment of the irrelevance of public opinion in international affairs is the belief that most people's attitudes toward foreign policy have little theoretical content. Lacking strong anchoring principles, individual attitudes are apt to oscillate rapidly. Contemporary world leaders thus have great latitude in formulating most foreign policies, since coherent constraints from grass-roots sources rarely exist.

The fundamental confusion about what is correct national policy is reflected in contemporary attitudes about many of the nation's wars. If no convincing framework exists for analyzing international relations beliefs, then we are not even sure how to properly interpret U.S. history.[3] A review of common arguments about America's conflicts reveals a wide diversity of evaluation criteria. Was Manifest Destiny reasonable? Did this historical law justify the annexation of Mexican, Spanish, and Native American lands? Do such historical laws have any status as fundamental principles? People's opinions on the morality of slavery and the value of preserving the Union strongly influenced how they viewed the Civil War. Should the United States have maintained an isolationist policy and not intervened in Europe during World War I? What about interventions in the Caribbean and Central America? What criteria determine whether U.S. actions in that region were wise or moral? If certain military actions profit us, is it right to destroy others and promote our self-interest at their expense?

In particular, what are the lessons of Vietnam? During that conflict everyone claimed that either God, morality, or prudence was on their side in the debate, and during his presidency Ronald Reagan went out of his way repeatedly to praise the Vietnam War as a noble cause. Was he right? Did the Vietnam War shatter an American consensus over foreign policy? If so, what were the parameters of that consensus? Our lack of generally accepted, systematic criteria for judging the morality, or even the utility, of that war is illustrated by a promotion for *American Heritage* magazine that promised to inform Americans about what we should tell our children about Vietnam. But over fifty quite different answers were given.

Despite the failure of scholars to find a comprehensive and coherent structure to attitudes about international relations, there is growing evidence that such a structure exists, although its nature is still debated. Some research suggests that people have broad postures regarding how governments should behave in foreign affairs. These postures are abstract beliefs that constrain attitudes in a hierarchical fashion based on core values. What is methodologically fascinating about this approach is that one's cognitive structure cannot be discerned if a researcher examines attitudes held at the same level of generalization—which is, of course, how pollsters usually examine attitudes. Only if attitudes are examined at different levels of generalization does an underlying structure become apparent. According to the revisionists who support this thesis, it is precisely the unsophisticated character of common people, which older writers argued precluded coherent beliefs, that might allow mass coherence in foreign policy attitudes.

Consider more closely the problem of being well uninformed. An earlier generation of scholars held that a lack of information on public affairs made it impossible for people to develop coherent policy attitudes. The revisionists make the opposite claim, arguing that for most people the amount of information they possess is irrelevant to the coherence of their attitudes. If this view is correct, then the unsophisticated should have about as structured a set of attitudes as many policy specialists. The revisionists cite Ronald Reagan as an excellent example of someone who lacked a detailed knowledge of almost everything but had an overarching theory of politics that allowed him to integrate diverse events into a coherent decision-making framework. Using such a hierarchical model to describe Reagan's thought processes, one can move from the few general principles he deeply held to their specific applications.

For those who use such a hierarchical cognitive approach, the lack of a large amount of specific information is not an impediment to the application of general principles. Rather, it may promote it. But if one acquires a large quantity of empirical evidence in an attempt to generate an inductive theory, there may be little apparent coherence to the structure of the observed policy attitudes. Of course, this is exactly the approach used by most behavioralists in their research, and their strategy may explain why they have failed to discover morally based policy attitudes.

If, as we suspect, the revisionist thesis is correct, the question becomes: What are the fundamental motivating principles that guide the formation of foreign policy attitudes? An obvious set of candidate principles for issues involving the use of military force are the normative prescriptions found in traditional writings, but this is a set that has never been examined in great detail by empirical social scientists. The imposing problem facing anyone who investigates the normative literature on conflict is the long litany of criteria for judging the rightness and wrongness of war. This diverse collection of moral and amoral standards can be combined in many ways to produce varied rules for deciding issues of right and wrong. In practical application, these standards can create radically different policies, depending on what values are most prized by decision makers. Application of these varied criteria in different situations seems to provide a fertile field for discussing the fine distinctions and obscure rules that intrigue so many normative philosophers.

SOCIAL CHOICE

Over the past three decades, social choice modeling has become increasingly important to our understanding of political behavior, but it has had major detrimental effects. In sociological studies of the law, the perspective has led to the view that individuals react to their environment almost totally in a self-interested way, and the principal means whereby governments can alter behavior is to change the structure of short-run rewards and punishments. The importance of fundamental moral beliefs in shaping attitudes and behavior has been denigrated by this perspective, which sees everything in purely cost-benefit terms.

Despite the obvious successes of the social choice approach, these models also have been unsuccessful in explaining important types of political activities. The successes and failures of social choice are well illustrated by the literature on voting behavior. While the formulations of Anthony Downs in *An Economic Theory of Democracy* (1957) and later theorists are useful in explaining the direction of people's voting decisions, they have had much less success in explaining why people choose to vote in the first place. The reason for this lies in a key assumption of such models. As Downs puts it, "General theories of social action always rely heavily on the self-interest axiom" (29).

While most later social choice modelers fully embraced the self-interest axiom, many early economists clearly saw it as an assumption of convenience that did not apply equally in all situations (Sen 1978). Indeed, Jeremy Bentham had to invent the word *maximization* to categorize such conscious calculations, which changed the way scholars and eventually policy elites looked at human behavior. Concentrating on maximization shifted attention away from such human characteristics as devotion, benevolence, and maliciousness (Mansbridge 1990, x–xi).

Gordon Tullock was a leading proselytizer of the self-interest viewpoint, and by the late 1970s proclaimed that the public interest view had become obsolete in political science.[4] While the study of altruism may have been in hibernation, it certainly was not dead, since social choice theory faced important internal contradictions. In particular, there was the problem of why people voted, which almost always is irrational from a self-interest perspective. Morris Fiorina later referred to the problem as the "paradox that ate rational choice theory" (1986, 10). Early economic modelers of political behavior assumed that voters act solely to maximize their utility, which generally allows prediction of the direction of a vote.

But these modelers also assumed that one's utility calculus can be represented by a comparison of short-run benefits minus costs. Although the costs of voting usually are moderate, so too are the benefits, and the chance that one's vote will be crucial to an outcome is almost always astronomically small. Therefore, ceteris paribus, voting ususally is irrational, since its expected utility is negative. However, this is a contradictory conclusion because we began by assuming that voters are rational, self-interested actors.

Further examination of the social choice literature on voting behavior shows that the normative concepts of right and wrong actions are often excluded from consideration.[5] If anything, this antipathy toward normative concepts is even greater among behavioralist political scientists. Michael Walzer notes this truism when he observes that behavioralists consider all moral terms to have "no proper descriptive use and no objective meaning"; consequently, "moral discourse was excluded" from the social sciences (1977, xi–xii). Another summary of the situation is even more succinct: "Among political scientists it is almost a point of pride for philosophers and students of behavior to ignore one another" (Wilson and Schochet 1980, xvii).

What should be noted at this juncture is that if the models used by the classical social choice theorists present distorted views of reality, then their predictions are misleading as well. Leaving out the moral component of human behavior may mean that predictions of important classes of events will be wrong. Until now, an important reason that some of the incorrect predictions of hard-line social choice models and their close cousin in international relations, reason of state theory, have been dismissed as unimportant anomalies is that moral matters do not fit nicely into an egoistic, cost-benefit paradigm.

Such modeling limitations, however, only characterize hard-line social choice approaches that adhere strictly to the self-interest paradigm. A number of scholars have become interested in integrating normative values into deductive and empirical models of behavior. In pursuing this goal, they have loosened the restraints on the concept of individual rationality by untying the knot that joined it so tightly with short-run self-interest. Robert Axelrod's *Evolution of Cooperation* (1984) is an excellent example. Other writers who take this same path argue that particular normative values are adopted by people because they are utility-maximizing in the long run. Accordingly, a normative rule is propagated when those who adopt it are viewed as successful and the rule is copied by others.

A less commonly cited explanation among political scientists for the development of moral norms is taken from biological and cultural studies. It looks at moral values as the basic inputs that structure attitude formation and decision making. According to this view, people's moral sensibilities are largely developed before adulthood. Since there is a consistency requirement to cognitive thought, these sensibilities both direct people toward particular types of careers and broadly structure the types of public policies they favor.

In closing this overview of decision-making models and explanations of attitude formation, we should emphasize that deductive approaches are not inherently amoral, nor do they have any inherent ideological bias. In the past, social choice was most often associated with a conservative political viewpoint. This is because such models generally were based on the assumption of short-run, individual self-interest, which steers people toward particular ideological conclusions. But the nature of any model fundamentally depends on its assumptions, and if the axioms of social choice models are modified, so too is their ideological tilt.

Most contemporary economists argue that ethics are comparatively unimportant in explaining human behavior and consequently moral constraints on human actions can be ignored without a great loss of predictive generality. As we will see, that is not the case in examining foreign policy attitudes. Moral constraints on military actions are quite important in shaping the attitudes of some decision makers and policy elites, and moral beliefs are often fundamental to explanations of attitude change. Nevertheless, such moral factors can be incorporated into social choice type explanations by modifying their basic assumptions, including a redefinition of whose goals are maximized from the strict self-interest of the individual to a more broadly defined reference group.

ETHICAL PRINCIPLES AS MORAL HEURISTICS

Scholars often respond to the apparent paradoxes generated by social choice models in two basic ways. First, numerous patches have been proposed to explain why observed, but seemingly nonrational behaviors really are self-serving. Second, attacks are launched on the methodology of deductive modeling itself, and many normative political scientists have declared in frustration that such models are of little use to anyone who wants to understand what "really is important" about politics.

Our approach departs from these patterns. We begin with the hypothesis that at least some people are strongly motivated by moral sensibilities that are not totally self-serving. We also assume that moral precepts can be usefully described and studied quantitatively from a heuristic perspective. Indeed, we view the proverbs of war as informal rules of thumb that offer people guidance in complex conflict situations. From this perspective, much of traditional ethics can be interpreted as a quest for a maximizing set of rules that promote long-run goals in a manner consistent with one's basic sensibilities. This heuristic approach is particularly useful as a re-search strategy because people's cognitive limits do not allow a close eval-uation of every situation. Instead, individuals try to develop general rules, called heuristics, to cover broad categories of potential situations. To be moral from the viewpoint of a particular outlook is to follow these rules when one's short-run advantage can be increased by violating them.

Can a heuristic approach account for the complexity frequently en-countered in policy matters? While we cannot give a definitive answer in advance of substantial empirical work, we are encouraged by current research. Heuristics have been used successfully in the development of the hard sciences (Kuhn 1962), as well as in statistical analyses (Brunk 1989). In iterated prisoner's dilemma contexts, heuristic methods have been used to explore the evolution of cooperation (Axelrod 1984) and the robust-ness of different moral strategies in competition with amoral ones (Van-berg and Congleton 1992). In questions concerning the morality of nu-clear deterrence and war, Joseph Nye concludes that heuristics, or what he calls maxims, are important in focusing people's moral judgments in complex, applied policy situations (1986, 97–100). Heuristics are also useful in analyzing diplomatic statecraft and defense policy (Tamashiro 1984; Tamashiro and Brunk 1985; Kanwisher 1989). All this suggests that a heuristic-based survey offers promise for the study of public policy attitudes.

If we assume that people view ethical rules as moral heuristics, the fun-damental question they focus on becomes: what rules should be adopted to produce good outcomes for my reference group? How people answer this question structures their attitudes toward society, government, public pol-icy, and the international political system. Since the precise future is un-known, people should adopt the rules they believe will maximize the chances of realizing their desired outcomes in the long run.

The first crucial matter that one must decide is whose good one wants to promote. The three possible responses are my own, my group's, or everyone's. Among decision makers in international relations, the first response usually is impossible to implement for anyone but a dictator. In the United States, most people instead ask: do only Americans matter, or do I care about all of humanity? Religion, philosophy, and political ideology all offer different solutions to the problem of choosing the morally correct rule system, but as we will see, this quest is elusive. It certainly has not been answered for many people by adopting the assumption of short-run individual utility maximization (see, e.g., Lau, Brown, and Sears 1978).

Nevertheless, we do know that many actors try to act systematically when making policy decisions because doing so offers many advantages. Actions can be explained in terms of general principles or specific justifications for particular acts. The first course is likely preferred by many people because it follows the heuristic of simplicity. In international politics, consistent adherence to ethical norms signals a nation-state's trustworthiness and reliability, making cooperative arrangements and alliances easier to establish (Keohane 1990). In domestic politics, systematic reasoning about public policy reduces the time politicians need to explain their actions to constituents and eases the task of garnering public approval. Because of the advantages offered by systematic reasoning, simple moral prescriptions, such as "Do unto others as you would have them do unto you," have become incorporated into many decision-making heuristics. In this way, such traditional approaches toward conflict as just war thinking may also have come to affect foreign policy attitudes.

PLAN OF ATTACK

This is a book about morality and public affairs, but it does not advocate any particular approach to decision making. Instead, our research focuses on how people actually form their opinions about international conflict. We want to know why people believe certain things and why they advocate certain actions. To better understand these problems, we have combined traditional, normative studies with metaethics, deductive modeling, and statistical methodologies. To construct the normative component of our study, we went to the religious, philosophical, political, and military writings on warfare to discover what they say about war, and we found that many of their teachings appear in the form of stories and proverbs. From this literature we distilled the essence of the varied approaches toward war.

In complex situations, people find it difficult to manage consistent moral sensibilities, attitudes, and belief systems. It may be for this reason that practical moral guidance is often offered in the form of proverbs, such as the story of the Good Samaritan, or short sayings like the golden rule. These prescriptions serve as moral heuristics that can be called upon when one makes specific decisions. Likewise, the literature about social cognition assumes that people are often misers who attempt to minimize their cognitive effort and argues that the use of such simplifying heuristics increases with the complexity of the environment. Since the international system is a very complex environment, such heuristics may be of particular importance to the policy makers operating there.

Having established the broad parameters of our project, we then turn to statistical techniques to try to answer three basic questions. First, do U.S. attitudes about war reflect any of these traditional concerns? Second, how much of contemporary thinking can be encapsulated by these normative precepts? Third, what is the structure of the cognitive landscape encompassing beliefs about the use of military force?

Armed with our statistically derived information, we develop a cognitive model of international conflict attitudes.[6] The success of the model is evident in its ability to explain both the modal patterns of elite attitudes and many of the paradoxes about public opinion and decision making that puzzle those who operate from any particular viewpoint. Our model not only explains which sorts of beliefs about conflict particular groups are likely to adopt but also the circumstances under which attitudes are likely to change.

Behavioralists often assume that the predominant interest of individuals centers on policy outcomes, but in practice the decision-making rules we document may serve as constraints on both attitudes and behavior, making certain outcomes unattainable. As we will see, as well, only certain actors are primarily concerned about outcomes. Others are principally concerned with decision-making procedures, which reflect commitments to particular ethical rules. An even larger group of people attempt to balance the application of general rules with their search for desired outcomes.

The model we propose also offers insights into how individuals form their attitudes and make decisions about international conflict. It shows how leaders structure their thinking about morality and war. In exploring these matters, we will discuss a number of diverse issues. Do people think about policy outcomes or decision-making rules when judging the reasonableness of a policy? What are the bases of decision making in foreign policy? When is risk assessment important? When do the interests of others dominate our own interests? As time passes, why do some people shift their opinions on the reasonableness of particular wars and other foreign policies?

A recurrent problem in the study of belief systems has been how to specify the conditions governing dramatic changes in attitudes. To refer to changes in foreign policy attitudes simply as shifts in moods is not satisfactory. The model we propose makes predictions about when attitudes will change and why they will change. The same model also suggests what kinds of wars will cause the most domestic discord. Why did Vietnam cause so much dissension, while the Gulf War did not? What is the importance of an in-group concept for decision making? Are people's policy beliefs conditioned more by their official roles in society or by political ideology? What accounts for the adoption of conflict belief systems? Our model offers answers to a number of these puzzles.

TWO

Traditional
Frameworks

The traditional literature on the morality of war is vast and wide ranging. It includes the writings of moral philosophers, theologians, political theorists, international relations scholars, jurists, military strategists, and statesmen. Unfortunately, for over two thousand years their discussions have been conducted in largely independent intellectual streams of thought that still are not well integrated. This historical circumstance produces some major problems for those concerned with the ethical terminology of warfare. Some of the concepts in the traditional literature are broad principles, such as the golden rule, while others are complex formulas. Particular value systems are referred to variously as ideas, theories, concepts, traditions, and doctrines. In this book, we use *framework* as a generic term to refer to any moral principle, perspective, formula, or outlook, while *doctrine* refers to the more specific approaches advocated by identifiable schools of thought. Much later, we will introduce the term *belief system* to designate an empirically identified orientation uncovered in our study.

For purposes of this discussion, ethics can be usefully divided into three types: normative ethics, metaethics, and descriptive ethics. Ethicists in the first category concentrate on the development and content of systems of moral values and principles that should guide thought and behavior. They also may apply their moral principles and values to solving particular problems, such as those posed by war. In contrast, metaethicists analyze the nature of moral reasoning and focus on how normative ethicists and common people define and justify their values and behaviors.

Metaethics thus deals with the development of decision-making rules. The goal of descriptive ethics is to identify people's moral values, which is an activity carried out mostly by social scientists rather than philosophers. In the earlier chapters we approach the problems posed by international conflict from the standpoint of descriptive ethics, and in later chapters move to a metaethical perspective, but because it is not our purpose to advocate any prescriptions for correct conduct, we never adopt the position of normative ethicists.

In the terminology of economics, ethical rules are so highly prized that they cannot be traded for normal goods or services (Levy 1981). Their application can legitimately be suspended only when the prescription of one rule conflicts with the prescription of another. Only recently have analytical and quantitative political scientists started to examine the characteristics and the development of ethical systems from such a perspective, which further aggravates the problem of inconsistent terminology.

Most early Western philosophers gave little attention to studying the moral issues concerning war. By the time of Socrates, philosophers had become more interested in defining the supreme value of a good life, and their principal focus became what was a good life for a particular community. In contrast, many theologians and their followers started with a commitment to the supreme value of a universal right to life. From early medieval times, Judeo-Christian scholars recognized a need to reconcile the supreme value of human life with the problem of whether to allow forceful resistance against violence directed toward innocent individuals or innocent nations.

Whatever the bases used by these nonphilosophers in constructing their moral doctrines on war, it is difficult to classify them using the metaethical schemes of contemporary moral philosophers, who primarily address questions other than those concerning the use of deadly force. Nevertheless, most of these doctrines can be classified according to their moral and nonmoral values and their moral obligations. Theories of moral value identify the intentions individuals and groups should have toward others. Theories of nonmoral value identify legitimate interests. Theories of moral obligation define the nature of right and wrong actions.

ETHICAL CONSTRAINTS

Philosophical theories of moral value require concern for the needs and interests of others. This moral requirement can be contrasted with self-interest, which economists assume is the basic motivation of human behavior and has been incorporated into most past social choice models of politics. Ethicists classify such a motivation as egoism.[1] The egoism of "economic man" is also consistent with the value system of nationalism when the state is viewed as the relevant actor.

Although a few all-inclusive social choice modelers believe that some expression of concern for others is necessary to explain many important human behaviors, they remain a minority. In a similar contrast to their field's dominant paradigm, some normative international relations theorists assert that the distinction between egoism and morality is important for understanding people's attitudes toward conflict, but the truth of this assertion remains unproven largely because we have lacked sufficient empirical evidence to test it adequately. If most decision makers are motivated by an unrestrained egoistic nationalism, and if public opinion is driven by egoistic self-interest, then social choice models should be quite adequate to explain attitude formation and decision making, and moral constraints can be ignored without a loss of predictive generality.

One example of this debate is the controversy among international relations theorists about the practical importance of the just war criteria. Its critics argue that just war theory is too nebulous to provide real-world guidance (see, e.g., Yoder 1984). If this is the case, then just war thought can be ignored by policy makers, for it is irrelevant to how people make their decisions and how nations act in the international system. But we know that by concentrating exclusively on the goal of egoistic self-interest, the social choice approach is unable to explain the sources of some important types of attitudes and behavior, and normative ethicists argue that this is the case in international affairs, as well. In certain situations people do not behave in a purely egoistic manner, and the moral constraints of traditional ethics might even be reformulated in a way to assume major importance in social choice models.[2] This could be done by making only a few changes in fundamental assumptions. Chief among these is a redefinition of whose utility people seek to maximize.

THE JUDEO-CHRISTIAN TRADITION

Judeo-Christian ethics are particularly important for the study of Western policy attitudes, but they have been interpreted to yield a wide variety of different theories of moral value. This illustrates the complexities involved in understanding the moral derivation of prescriptions regarding conflict. One version of Judeo-Christian ethics is the ethic of self-abnegation, which stresses the principle of love and is the source of the doctrine of pacifism. Focusing on love requires that individuals have a total concern for others that overrides even their own physical survival.[3]

Another approach, the ethic of self-fulfillment, advocates the moral principle of justice, and this is the source of the just war doctrine. It allows concern for self-interest, but only as long as there is a concern for the similar needs of others. This ethic does not condemn all self-interest as immoral, only totally selfish conceptions of self-interest. The ethic of self-fulfillment is advocated by some inclusive social choice modelers, who allow for motivations other than egoistic self-interest.[4]

Since decisions concerning deadly force have such potentially dire consequences, moral theorists who have addressed these issues have focused on defining which nonmoral values are sufficiently important to justify taking another's life. The theories of nonmoral value that underlie moral positions stress the sanctity of life, while amoral and immoral positions stress other values, including survival, order, power, and protecting important national interests.

Interrelated with theories of value are theories of moral obligation that define what are right and wrong actions. Such theories embody three basic types of reasoning. In judging the rightness of acts, a deontological approach focuses on the nature of specific actions, which are evaluated without regard to particular circumstances and consequences. Deontological reasoning is associated with the argument that no end can justify certain types of means and with advocacy of rule-based principles such as "Thou shalt not kill" and "Do no murder." Teleological reasoning evaluates actions based on their consequences for the attainment of particular ends — that is, nonmoral values — which can be advocated either for universally or nonuniversally defined others, depending on the interrelated theory of moral value. Teleological reasoning is an end-justifies-the-means approach. Finally, mixed-deontological reasoning stresses deontologically derived principles but holds that the circumstances and consequences of achieving one's valued ends are important for determining these principles.

GENERAL APPROACHES TO CONFLICT

Over a dozen major approaches to international conflict are found in the traditional literature. At the broadest level are the golden rule, moral perfectionist reasoning and moral nonperfectionist reasoning. At a more specific level are the doctrines of fatalism, the moral crusade or holy war, pacifism, just war theory, the supreme emergency doctrine, nuclear paci-

Table 2.1 **Conflict Doctrines, by Metaethical Characteristics**

Theories of Value	Theories of Obligation		
	Deontological: Focus on nature of acts	Teleological: Focus on circumstances and consequences	Mixed-Deontological: Circumstances and consequences are relevant for determining deontological rules
Moral Values			
Love: Total concern for others	Universal pacifism	Moral crusade	
Justice: Concern for others and oneself			Antiwar pacifism Just war Retaliatory ethic Supreme emergency Nuclear pacifism
Egoism: Total concern for oneself or one's group		Moral crusade Legalism Reason of state Supreme emergency	Retaliatory ethic Supreme emergency Nuclear pacifism
Nonmoral Values			
Universal needs for human survival and well-being	Universal pacifism	Moral crusade	Antiwar pacifism Just war Retaliatory ethic Supreme emergency Nuclear pacifism
National interests		Legalism Reason of state	Retaliatory ethic Supreme emergency

fism, the retaliatory ethic, utilitarianism, legalism, and reason of state. These conflict doctrines are categorized in table 2.1 according to their theories of value and obligation.

The Golden Rule

The essence of morality according to the golden rule is "Do unto others as you would have others do unto you." Versions of the golden rule are found in all the world's major religions, and it is a proverb in most languages.[5] The golden rule is such a pervasive prescription that some scholars consider it a principle with universal validity. In fact, the golden rule is a remarkable concept. Although seemingly general and vague, it relates theories of moral and nonmoral value with theories of obligation. It views the essence of morality as a concern for others. This can be contrasted with the pure egoism embraced by the self-interest axiom of social choice.

While the golden rule does not specify the content of a theory of nonmoral value, it does indicate that however one defines such a theory, the same ends must be desired for oneself and others. The requirement of acting toward others in the same way that you want them to act toward you is the golden rule's theory of moral obligation. In Christian ethics, the requirement "Love thy neighbor as thyself" is analogous to the golden rule. A secular version of the golden rule is Immanuel Kant's categorical imperative, which defines justice as treating others as ends in themselves and not just a means to your own ends.

Experimental studies in game theory often find that some people stubbornly refuse to adopt purely egoistic strategies. Researchers from the self-interest paradigm have looked at such evidence and dismissed the actions of these apparent altruists as irrational, sometimes reporting that their subjects who act in a golden rule fashion must not be intelligent enough to determine their own self-interest (see, e.g., Rapoport and Chammah 1965, 29). Other writers argue that a better interpretation of such data is that these apparent altruists in game theory situations are really more sophisticated than the self-interested rationalists of social choice theory (e.g., Sen 1974, 1978). Rather than looking at the short-run benefits of adopting an egoistic strategy, these sophisticated people adopt the strategy that they would like others to adopt in hopes of achieving long-run benefits. Seen from this perspective, the experimental evidence suggests that real-world people sometimes do adopt an applied version of the golden rule.

Lying behind the surface generalization that one should value the good of others, the golden rule hides many complexities. The Judeo-Christian command against lethal violence can be interpreted in two ways. Is it "Thou shalt not kill" or "Do no murder"? These contrasting interpretations provide quite different policy prescriptions. When combined with the love-thy-neighbor principle, different theories of moral value, nonmoral value, and obligation are derived, which generate pacifism or the just war doctrine.

While important to Judeo-Christian ethics, the golden rule, the "Love thy neighbor" principle, and other normative prescriptions concerning the use of deadly force did not originate with Judaism or Christianity. War was a common feature in primitive societies, and its consequences had to be incorporated into their beliefs (see Davie 1968; Green 1988). Ancient political communities generally had religiously based moral systems that included norms concerning the use of force. These early societies were often organized along bloodlines, and kinship factors were steeped in ancestrally based religious belief systems. While their value systems often stressed a concern for others, that concern was primarily a collective one for others in a kinship group. It was not so much a concern for individuals as for the survival and well-being of the group.

Because of the constant threat of war, most primitive value systems were geared to promote in-group unity. The primitive ethical systems that evolved in these societies served particular utility-maximizing purposes: they increased group strength and enhanced a group's often tenuous chances for survival and victory in intergroup conflicts. Accordingly, these value systems condemned in-group murder, stealing, and other acts of violence that destroyed the unity of one's society. However, as with contemporary nations, certain actions prohibited among members of the bloodline were permissible, or even considered honorable, when committed against outsiders.

Generally in these primitive ethical systems, murderous acts against one's kin were condemned; killing murderous kinship others in self-defense was acceptable; and wars waged against external groups were given free rein. Another common characteristic of the value orientation found in many traditional communities was the duty of blood revenge. Although methods existed for minimizing the problem of revenge in the case of in-group murder, an endless series of revenge and counterrevenge attacks could ensue if the blood of one's kin was spilled by outsiders. The result might be the virtual annihilation of the bloodlines, which is why norms safeguarding against such precipitory acts were so important.

While the principles of "Do unto others" and "Love thy neighbor" were fairly well established in pre-Christian communities, the ancient definitions of others were extremely limited by kinship factors. Prohibitions frequently rested upon religion-based definitions of one's group and one's duties to the group. These concepts were reinforced by interaction with members of similar groups in a primitive international system governed by principles generating fierce and vengeful attitudes toward outsiders. These older and narrower definitions of others required a total concern for kinship others and potentially a total hatred of outsiders.

When seen in this sense, the "Love thy neighbor" principle becomes a cause, rather than a solution to the problem of intergroup conflict. Accordingly, progressive Christian interpretations of Jesus Christ's teachings may be seen as an effort to rechannel moral values toward universal others as defined by the concept of a holy family and away from restrictive bloodline definitions of neighbors (Chamberlin and Feldman 1950, 965–66; Stout 1990, 24–25). The parable of the Good Samaritan is associated with this transformation, and the following example of the "Love thy neighbor" principle is a reflection of this enlarged characterization: "Ye have heard that it hath been said, Thou shalt love thy neighbor, and hate thine enemy. But I say unto you, Love your enemies. . . . For if ye love them which love you, what reward have ye? . . . And if ye salute your brethren only, what do ye more than others?" (Matthew 5:43–47).

A corollary to the golden rule in many Eastern philosophies is based on the utility gained by following a particular rule system, rather than single-mindedly striving directly for personal gain. According to Taoist and Buddhist thought, one obtains a thing by wanting it less, not more. The outcome you desire is most likely when you abandon a direct search for it and devote yourself to following more general rules for the good life. In doing so, you employ the Kantian principle of treating others as people who are valued in their own right, rather than as a means for advancing your own ends.

Moral Perfectionism

Moral perfectionism and moral nonperfectionism are broad forms of thought. When applied to the golden rule and other fundamental principles, they yield different theories of value and obligation. In turn, these underpin such contrasting doctrines as pacifism, holy war, and just war theory. Moral perfectionists argue that certain fundamental principles and values are binding without exception. Such thinkers do not compromise their fundamental principles for the sake of any practical or political considerations.

Those who follow moral perfectionism generally fall into two categories whose precepts consist of combinations of theories of value and theories of obligation, which generate different doctrines regarding war. One combination leads to universal pacifism, which consists of total concern for all others, even if one's own life must be sacrificed in this pursuit. Pacifists believe that the supreme value is a right to life for universally defined others. They hold deontologically derived, rule-based norms that condemn all killing and all war regardless of the consequences of not acting to protect the lives of innocent parties.

A second type of moral perfectionism reflects teleological reasoning. It advocates total concern for others by stressing the supreme importance of the nonmoral value of advancing a particular theological or secular set of beliefs. One should do unto others and show your love for them by converting them to your beliefs. This may be accomplished by using deadly force, in the case of holy war and moral crusading outlooks. Religious examples of this approach include Islamic jihads and Christian crusades. Secular examples abound, as well. Included here is the nineteenth-century American ethic that allowed the theft of land and murder of Native Americans in the name of Manifest Destiny. Of a similar nature are the irredentist movements that have swept former communist states. Such outlooks can call for the annihilation of intractable nonbelievers and those thought to be inherently evil. In the disputed territories of Bosnia, this is called ethnic cleansing.

The morality of aggressive war and unrestrained warfare in such situations can be justified because these actions increase the chance of advancing a valued set of beliefs. Therefore, certain ends can be claimed to justify any useful means. Some versions of this outlook parallel the group-based attitudes of ancient societies. In doing so, they reflect characterizations of the others who are to be valued in exclusive in-group terms. This dehumanizes nonbelieving others and involves defining one's neighbor in nonuniversalistic terms.

Moral Nonperfectionism

Nonperfectionism considers the theories of obligation underpinning such moral perfectionist doctrines as pacifism and holy war as too restrictive. Pacifism is derived from deontological reasoning to the total exclusion of teleological factors including national survival. Holy war is derived from teleological reasoning to the exclusion of the deontological factors of constraints on the resort to war and how it is waged. Accordingly, nonperfectionist thought considers perfectionism as a source of moral approval for the undesirable extremes of nonviolence and unrestrained violence.

Moral nonperfectionism favors mixed-deontological reasoning, and it underpins such doctrines as situation ethics, just war, the retaliatory ethic, and supreme emergency. Two factors common to these doctrines are their rejection of moral perfectionism and their use of mixed-deontological reasoning; they differ in their specificity of substantive value content. For example, just war doctrine has relatively clear-cut content, while situation ethics is more a process for examining the morality of war.

In theory, situation ethics holds that decision makers should choose the most moral or the least immoral alternative available to them. However, the application of situation ethics requires knowledge of all the important situational factors. These include knowing what an individual believes to be important, what are the realistic policy options, and what is the degree of immorality of each. Consequently, there are no specific standards of morality associated with this approach, and one cannot unambiguously assess the degree of morality of any particular action. Instead, the door is open for the application of different theories of moral and nonmoral value, which often yield contrasting judgments about the same action. This is particularly the case when teleological reasoning is combined with nonspecific valued ends for nonspecific others. The vagueness of situation ethics can be seen in the contemporary debate over the morality of using the atomic bomb on Japanese cities. Those who stress the value of saving American lives consider U.S. actions the lesser of evils, while those who stress the value of protecting innocents among the enemy state condemn the bombings as the greater evil. Another practical consequence of applying situation ethics may be a moral morass where leaders can claim their national policies are the most moral alternatives, when they really were chosen for self-serving purposes.

In contrast, just war doctrine is the main example of the application of nonperfectionist ethics that has produced explicit norms regarding warfare. Here the consequences of actions are stressed, but with the application of deontologically derived norms concerning resort to war and the conduct of warfare. Just war constraints cannot be overridden through an appeal to teleological concerns.

CONFLICT DOCTRINES

To understand contemporary attitudes toward international conflict, it is useful to describe the major doctrinal positions found in the traditional literature and to identify their underlying theories of value and forms of reasoning. This provides a foundation for our later empirical analysis, allowing us to determine whether any of the moral and amoral concepts developed by traditional thinkers are employed by contemporary American elites. Because of their historical importance, a dozen specific approaches to international conflict deserve review. When one examines these doctrines, it is particularly important to identify their *ad bellum* rules for the resort to war and the *in bello* rules for war conduct.

Just War

The wise man, they say, will wage just wars. Surely, if he remembers that he is a human being, he will lament the fact that he is faced with the necessity of waging just wars; for if they were not just, he would not have to engage in them, and consequently there would be no wars for a wise man. For it is the injustice of the opposing side that lays on the wise man the duty of waging wars. — Augustine

If someone is commanded to join a war, as often happens, knowing that the war is unlawful, then they should abstain. That God is to be obeyed rather than men not only have the Apostles decreed but Socrates as well. — Hugo Grotius

In contemporary times, the Catholic Church and virtually all of America's Protestant denominations have supported some version of the just war doctrine. In substantive content it is similar to contemporary international law, and its prescriptions enjoy substantial credence. One example of its importance as a constraint on international conflict is the moral check list used by Chief of Naval Operations James Watkins in advising President Reagan on possible U.S. responses to terrorism. His criteria for military action included a number of just war provisions. Similarly, during the debate before the Gulf War, George Bush used just war doctrine to defend his policies, and many of his supporters, as well as his opponents, used it as a framework to organize their thoughts on the conflict (Johnson and Weigel 1991).

As often defined, contemporary just war doctrine consists of a series of rules that must be satisfied regarding the reasons for war and its conduct. According to the principle of just cause, a resort to military force must be defensively motivated and must be a last resort in response to an actual armed attack constituting a threat of substantial harm. The principle of right intention holds that the purposes of war should be limited to restoring peace and defeating an enemy's military force; it condemns the motive of revenge and wanton violence. According to the hope of success criterion, there should be a reasonable chance of achieving victory in defense of one's nation. Wars can be ordered only by a competent authority responsible for public order and safety, not by private individuals or groups. A proportionality requirement holds that the likely overall good to be achieved by a war should outweigh its estimated evils.

The good that flows from a conflict is defined by just war theorists as protecting the innocent from unjust attack and protecting commonly recognized community values, such as national independence and freedom. The evils of a war are measured in terms of the casualties and the material damage that will be suffered by both sides during the conflict. The amount of destruction caused by attacks against military targets must be proportional to the importance of a military objective, and wanton violence and unnecessary destruction should be avoided.

Collateral harm to civilians from attacks on military targets must be evaluated according to similar calculations, which is the rule of *in bello* proportionality. Military attacks intentionally aimed at civilians are strictly forbidden by the principle of noncombatant immunity. Only two types of people in an enemy state are legitimate targets. The first is the soldier. The second is the civilian who provides support for the military and can cause indirect harm through such actions as producing munitions, but such civilians are legitimate targets only when in their munitions factories. Other civilians are considered noncombatants. Unlike the situation in a holy war, these noncombatants are immune from intentional attack.

The theory of moral value embodied in just war doctrine requires a concern for universally defined innocent others. This can be contrasted with the concern for all others that is embodied in pacifism. On the one hand, war is permitted for the just cause of defense to protect the victims of aggression. On the other, the principles of right intention, proportionality, and noncombatant immunity place restrictions on the overall purposes and conduct of war to protect civilian innocents among the enemy state and even enemy combatants.

The theory of nonmoral value embodied in just war doctrine stresses the importance of biological survival, but it also includes other values, such as national independence and freedom, as part of the good that can be achieved by war. However, in rejecting differences in ideology or the goal of protecting all national interests as justifications for war, just war theory rejects the nonmoral values stressed by the moral crusading and reason of state doctrines.

The just war approach is shaped by a mixed-deontological theory of moral obligation. Unlike pacifism, just war reasoning is teleological in taking into account not only the circumstantial factor that violent aggression can occur, but also the consequentialist factor that practicing nonresistance cannot always protect innocent lives. Another teleological element of just war theory is the *ad bellum* proportionality requirement that war should produce, in the balance, a preponderance of good over evil. The most teleological principle of just war is the proportionality requirement. As defined by the American Catholic bishops, "Proportionality means that the damage to be inflicted and the costs incurred by war (including to the adversary) must be proportionate to the good expected by taking up arms. Nor should judgments concerning proportionality be limited to the temporary order without regard to a spiritual dimension in terms of 'damage,' 'cost,' and 'the good expected'" (quoted in Castelli 1983, 220).

However, just war doctrine also reflects deontological reasoning by stressing that injury and damage to the civilian sectors of *both* sides in a conflict are the main evils of war. Deontological reasoning is central in determining the content of the discriminate means principle, and it also shapes the principles of right intention and proportionality. If the conduct norms of just war were guided only by teleological reasoning, they likely would have little effect in establishing constraints on warfare and particularly the fate of noncombatants (Walzer 1977, 129–33).

The term *just war doctrine* usually refers to its Judeo-Christian version, which is embodied in seven more or less standard principles that determine whether a war is just. The just war tradition is a broader, looser, evolving concept that includes contributions from a wide array of sources. The beliefs of doctrines such as the retaliatory ethic and supreme emergency can be considered candidates for inclusion in the just war tradition, but not in the just war doctrine. The basic notion of the *in bello* component of the tradition is restraint in the conduct of warfare beyond that justified by a belligerent's narrowly conceived self-interest or expediency. The doctrine's component is more specific and more restrictive. James Turner Johnson regards the just war tradition as the "fundamental way we in the West think about the justification and limitation of violence" (1981, 329). However, as Johnson notes, it is important to distinguish between the tradition and the doctrine, since the former includes positions that are very different from the latter and from each other, despite their relatively moderate content when compared to the doctrines of the moral crusade and amoral reason of state.

Supreme Emergency

Should I wager this determinate crime (the killing of innocent people) against that immeasurable evil (a Nazi triumph)? — Michael Walzer

This doctrine holds that constraints on the conduct of war may be suspended during a supreme emergency, a situation in which a military defeat appears to be imminent at the hands of a very evil enemy (such as Nazi Germany or Stalinist Russia) that threatens a society's fundamental values.[6] The supreme emergency doctrine is supported by some just war theorists and is similar to just war thinking in advocating constraints in all situations other than a supreme emergency. Michael Walzer, for example, considered the British terror bombing of German cities to be justified during the early part of World War II, when it appeared likely that Germany might be triumphant, but the strategy could no longer be justified in his eyes as soon as the Allied victory in Europe seemed likely, and such terror bombing never was justified against Japan (1977, 255–68).

Since the justifications for suspending constraints on the conduct of war offered by supreme emergency advocates stress circumstantial and consequentialist factors, perhaps the supreme emergency doctrine should be classified as mixed-teleological rather than mixed-deontological reasoning. The deontological conduct norms of just war are sacrificed to proportionality considerations and teleological reasoning by supreme emergency theorists. The supreme emergency doctrine also displays aspects of nonuniversalistic in-group thinking as a theory of moral value; for example, one might want to protect the values of Western civilization (Kurtz 1988, 56–58).

Legalism

Legalism asserts the primacy of governmental authority and law.[7] It holds that discharging one's duty takes precedence over personal, political, and moral interests. The doctrine's focus is on legal duties. If addressed at all, matters of personal conscience derive from them. Legal duties are not derivative from moral considerations. With respect to an international conflict, a war's justness is not for an individual to judge. One's only duty is to obey the commands of higher government officials.

Legalism may develop as a natural outgrowth of bureaucratic behavior, which Robert Merton described as the process whereby a person's "adherence to the rules, originally conceived as a means, becomes transformed into an end-in-itself" (1956, 253). In bureaucratic organizations, there is a presumption that one should obey the orders of superiors since they hold legitimate positions of authority. This norm of proper behavior is reinforced by a reward system that tries to drive out anyone unwilling to support an organization's goals (Weber 1946). Toward the end of the Second World War, the British newspaper the *Observer* published a description of Albert Speer that captured the essence of the bureaucratic transformation of pubic affairs.

> Speer is not one of the flamboyant and picturesque Nazis. Whether he has any other than conventional political opinions at all is unknown. He might have joined any other political party which gave him a job and a career. He is

very much the successful average man, well-dressed, civil, noncorrupt, very middle-class in his style of life, with a wife and six children. Much less than any other of the German leaders does he stand for anything particularly German or particularly Nazi. He rather symbolizes a type which is becoming increasingly important in all belligerent countries: the pure technician, the classless bright young man without background, with no other original aim than to make his way in the world and no other means than his technical and managerial ability. It is the lack of psychological and spiritual ballast, and the ease with which he handles the terrifying technical and organizational machinery of our age, which makes the slight type go extremely far nowadays. . . . The Hitlers and Himmlers we may well get rid of, but the Speers, whatever happens to this particular special man, will long be with us. (April 9, 1944, quoted in Wintle 1989, 57)

In strongly bureaucratic situations such as military service, people often feel responsible to those giving orders but not for the order's consequences (Milgram 1974). Reflecting this predisposition during his trial for war crimes, Adolf Eichmann embraced the legalist position by arguing, "So far as my participation is concerned, I must point out that I do not consider myself guilty from a legal point of view. I was only receiving and carrying out orders" (quoted in Faulkner 1973, 135). This also was the argument of Lt. William Calley in defending the massacre at My Lai (Kelman and Lawrence 1972; Cockerham and Cohen 1980). Calley contended that he had been ordered to destroy everything in the village and that the Vietnamese civilians found there were covered by the order.

Augustine and Thomas Aquinas, key developers of the Christian just war doctrine, adhered to a version of legalism in asserting that it was the duty of soldiers to obey competent authorities on matters of war conduct. Moreover, their doctrine of just war did not contain an explicit *in bello* position (Johnson 1981, 230–37; Hartigan 1982; Miller 1991, 27). Historically, some Christian holy wars have demanded an unrestrained warfare that is implicit in the orders of superiors to their soldiers, while other Christian holy wars were fought according to the constraints of current just war doctrine.

Legalism is a position that pertains primarily to the *in bello* issues of war as opposed to their *ad bellum* issues. Legalism variously can be considered a component of the reason of state and other doctrines, such as the moral crusade or supreme emergency positions, when they take on an in-group value orientation. The legalism philosophy cannot incorporate a direct concern for others who are outside one's community, since it relegates such considerations to superiors.

In practice, legalism is a vague and uncertain position regarding the legitimate conduct of war. It calls for obedience to the commands of superiors but does not address the substantive issue of what those commands should be. In contemporary usage, the legalist doctrine is most often associated with obedience to the orders of superiors as a justification for the commission of war crimes.

Moral Crusade and Holy War

When ye encounter the unbelievers, strike off their heads, until ye have made a great slaughter among them. Verily, if God pleased, He could take vengeance on them without your assistance, but he commandeth you to fight his battles.
—Koran, sura 47

The Albigensian War, in the beginning of the thirteenth century, commenced with the storming of Bezieres, and a massacre in which fifteen thousand persons . . . were put to the sword. Not a living soul escaped. . . . It was here that a Cistercian monk, being asked how the Catholics were to be distinguished from the heretics, answered, "Kill them all! God will know his own."—Percy Anecdotes

We must act with vindictive earnestness against the Sioux, even to their extermination, men, women, and children. Nothing less will reach the root of the case.
—William Tecumseh Sherman

Moral crusade and holy war doctrines reflect theories of moral and nonmoral value that stress the supreme importance of religious or ideological beliefs.[8] Through forced conversion, their proponents seek the desired ends offered by their own ideologies not only for themselves, but for others as well. The associated theory of moral obligation is teleological in that the rightness of a war and its conduct are judged solely in terms of consequentialist factors centering on the protection or advancement of one's valued beliefs. Crusading sentiments are found in numerous religious writings, including the holy books of the Moslems and Sikhs. Many scholars feel this type of outlook has been a major source of aggressive and unrestrained warfare throughout history, but the direction of causation has not been empirically established. Do these outlooks cause war, or does prolonged conflict cause people to adopt such justifications, which, consequently, always accompany prolonged conflict?

It is suggestive to note that while game theory simulations have found that "nice" strategies often decline quickly, "not-nice" strategies, like the aggressive use of force to further self-interest at the expense of others, may take many generations to be extinguished (see, e.g., Vanberg and Congleton 1992). This presents the leaders of countries in "not-nice" neighborhoods with the pressing problem of what to do with their "not-nice" opponents. In such cases, a holy war of ethnic cleansing might be a rational strategy if one's opponents are particularly annoying, unrepentant, and dangerous. If a society does not have the patience to wait generations for the evil embodied in its enemies to be extinguished through some sort of natural evolution, then from the standpoint of the holy war and moral crusading doctrines, the genocidal extermination of one's enemies becomes not only a rational option but a moral one as well.

Some Americans perceived that just such a situation existed during the Civil War. This logic was reflected in the comments of William Tecumseh Sherman in a letter to Ulysses S. Grant written from Atlanta. "Until we can repopulate Georgia, it is useless for us to occupy it; but the utter destruction of its roads, houses and people will cripple their military resources" (quoted in Wintle 1989, 281). The frustration of another northerner upon realizing that even the massive devastation of the Civil War had caused no fundamental changes in southern attitudes was reflected in a speech by the abolitionist W. P. Brownlow. "If I had the power, I would arm every wolf, panther, catamount and bear in the mountains of America, every crocodile in the swamps of Florida, every negro in the South, every devil in Hell, clothe him in the uniform of the Federal Army, and then turn them loose on the rebels of the South and exterminate every man, woman and child south of Mason and Dixon's Line" (quoted in Wintle 1989, 283).

In our survey of the traditional literature on war, we noted many similar expressions of moral crusading. They seem to be ubiquitous after extended conflicts and reflect extreme personal frustration, but this frustration often declines quickly with the coming of peace. A thoughtful reflection on the origins of this frustration also is found in the writings of General Sherman:

> We of the North are beyond question right in our cause, but we are not bound to ignore the fact that the people of the South have prejudices which form part of their nature, and which they cannot throw off without an effort of reason or the slower process of natural change. The question then arises, should we treat as absolute enemies all in the South who differ from us in opinion or prejudice, kill or banish them, or should we give them time to think and

gradually change their conduct so as to conform to the new order of things which is slowly and gradually creeping into their country? (quoted in Wintle 1989, 280)

A central feature of moral crusades and holy wars is approval of the aggressive use of force to export one's beliefs or punish the infidel. This approach reflects an assignment of a higher priority to beliefs than to human life. By way of contrast, the theory of nonmoral value stressed by pacifism asserts a supreme importance to all human life, while just war theorists stress that only the lives of innocents should be given such a high value. Holy war and moral crusading outlooks stress the nonmaterial characteristics of this life or the afterlife, and they demand an attitude of self-sacrificial love analogous to the love of the pacifist doctrine. While pacifism requires a willingness to sacrifice one's own life out of a concern for higher values, the same is also true for some holy warriors and moral crusaders.

The norms of a holy war or moral crusade can call for unrestrained and total warfare against the enemy. This advocacy partly stems from teleological reasoning, whereby a supreme end can justify the use of any means to achieve victory. Another supporting factor for this assertive approach is a theory of nonmoral value that generates subjectivist and collectivist definitions of an enemy's guilt and culpability for moral evil. For a holy warrior, the enemy is not just a group of combatants in a physical sense. Instead, the entire enemy's society is deemed to possess a collective guilt, since it has committed the sin of evil beliefs. From this perspective, war often becomes a moral act and sometimes even is a moral duty. Waging war may be necessary to promote a supreme good or to punish a supreme evil. To do otherwise is to tolerate an evil that should be opposed.

Although Augustine and Thomas Aquinas were the main developers of Christian just war doctrine, they also adhered to such subjectivist and collectivist notions of guilt. The just wars of medieval Europe were not unlike modern holy wars. While the *in bello* constraints of contemporary just war doctrine strictly forbid intentional attacks against civilians, this prohibition came from other sources. Such prohibitions were developed by later Catholic canonists, the developers of the medieval code of chivalry, soldiers, statesmen, later philosopher-theologians, and international lawyers who adhered to natural law thought (Johnson 1981; Hartigan 1982).

Pacifism

Thou shalt not kill. — Exodus 20:18

Nonviolence is not a garment to be put on and off at will. Its seat is in the heart, and it must be an inseparable part of our very being. — Mahatma Gandhi

In its universal and most all-encompassing form, the universalist pacifism doctrine condemns all killing and all wars.[9] Another version, antiwar pacifism, allows killing for individual self-defense and condemns only organized warfare between nations. Private pacifism, on the other hand, condones wars of public defense but condemns private killing for one's own self-defense. Antiwar pacifism allows killing by an individual as a response to a murderous attack but argues that soldiers and civilians on both sides are inevitably the victims of war; therefore, all war is wrong. The loss of life in combat in a war that pursues the ends of a political community violates both the moral and nonmoral values of the pacifist. In some ways, private pacifism is closely linked with just war thinking. Private pacifism condones killing if it is motivated by a concern for others who are the victims of aggression but condemns killing motivated by a concern for one's own survival.

Christians at first advocated universal pacifism, but under the influence of Augustine turned toward private pacifism combined with the just war position and, at times, a holy war approach. Following dissemination of the writings of Thomas Aquinas, medieval Catholic theologians incorporated an allowance for private defense into their position.

Advocates of universal pacifism stress the supreme nonmoral value of human life and a theory of moral value that emphasizes self-sacrificial love for universally defined others. No other goals, such as personal or group survival, or other ends valued by individuals or groups, such as freedom or economic needs, can justify taking another person's life. Consequently, the Christian pacifist adheres to deontological moral perfectionist reasoning in interpreting the fundamental principles of the golden rule, "Thou shalt not kill," "Love thy neighbor as thyself," and "Resist not evil." Judeo-Christian theologians cite the ethic of self-abnegation as reflecting these pacifist interpretations (Gordis 1964; Ramsey 1961; Thomas 1955, 505–21). Accordingly, universal pacifists should have total concern for their neighbors, including their mortal enemies, and should have no concern for their own needs or even their personal, physical survival in life-threatening situations.

The early church fathers likely supported pacifism because they expected the imminent arrival of a new age that would replace the material world (Johnson 1981, xxvii-viii). Early Christians thus advocated universal pacifism because of their disdain for earthly life. Their disdain was directed not so much against earthly violence but against all material activities. Mahatma Gandhi is respected for his concern with the spiritual side of mankind.[10] He considered a resort to deadly force, even for defensive purposes, to reflect man's animal nature. It was just this animal component that was protected through defense by force. If motivated by spiritual goals to practice nonviolence, one feels the loss of one's material self as no loss at all. Because of its onerous demands, the practice of the pacifist doctrine rarely is survival maximizing, and few Christians followed it after Christianity became the state religion of the Roman Empire.

Nuclear Pacifism

> *Thus far the chief purpose of our military establishment has been to win wars. From now on its chief purpose must be to avert them. It can have almost no other useful purpose.* — Bernard Brodie

The recently developed doctrine of nuclear pacifism is a response to a contemporary historical circumstance and is independently derived from both universal pacifism and some applications of just war logic.[11] Nuclear pacifism condemns nuclear war. Since universal pacifists reject all war, naturally they reject the idea of nuclear war. The more interesting derivation of nuclear pacifism is from just war theory. While the just war doctrine does not reject all war, almost all just war theorists reject nuclear war.

Contemporary just war scholars have extensively examined the morality of retaliatory nuclear warfare in assaults against cities, counterforce nuclear warfare, and threatening nuclear warfare as a deterrent strategy. While just war scholars agree almost unanimously on some nuclear warfare issues, they are divided on others. Just war theorists generally condemn counterforce nuclear warfare if it causes substantial civilian casualties, which is presumed to be the case in most counterforce scenarios. All just war theorists reject countercities nuclear warfare, even in response to a similar nuclear attack against our cities. Such retaliatory warfare is labeled a crime against God and mankind and mass genocide. It also is considered by just war theorists to satisfy the unacceptable motive of revenge. As for the morality of various nuclear deterrent strategies, most just war theorists adhere to the Pauline injunction that it is wrong to do evil that good may come, and so too it must be wrong to threaten evil that good may come. Accordingly, theorists who reject counterforce and countercities nuclear warfare also reject the threat of using such warfare for deterrence purposes.

Reason of State

Laws are dumb in times of war. — Marcus Tullius Cicero

We see, therefore, that war is not only a political act, but also a real political instrument, a continuation of political commerce, a carrying out of the same by other means. — Karl von Clausewitz

I cannot forecast to you the action of Russia. It is a riddle wrapped in a mystery inside an enigma. But perhaps there is a key. That key is Russian national interest. — Winston Churchill

Next to pacifism, reason of state is the conflict doctrine easiest to put into words, and we find many examples of its use throughout history. It is often viewed as a prescriptive rule that leaders should be guided only by reasons of state when deciding whether to resort to war and how to fight a war.[12] Moral constraints are considered irrelevant. While many other schools see national policies in terms of good and evil, reason of state adherents judge them as wise or foolish.

From this perspective, morality may be a hindrance to the advancement and protection of our country's interests and the fundamental goal of achieving victory. As one journalist commented, "Where do morals come in when you are fighting for your life?" A similar sentiment was expressed by a diplomat who said that the term *moral war* is an oxymoron. Another commented, "Most would say that war is a temporary suspension of moral concerns allowing a government to pursue its national interests. War is more amoral rather than immoral." Quite a few military officers stated a version of this sentiment: "There is no such thing as a moral war. All war is immoral."

The amoral reason of state approach also is called Machiavellianism, realism, realpolitik, *raison d'etat, kriegsraison,* military necessity, and power politics. Expediency and necessity must be the reigning guidelines of nations. Machiavelli states in *The Discourses,* "When the entire safety of one's country is at stake, there should be no consideration of just or unjust, merciful or cruel, praiseworthy or disgraceful; on the contrary, putting aside every form of respect, that decision which will save her life and preserve her liberty must be followed completely" (1979a, 411). This was echoed by a military officer in our study: "When it's your ass or his, morality is not a consideration." Similarly, an admiral expressed the reason of state approach: "Survival of our country is paramount; thus acting in our national interests should govern our foreign policy."

The atomic bomb challenged the rationales and justifications of all the traditional doctrines. Anatol Rapoport succinctly described the predicament facing reason of state theorists regarding the nuclear dilemma:

> Clausewitz's great achievement was in having made people aware of the way war can be used as an arm of national policy in the sense of accepting its legitimacy. In his day the question of the legitimacy of war did not arise. In our day this question is forced upon us. The disciples of Clausewitz in effect plead for "recognizing" war as an arm of national policy in the sense of accepting its legitimacy. And since war in the nuclear age has become a political absurdity, a vast amount of discussion is devoted to theorizing about "limited wars," controlled escalation, the game of threats, self-terminating "nuclear exchanges" and the like. All this investment of intellectual effort seems to be motivated to a considerable degree by a determination to preserve the struggle for power as the theoretical bedrock of political reality (1968, 412).

Retaliatory Ethic

Though I walk through the valley of the shadow of death, I fear no evil, for I am the biggest son of a bitch in the valley. — Vietnam War slogan

The retaliatory ethic holds that a country has a right to suspend any norm of constraining behavior that an enemy has violated.[13] Constraints on war conduct are limited to their reciprocal observance. The retaliatory ethic is analogous to tit-for-tat, which has been shown to be a successful strategy in computer simulations (Axelrod 1984). It also is similar to the international legal concept of reprisal, although international law requires that the purpose of a reprisal be to compel an enemy to cease its illegal behavior.

The retaliatory ethic offers the least restrictive set of criteria on war conduct of the several doctrines that fall generically within the broadly defined moral tradition. The retaliatory ethic accepts specific constraints only if an enemy implements them as well. In contrast, the supreme emergency doctrine sanctions the abandoning of constraints only in cases of a supreme emergency, while just war doctrine considers enemy violations of the norms of war conduct and supreme emergencies as irrelevant to how wars should be fought. Arguments reflecting the retaliatory ethic were used by British and U.S. officials to justify the terror bombing of Germany during World War II and the use of the atomic bomb against Japan. The nuclear strategy embodied in the doctrine of MAD (mutual assured destruction) also rests on the retaliatory ethic (Walzer 1977, 263–68; Cohen 1989, 94–99).

The value systems of primitive societies usually condemned murder and other antisocial acts within their group, but not toward outsiders. A norm of negative reciprocity, such as the retaliatory ethic, may be the first step away from this ancient pattern. While social norms such as the golden rule and the positive reciprocity principle of returning good with good develop most often among members of a group, they also have been seen to develop on the battlefield (Axelrod 1984, Kurtz 1988, 55–58).

Fatalism

> And ye shall hear of wars and rumors of wars: see that ye be not troubled: for all these things must come to pass, but the end is not yet. For nation shall rise against nation, and kingdom against kingdom: and there shall be famines, and pestilences, and earthquakes, in diverse places. All these are the beginning of sorrows.
> —Matthew 24:6–8

Fatalism is a passive, resigned view that sees war and its accompanying cruelties as integral and perpetual features of human existence.[14] The evils of war are neither policy consequences nor the products of political intentions. The evils of war are a condition without end; they are eternal and unavoidable. Although fatalism is thought to be more prominent in Eastern societies, it still can occasionally be seen in some Western explanations of warfare. A fatalist outlook was expressed retrospectively by some American officials in discussing their decision to use the atomic bomb on Japan (Walzer 1977, 265–66). In a similar vein, Robert Oppenheimer recalled his thoughts shortly after the first atomic bomb was tested.

> We knew the world would not be the same. A few people laughed. A few people cried. Most people were silent. I remembered a line from the Hindu scripture — the *Bhagavad-gita*. Vishnu is trying to persuade the prince that he should do his duty, and to impress him, takes on his multi-armed form and says, "Now I am become Death, the destroyer of worlds." I suppose we all felt that, one way or another. (Quoted in Wintle 1989, 353)

Fatalism constitutes a type of deterministic outlook that denies the possibility of individual moral choice and value. By definition, it lacks theories of moral and nonmoral value and of moral obligation and responsibility in the context of war. The tenets of this doctrine were rarely cited by the more than two thousand U.S. elites who participated in our study. In fact, we could identify only two specific statements that seemed to express such a fatalistic outlook. One junior military officer commented, "War is hell, and it hasn't changed since the hordes from the North decimated the conquered populations of Europe. Nor will nuclear weapons be done away with on the morality issue, they will be reduced because they will become inefficient." A captain was even more pessimistic when he made the following comments during the closing days of the cold war: "I fear a nuclear holocaust is inevitable, given the ignorance and wishfulness of the people and our leaders. Laymen and politicians simply have no concept of the destructiveness of nuclear weapons. . . . I am very bitter about the hawks . . . who by design avoided service in the Vietnam War and, now, in order to save their consciences beat the drum for confrontation with the USSR."

Utilitarianism

This is a philosophically derived, teleological theory of moral obligation that has been particularly important in the history of economic theory. Utilitarianism judges acts by the standard of promoting the greatest possible degree of good over evil for humanity. As such, it advocates a universalist theory of moral value. Its focus is on collective considerations, not on individual rights or needs, but the definition of what constitutes the important nonmoral good varies greatly among utilitarian ethicists.

In economics, it often is associated with Jeremy Bentham's admonition that we should try to achieve the greatest good for the greatest number of people — or with its more sophisticated version, as advocated by John Stuart Mill, which seeks to move beyond Bentham's emphasis on material pleasures to include the higher quality pleasures of the arts and intellect. But its practical implementation in public policy has been handicapped by difficulties in measuring interpersonal utility. Many war doctrines avoid this issue by positing a set of rules that determine what factors people should examine when evaluating conflict.

When applied to issues of war, this doctrine holds that morally justifiable wars and the rules for waging war are those that maximize the long-range expected benefits of the warring states or the world as a whole.[15] While there is no identifiable utilitarian doctrine on the moral issues of war, its teleological focus on utility is embodied in such doctrines as just war, supreme emergency, and reason of state. While nationalism is a form of nonuniversal utilitarianism, it is classified as egoistic by most ethicists. The proportionality principle of just war doctrine also reflects utilitarian calculations.

REALIST THOUGHT

The most important stream of thought in contemporary international relations theory is realism. In shaping the structure of American cold war policy, George Kennan (1951) dismissed the roles of both morality and ideology and tried to insulate the diplomatic community from what he believed were their detrimental influences. In general, realists like Kennan view themselves as pragmatists who are unencumbered by what they see as outmoded moral beliefs. Such a perspective rests on the dubious assumption that morality is a superficial problem for governments that can be overcome by properly educating the policy elite (see, e.g., Hunt 1987). But on close inspection, it can be seen that such realists as Hans Morgenthau and Reinhold Niebuhr advocated substantive positions that are close to the just war doctrine. The differences among the giants of realist thought can best be understood by noting their definitions of morality and the historical context of their works.

Niccolò Machiavelli

Although generally linked with political realism, the amoral reason of state approach is best associated with the Machiavellian version of realism. The author of *The Prince* defined morality in terms of Christian ethics, but associated morality only with the ethic of self-abnegation. Machiavelli used utilitarian logic in arguing that the establishment of a unified Italian state was necessary to overcome the weaknesses of a chaotic community faced with external domination. In holding this position, he was forced to reject the standard Christian ethics of his day. Machiavelli considered Christian ethics to be the source of a value system that oriented people toward meekness and otherworldly concerns, and away from the values of power, glory, material wealth, and success. Such aggressive values had been embodied in ancient pagan religions and had been crucial to the Roman Empire's success.

Machiavelli equated morality with pacifist values and weakness, which he felt were incompatible with achieving reasons of state. To be successful, the ruler had to learn how not to be good. He did this by rejecting self-abnegation ethics as the first step toward defeating his ruthless domestic opponents, establishing order, repelling external threats, and expanding the state's power through aggressive war. Nevertheless, Machiavelli advocated a domestic resort to amoral means only when necessary. He also thought that it was vital for a ruler to have the loyalty of his subjects and troops, since loyalty was a better source of power than reliance on mercenary forces. While it is more advantageous to be feared than to be loved, it is best to be both feared and loved. The worst situation for the prince is to be hated. Accordingly, however amoral a government is in practice, a ruler should try to appear to be moral, and a leader should resort to ruthless means only as dictated by necessity.

Machiavelli appears to have been unaware of both the just war doctrine and the Christian ethic of self-fulfillment. The latter considers the self-interested concern for one's own survival and basic interests as morally legitimate as long as they are not pursued at the expense of others. While following self-fulfillment ethics might not have been successful in creating the Italian nation-state that was Machiavelli's overriding goal, he was incorrect in attacking all Christian ethics as fundamentally pacifist.

Hans Morgenthau

Hans Morgenthau associated morality with both the pacifist and holy war doctrines. He equated universal moral principles with Judeo-Christian ethics and, like Machiavelli, defined them in terms of the ethic of self-abnegation and its moral principle of love. Unlike Machiavelli, Morgenthau adhered to the Judeo-Christian tradition, but he considered its moral requirements to be an unrealistic standard for national leaders in the jungle of international power politics. It was this difference that led Machiavelli, but not Morgenthau, to allow reasons of state to include unlimited national goals and unrestrained means.

Morgenthau considered only certain national goals and means to be legitimate. The substance of his position was analogous to the ethic of self-fulfillment and the general content of the just war tradition. Morgenthau argued that leaders should pursue the national interests of survival and economic well-being, and force should be used only as it was necessary to achieve moderate goals. At the same time, leaders should recognize these same legitimate interests of other nations and not violate them.

Seemingly unaware of the self-fulfillment version of Christian ethics, Morgenthau labeled his prescriptive positions as prudential policies or wise statesmanship and generally avoided using the word *morality* in their context. His *Politics Among Nations* contains only one brief passage on Christian just war doctrine, and he pejoratively equates the just war approach with the holy war outlook (1967, 352). In addition to defining morality in terms of the pacifist tradition, Morgenthau was acutely aware of the central role of moral claims in holy war doctrines. He considered such claims to be gross distortions of the universal law of love for God and mankind.

Morgenthau asserted that man has a two-sided nature. On one hand, people are motivated by the goals of physical survival and material well-being. This aspect of their behavior generates a drive for power, since controlling others is a rational means of achieving these goals. Morgenthau made the standard economic assumptions that life is dominated by scarcity and that there is an intense competition for scarce resources. Political and military power are valued in such a world as means that can be used to achieve desired material ends. Morgenthau believed that the more success one had in the worldly competition for scare resources, the more one violated the moral requirement of having total love for others.

The other side of man's nature is spiritual. According to Morgenthau, people are morally oriented toward others through a desire to treat them as ends in themselves, which is the Kantian version of the golden rule. Accordingly, our material side orients us toward considering others as a means and as objects of power that can be used to realize our own goals of survival and material well-being. The moral side of human nature predicates the dilemma that moral behavior directly conflicts with survival concerns. This dilemma generates the need to justify a social existence where one either rules or is ruled by others.[16] Members of a group that is ruled need to justify their being dominated. As for the rulers, they have to morally justify their rule and their assignment of a priority to their own group's survival and well-being at the expense of others.

Because Morgenthau adhered to universalistic ethics, such moral justification was impossible for him. Instead, he was forced to conclude that all politics is morally evil. At best, moral evaluation consists of prudence, which he defined as choosing the lesser of evils. Morgenthau objected to any utilitarian ethical theories and teleological reasoning that labeled the lesser of evils approach as achieving, in balance, the greatest preponderance of good over evil in terms of satisfying human needs. Moreover, by denying that the only possible end was total love for God and mankind, utilitarianism opened itself to value systems that defined the nation as an end in itself and to teleological reasoning that justified actions promoting the greatest net good for the nation. Morgenthau considered all this to be in conflict with the universalist and deontological character of traditional Judeo-Christian ethics as he perceived them. A senior diplomat in our study expressed a similar view: "In full-scale war, morality becomes largely impracticable. I basically view morality as an individual rather than a collective consideration. As Morgenthau believed, but did not make sufficiently explicit, any shared values get plugged into a broadly defined, long-term national interest."

Reinhold Niebuhr

In contrast to Morgenthau, Reinhold Niebuhr (1932) defined morality in terms of the principles of love and justice. Like Morgenthau, he rejected love as an unrealistic standard for the moral evaluation of political actions. However, defining morality as including justice in the sense of the self-fulfillment ethic and the Kantian categorical imperative, Niebuhr considered national ends centered in survival and well-being to be morally correct so long as they were pursued in ways that did not violate the similar legitimate interests of other nations. Moreover, he regarded the use of deadly force as sometimes necessary to establish and maintain justice. Unlike Morgenthau, Niebuhr did not consider the exercise of power to be inherently immoral.

Morgenthau and Niebuhr generally agreed on the basic substantive content of the legitimate ends and means of states, always stressing moderation. However, they used different terminology in their discussions because of their different definitions of morality. While Morgenthau declared that national survival was a valid moral principle, his use of such terminology was rare. More often, he used the words *prudent* or *wise* to characterize the moderate policies that he favored. Niebuhr was more willing to use moral terminology, mainly the words *just* or *justice,* to characterize these policies. Moreover, Niebuhr even advocated the substantive content of the just war doctrine, although his derivation and terminology differed from the classical just war positions. Accordingly, he considered war and certain types of conduct as sometimes just and not, in substance or terminology, the amoral expedients Morgenthau found them to be.

Friedrich Meinecke

In the case of moral crusading and holy wars, rulers and religious prophets justify their goals in the terms of universalistic ethics. Morgenthau considered the ethic of mass nationalism as the main example of this corruption of the fundamental meanings of good and evil and right and wrong. Friedrich Meinecke (1957) examined the source of this transformation. He observed that by the nineteenth century the process of nation building, which was in its infancy during Machiavelli's time, had resulted in the establishment of industrialized economies and mass armies. In the process of this historical evolution, rulers had discovered that the maintenance of these systems required popular identification and loyalty to the nation. Accordingly, these goals were furthered by the creation of the welfare state. By the twentieth century, both rulers and ruled had come to see ethical qualities in their nation-states and routinely made nationalistic claims held to have universal moral validity. Morgenthau referred to this as the ethics of nationalistic universalism (1967, 235–49).

Along with the other realists, Meinecke argued that the Western concept of universalistic ethics had been captured and distorted by the process of state building and it now served national power goals rather than constraining them. According to this reasoning, nationalists ethnocentrically and falsely resolved the contradiction between a concern for others and the need to control others by claiming that the power of their nation served the good of everyone because of the universal validity of their nation's values.[17]

According to Meinecke, the tragic outcome of these historical forces was a fanatical nationalistic moral crusading. It was launched by individuals who had lost all understanding of the basic differences between right and wrong established in traditional ethics. Even Machiavelli acknowledged that certain state actions were morally wrong or amorally expedient. In the twentieth century, aggressive wars and unrestrained defensive wars were morally justified by the precepts of the new value systems of nationalistic ethics. The need to justify one's social existence had become coupled with an ethnocentric, power-oriented reason of state doctrine. This generated massive military establishments that could be used without restraint in the name of a morality that originally had insisted on restraint.

A MORAL REASON OF STATE?

With this comparison of the terminology and views of the leading realist thinkers, we can comment with greater precision on the various versions of reason of state doctrine besides its amoral branch commonly linked with Machiavelli. Some realist scholars argue that the reason of state approach can have a moral quality in seeking to protect a nation's legitimate and vital interests against its rivals. It is natural to see people who follow rules similar to our own as moral individuals since people often judge whether another person is moral by their own rules. Domestically, those who do not follow our most fundamental norms are deemed criminals if their behavior is too annoying. Externally, they are ignored, unless they become too obnoxious, in which case a war against them may be necessary.

Moreover, realists claim that prudence often acts as an ethical guideline through its stress on cost-benefit calculations and by insisting on moderation in the choice of goals and means. We associate this moral reason of state doctrine with the substantive positions of realists such as Hans Morgenthau, Friedrich Meinecke, and Kenneth Thompson, although we are mindful of their hesitancy in labeling such positions as moral. For the reasons noted above, we also associate Reinhold Niebuhr with the just war doctrine. Modern nationalism is another moral version of the reason of state doctrine but differs so much from a moderate realist position in substantive content and terminology that it more properly belongs with the moral crusading doctrine. In our subsequent discussion, we use the term *reason of state* only to refer to the purely amoral version of this doctrine.

The theory of moral value of the reason of state doctrine does not incorporate a fundamental concern for universal others. It asserts the primacy of national interests by explicitly disavowing the relevance of concern for the interests of other nations. Its theory of nonmoral value stresses national interests or reasons of state. However, when this doctrinal outlook is coupled with the existence of a large number of nations in the contemporary international system, the wide array of subnational actors operating in these nations, and teleological reasoning, the reason of state approach lacks specificity regarding its nonmoral values.

While Morgenthau criticized utilitarian ethics on these grounds, the same problem persists in any amoral advocacy of national interests as the proper guideline for national leaders. Realists who advocate prudence as an ethical guideline have been similarly criticized for not supplying the hierarchy of values needed to apply it (Smith 1986, 234–38). When viewed in this light, the doctrine is an empty vessel that can be filled in endless ways with various ends and means in the realm of nonmoral value. One way to make the doctrine moral is to assert that we are moral and those who do not follow our rules are immoral. The social psychology literature suggests that it is exactly this sort of justification that appeals to many people.

THREE

Investigating
Belief Systems

Many previous studies of foreign policy beliefs have lacked an explicit theoretical base. In large part, this has been due to data accessibility problems, which made theory development difficult. During the cold war, it was hard to gain access to elite actors, as many were reluctant to openly discuss such sensitive matters as the reasons the United States should go to war at a time when its nuclear weapons policy was in dispute. Consequently, social scientists often had to use inadequate data sources not well suited for theory building. To avoid these pitfalls, we draw much of our empirical evidence from a series of five surveys that were designed explicitly to tap elite beliefs about conflict.

Another impediment to theory building is the commonly encountered confusion in the international relations literature between belief systems and cognitive factors of evaluation. We use the term *belief system* to represent an empirically verifiable configuration of ideas and attitudes connected in some organized manner that is stable and general enough to provide an individual broad guidance on more specific matters. Cognitive factors of evaluation are components of belief systems.

Among elites, such belief systems may be complex and wide-ranging outlooks that organize large amounts of knowledge, ideas, and attitudes, while the belief systems of the mass public are likely to be information poor. In consequence, until recently most public opinion researchers have thought that the attitudes of nonelites on foreign policy are only weakly organized (see, e.g., Almond 1950; Converse 1964), but recent scholarship argues that a lack of detailed information might actually enhance the importance of core beliefs in shaping attitudes (see, e.g., Hurwitz and Peffley 1987, 1990). If the revisionists are correct, then even many information-poor members of the general public might have relatively coherent belief systems.

NORMS AND BELIEF SYSTEMS

When investigating the structure of belief systems, one may usefully begin with the concept of norms. A norm is an expectation about correct behavior that is shared by most members of a group. Norms are group characteristics and not individual properties, and while they are standards for conduct and guidelines for behavior accepted by most members of a group, they are not actual behaviors. Over the centuries, the norms of proper behavior in the international system have shifted many times.

An investigation of contemporary elite norms might be particularly useful in identifying the component principles of their belief systems. In the case of beliefs about international conflict, it seems likely that different types of actors will exhibit different norm patterns because they are trying to maximize different goals. Although different maximization principles can be proposed for various elite groups, and undoubtedly some individuals within these groups value different things, we can make the general nature of a norm-based research design clearer by suggesting a few obvious elite goals.

The armed forces are interested in countering foreign military action. Members of Congress are interested in preserving the country and being reelected. The diplomatic corps is concerned with furthering American interests and minimizing foreign conflict. The press wants a free flow of information so as to better inform the people about foreign policy and to maximize circulation. Religious leaders are interested in saving souls and increasing general human well-being. Consequently, we may find that different modal preferences toward foreign policy dominate among different U.S. elite groups. These differences may allow us to infer the components of real-world belief systems from the modal group values. If these inferred tenets seem to parallel the component principles of one or more of the traditional doctrines found in the literature (such as reason of state or just war thinking), we will be able to go further and ask whether U.S. elites subscribe to any of the traditional doctrines.

Norms have a wide variety of sources. Some are philosophically based, while others are prudential. An example of a prudential foreign policy norm is the prohibition against taking action against another country's diplomats, since such action might result in retaliation. In many circumstances, it could be useful in the short run to violate the ban on acting against individual diplomats (for example, the murder of a London policewoman by a member of the Libyan embassy staff or the use of a diplomatic pouch to smuggle drugs). However, the continuation of this norm is best seen as a problem of defining long-run, overriding national goals. Since the rule of noninterference with diplomatic personnel has a critical value to the international system, even the most serious action by a diplomat might not justify its violation. As another example, most nations were outraged when Iran seized Western hostages during the Carter administration, when Iraq tried to use hostages as human shields before the Gulf War, and when the Bosnian Serbs did likewise with United Nations personnel. Such actions are viewed as so serious that international law recognizes them as justifications for war.

Other types of norms are more short-lived and exist only because of chance fluctuations in the dynamics of social systems. Beginning with V. O. Key's (1949) study of the one-party state political systems of the American South, a friends-and-neighbors model has often been applied to voting behavior (see, e.g., Brunk, Adams, and Ramesh 1988). The friends-and-neighbors approach is generalizable as a model of contagion, which also explains the spread of fads. A faddish belief propagates when one's acquaintances believe something and every time they have a conversation about the matter one is more likely to believe it. A recurrent example that appears from time to time on the national news is the belief that Proctor and Gamble is controlled by the devil. In the same way that political support for a candidate spreads through a one-party political system, talking about the company's trademark of a witch and thirteen stars gives the rumor credence among particular sorts of religious fundamentalists. Their concern, in turn, increases the probability they will talk about the problem with their friends and neighbors, increasing the likelihood that others will also believe the rumor. As shown by Proctor and Gamble's repeated attempts to eradicate this public relations nightmare, such a faddish belief may proliferate through a system many times before being extinguished.

If a fad involving some physical action is observed by enough people, a precedent is set for the activity, but its continuance often has little purpose other than to express group solidarity. Many such norms, like "streaking" on college campuses by fraternities during the 1970s, are seen by most people as relatively harmless activities with no great usefulness. Most are quickly abandoned, but a few norms continue to be observed because their abandonment also may have costs. In diplomacy, the practice of giving gifts to foreign leaders once had great significance but now serves little purpose. But to be the first country to abandon the custom would offend others while gaining little benefit.

Belief systems are interrelated sets of attitudes that incorporate many normative prescriptions. Past behavioral research into political attitudes, particularly those held by the mass public, often concluded that belief systems consist of only weakly interconnected sets of predispositions that sometimes do not have strong logical links. In such systems, group norms can have a faddish and perhaps almost random nature. Nevertheless, there is ample reason to think that some important norms in public policy are more fundamental. We know, for example, that the sources of professional norms often lie outside one's workplace (Mosher 1982). When professionals hold attitudes that are critical to the normative rules they apply in their official positions, they see such beliefs as the only correct ways of doing things.

Altruism also may be an important source of many normative attitudes in public policy. Most researchers believe that social altruism develops more easily in small closed populations, where it is likely to be reciprocated, than in large societies with few sequential interactions (see, e.g., Trivers 1971). Nevertheless, even in ancient times when there were few large cities, purely altruistic behavior might have been rare, as is suggested by the Good Samaritan's uncommon generosity.

Personal contacts and informal decision making may be efficient in small organizations, but this probably is not true of complicated structures. As modern organizations have grown larger, it has become increasingly difficult for individuals to have a measurable impact on the general good. Therefore, an organization's size should have some effect on the type of ethical rules that are adopted by its members. As organizations become larger, the focus of decision making changes from solving particular isolated problems or helping individual clients to establishing a set of general rules that are appropriate for repeated use. Any rule that is accepted as a norm in such an institutional environment has to be appropriate for the repeated play of the organization's main game, or it will have little use to the organization. If altruism is important in structuring foreign policy beliefs, a rationale will have to be developed to explain how it can evolve in such a seemingly hostile environment.

Regarding attitudes toward international conflict, different sorts of belief systems are likely to evolve in different types of organizations. The level of formal institutionalization of an organization should affect one's beliefs, but an even more important factor should be an organization's goals. It seems likely that people with different goals and fundamental moral sensibilities drift toward membership in different types of organizations. If a person has a strong attachment to country, then military service is a valued career. If an individual has a strong spiritual belief that human life is a fundamental end, then a religious calling and career in the ministry is valued. A person who holds an antilegalistic position and believes that blindly following orders is an abrogation of moral responsibility should not choose a military life. Individuals with different beliefs about the proper bases for social rules consequently drift toward certain careers, but there are many intervening factors that affect such decisions, and we would not expect all those in similar situations to adopt identical beliefs.

With the notable exception of the literature on rational bureaucratic behavior, theories of elite norm adoption are not well developed.[1] Most administrative scholars have been more interested in studying bureaucratic than professional behavior. This is unfortunate, because the normative conflicts that surround whistle blowing illustrate what may be the fundamental difference between bureaucratic and professional behavior. Professionals often bring externally defined standards to their work and call upon these standards when making decisions.[2] Because of their reference to these external standards, professionals may be less responsive to an organization and more committed to their individual jobs or their profession. Similarly, we would expect some sources of elite attitudes toward conflict to come from outside government or outside one's work environment.

Laws, Customs, and Ethical Belief Systems

There is no scholarly consensus on the importance of norms in studying attitudes and beliefs partly because there are at least three different sources of norms: laws, customs, and ethical belief systems. Each provides different legitimizing justifications for behavior. The interaction among these three sources of normative attitudes potentially can make their empirical investigation difficult.

Laws are explicit governmental acts. In democracies, they are usually the product of voting systems and may be only loosely related in any logical way. In fact, upon close examination many laws are seen to be contradictory. Contemporary American examples include the prohibition against prayer in classrooms while the coins and currency of the United States read "In God We Trust"; the prohibition against many recreational drugs, while one of the most dangerous drugs receives official sanction through subsidies to tobacco farmers; and affirmative action laws that require the hiring of an equitable number of minorities, while governments fail to provide sufficient educational funding to train minority students.

Customs are informal standards that may be even more loosely related. Often they are associated only because of historical chance or social context. Here reside the faddish behaviors of college fraternities and youth gangs. Many of their norms are derived from unsystematic, random peer pressures.

When important policy matters come into dispute, it is difficult to justify to professionals a blind obedience to either laws or customs since these sources of norms lack much in the way of logical coherence. Upon thoughtful reflection, many elites realize that little more than chance has brought together such rules. The wide variety of paradoxes that flow from all methods of aggregating individual preferences and measuring interpersonal utility produce a dilemma. Unless one follows a group-centered ethical framework, legalism, or particular types of utilitarian logic that allow a person to ignore short-run contradictions to reach some long-run end, professionals cannot justify a blind obedience to either laws or customs.

The potentially incoherent nature of these two sources of norms is suggested by the voters' paradox, which was first noted by the French mathematician and political theorist Nicholas de Condorcet. He observed that in certain circumstances contradictory laws could be passed by a legislature in a random fashion. For example, in a certain policy area there are three alternatives, and each is supported by a third of the legislature. One-third of them prefers A over B over C, one-third prefers B over C over A, and one-third prefers C over A over B. The sequence of voting on paired alternatives determines public policy, and therefore A, B, or C can become law. One day a revolutionary legislature may vote to reinstate its former king as an elected ruler, a few days later it may vote to have him executed for his past acts, and still later it may apologize for his regrettable death and grant his widow a pension. Since the selection of all three policy alternatives is possible, and real-world situations of this sort likely abound, the voters' paradox shows that majority rule often has no real meaning.[3]

The last source of professional norms is the ethical belief system. Unlike laws and customs, ethical belief systems are sets of closely related platonic principles that may be deduced by thoughtful people from a few simple assumptions. One of the first explicit examples of such an ethical system toward international conflict was developed by medieval Catholic theologians. In particular, Augustine, Thomas Aquinas, and others argued that the component principles of just war theory will be derived independently by any skilled moralist who begins with the golden rule and a few other simple beliefs (see Secrest, Brunk, and Tamashiro 1991a). The argument is logically coherent, and today just war theory forms the basis of much of the international law on warfare. Part of its essence is expressed by Augustine in the following few sentences:

> There are . . . certain exceptions to the law against killing, made by the authority of God himself. There are some whose killing God orders, either by a law, or by an express command to a particular person at a particular time. In fact one who owes a duty of obedience to the giver of the command does not himself "kill" — he is an instrument, a sword in its user's hand. For this reason the commandment forbidding killing was not broken by those who have waged wars on the authority of God, or those who have imposed the death penalty on criminals when representing the authority of the State in accordance with the laws of the State, the justest and most reasonable source of power. (Quoted in Wintle 1989, 29)

Conflicts Caused by Ideals

There are only two classes who, as categories, show courage in war — the front-line soldier and the conscientious objector. — Basil Liddell Hart

It seems that these varied sources of norms will almost inevitably bring people into conflict about rules of the game. If acting professionally means bringing to one's work some standards of conduct that are derived from an outside setting, then the deviants in organizations that have "gone wild" in the manner of the Nixon White House may be highly principled individuals operating from their own strongly held beliefs about public morality. Instead of blindly agreeing with their colleagues and obeying the orders of their superiors, the most professional of these elites may follow platonic sets of norms developed by others outside their organization or derived independently by the elites themselves through logical thought. If conflict ensues, the result may resemble the "Saturday Night Massacre," when high officials were fired one weekend by President Nixon when Attorney General Elliot Richardson and others in the Justice Department refused to help the president cover up the Watergate scandal. Realizing the potential for such an outcome, elites may feel an opposite pressure to adopt a prudential norm of not disputing authority because to do so is to risk one's career.

Frederick Mosher expresses the difficulties involved in trying to re-solve the conflicts that face such government elites: "There is a built-in animosity between the professions and politics. . . . Most of the profes-sions . . . won their . . . spurs over many arduous years of contend-ing against the infiltration, the domination, and the influence of politi-cians (who to many professionals are amateurs at best and criminals at worst). . . . Professionalism rests upon specialized knowledge, science, and rationality. There are *correct* ways of solving problems and doing things" (1982, 118).

Ethical Belief Systems

Past studies of norms were based on many different and often conflicting approaches derived from perspectives based in sociology, theology, philos-ophy, history, psychology, game theory, and organizational behavior. In particular, since the mid-1970s sociobiologists have argued about why altruistic behavior does not quickly die out in all biological systems. Econ-omists and behavioral political scientists increasingly have become inter-ested in many traditional ethical problems, including altruism, loyalty, cooperation, ideology, reciprocity, deception, justice, charity, and conflict. Robert Axelrod provides one of the best known examples of this new line of research about ethical values in his *Evolution of Cooperation* (1984). There he shows how cooperation develops as a response to the repeated playing of non–zero-sum games, where the total payoffs can be increased if players adopt rules that respect the interests of others. Ethicists would call such rules moral. Such a game theory approach to the study of ethical belief systems potentially offers a way around the morass that economists have faced in attempting to measure interpersonal utility and formulate explanations based on short-run self-interest.

While recent research suggests that we may usefully study ethical belief systems using behavioral methods, the problems inherent in this endeavor are not trivial. In his classic discussion of political ideologies, Philip Converse writes: "Belief systems have never surrendered easily to study or quantification. Indeed, they have often served as primary exhibits for the doctrine that what is important to study cannot be measured and what can be measured is not important to study" (1964, 206). In fact, many researchers who examine belief systems find little stable attitude constraint among public policy opinions, and this is typical of the studies that follow Converse's methodology in examining the association among attitudes measured at the same level of abstraction. On the other hand, studies that examine hierarchically structured attitudes and search for core values observe more coherence in people's beliefs (e.g., Lane 1962; Conover and Feldman 1984; Hurwitz and Peffley 1987).

For many years, social psychologists have conducted substantial research into the nature of moral reasoning and behavior, although their work is usually conducted with ordinary people as subjects rather than a nation's elite.[4] Two broad schools of thought in social psychology are relevant to our endeavor here. Social learning theory argues that models and punishments are critical for the internalization of norms. The modal moral outlook of a person is believed to arise from a response to pressures for conformity. Since norms differ from society to society, it follows from this perspective that all moral norms are culturally relative and cannot universally be communicated between people of different societies. In contrast, cognitive development theory argues that there is a relation between moral and cognitive development, which follows from successive reintegrations of thinking and structures as one matures. Accordingly, there is an order to these stages of moral development, and the process is culture-free.

The social cognition literature provides a potentially useful framework for analysis, but it is only one of many frameworks that have been proposed to examine moral behavior.[5] These writers often assume that people are cognitive misers with limited abilities to store, retrieve, and use information (see, e.g., Fiske and Taylor 1984). In the real world, people search for ways to simplify their environment, and this is how moral heuristics evolve.

A general social-psychological model of the relation among reality beliefs, normative beliefs, attitudes, intentions, and behaviors is presented in figure 3.1. In this model, an individual's thought structure consists of two types of beliefs.[6] Reality beliefs concern what is thought to be the actual nature of the social and physical world. Normative beliefs concern the moral evaluation of that reality and what actions properly should be taken by individuals and groups. Specific attitudes may be generated through interactions between reality beliefs and normative beliefs. An individual's specific attitudes can, in turn, lead to intentions to behave, and eventually these intentions may lead to actual behaviors.

The doctrines on morality and war contain a series of reality beliefs, which are assumptions about the nature of the international system, and some indication of the likely interactions between one's reality beliefs and normative beliefs. Just war theorists, for example, have a different definition of who is an enemy within an enemy state from reason of state

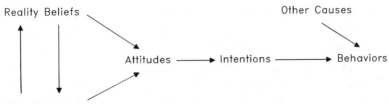

Figure 3.1 **The Social-Psychological Model**

theorists. These differing reality and normative beliefs generate different attitudes regarding whether civilians are legitimate targets for military action. A causal sequence is at work when one derives the policy prescriptions appropriate for each school of thought, but at every step the linkage to a doctrine's core beliefs becomes weaker. There are three reasons for this. First, one may follow many separate paths in forming attitudes. Second, all the logical derivations for consistent reasoning may not yet have been worked out by an individual. Finally, many other causes may have an impact.[7]

One example involves the complicated doctrines that have arisen in the traditional literature regarding legitimate justifications for the use of force. Many well-developed philosophical doctrines, such as pacifism, holy war, and just war, are directly derived from often conflicting interpretations of more fundamental beliefs and from the application of various methods of moral reasoning. As one example of this complexity, the normative doctrine of nuclear pacifism is derived by one group of contemporary scholars from the general doctrine of pacifism. In turn, pacifism stems from a moral perfectionist interpretation of fundamental principles. Other scholars derive nuclear pacifism from a particular application of certain parts of the just war doctrine, and their position has evolved from a nonperfectionist interpretation of those principles.

Moral Sensibilities

Our work builds on notions of attitudes, moral sensibilities, and belief systems. These organizing principles allow us to link underlying, not necessarily conscious motives to the conscious belief structures people use in reaching judgments. Moral sensibilities refer to such feelings as sympathy, guilt, gratitude, loyalty, and indignation. These are the emotional components of human conscience. One theory of moral sensibilities argues that these emotions reinforce biological altruism because such sensibilities are genetically adaptive (Trivers 1985). In turn, these sensibilities may have helped institutionalize morality in human society. We use the idea of moral sensibilities as a way of indicating certain powerful foundations of social morality, which implies that these feelings precede the formation of belief systems.

It is useful to note further some features of moral sensibilities, attitudes, and belief systems. Moral sensibilities are products of temperament and culture, enduring and fundamental. Since these sensibilities are largely matters of feeling rather than cognition, they are often unfocused. Alone, they cannot provide practical guidelines for policy making, but moral sensibilities do provide the motivation to move in certain directions. Our empirical work uses attitudinal data and observed elite norms to build a model of policy preferences. It is based on the concepts of moral sensibilities and belief systems and asks whether certain empirically observed patterns of U.S. elite beliefs appear to fit any of the traditional schools of thought found in the literature on conflict. If so, this will further allow us to infer the fundamental motivations and sensibilities held by American elites.

Research Limitations

The limitations of our empirical work should be made explicit. First, we make no claim that moral sensibilities are the only cause of attitudes or behaviors. Nor do we claim that the absence of moral sensibilities implies the presence of immoral attitudes or behaviors. Some people argue that much of statecraft is outside of the realm of morality. According to this view, international conflict is neither moral nor immoral. Examples of other influences on attitudes and behaviors having little to do with moral sensibilities are obvious, even among moral actors. They include misperceptions, organizational influences, political pressures, lack of personal steadfastness, stress, surprise, fatigue, and cultural factors.

Second, our research centers on attitudes and judgments, and it is not directly concerned with behavior. Our methodological focus is on what people say about policy issues. Possessing an attitude and displaying it may not be the same thing. People's attitudes can sometimes be correctly identified in the absence of predictive power about their behavior, partly because in bureaucratic situations people's actions often are controlled by an organization. Still, while people may not always act according to the attitudes they express, it seems a safe assumption that elites are, for the most part, consciously aware of their basic attitudes on such crucial matters as war and peace. If given the opportunity, their attitudes will influence their decisions.

Third, our effort focuses on the attitudes of elites, not of the mass public. For decades most public opinion scholars have argued that one cannot go directly from models of elite judgment to the attitudes of the mass public. Recently, however, the general perception of unstructured public attitudes has begun to change as the importance of core beliefs in attitude coherence has become apparent. Jon Hurwitz and Mark Peffley argue that for the average citizen, "paucity of information does not impede structure and consistency; on the contrary, it motivates the development and employment of structure. . . . [We] see individuals as attempting to cope with an extraordinarily confusing world . . . by structuring views about foreign policies according to their more general and abstract beliefs" (1987, 1114). So while our results for U.S. elites cannot automatically be generalized to the American public, it is important to note that the idea of core beliefs is at the heart of our model as expressed in a person's fundamental sensibilities.

Finally, our work focuses on motivations but does not provide unique criteria for judging whether a particular action or motive is morally justified. It is not our intention to provide general, principled rationales for conduct. Indeed, our research suggests that many people are subject to incompatible moral and practical pressures. Rather than using one single measure for moral judgment, substantial portions of U.S. elites accept a small number of different belief systems. While these belief systems have certain shared basic elements, they differ in some of their specific rationales for engaging in conflict and on the types of military actions that can be justified once a war has been engaged. Consequently, a nation's people may be almost unanimous in their conclusions about some issues in international affairs, while intense debates will rage about other policies.

DIFFICULTIES IN INVESTIGATING BELIEFS

The religious and philosophical literatures have produced many ethical conjectures about the nature of conflict, but these often are a mix of different levels of discourse and claims to knowledge. The sorts of philosophical, theoretical, empirical, and semantic issues that typically demand resolution in such investigations have seen little discussion in the quantitative social science literature.

An empirical approach requires operating from a particular research tradition, behavioralism, that rests on certain broad presuppositions. A fundamental question can be raised about studying normative belief systems in this way: Are the philosophical presuppositions of behavioralism, and particularly survey research as a methodological technique, sound enough to allow such study? Two core questions stand out among the possibilities. First, are there any reasons to suppose that a behavioral study cannot tap elite moral attitudes? Second, are there any major philosophical perspectives in ethics that are incompatible with the fundamental presuppositions that underlie survey research?

The Issue of Meaning

Justifying the use of behavioral techniques to study ethical belief systems requires that we address some deep issues of language meaning. At least three broad views exist regarding the proper interpretation of language that bear upon the difficulties involved in discovering the meaning of people's moral beliefs.

An objectivist view understands moral sentences to have determinant meanings that can be uncovered and empirically investigated. In other words, there is no essential difference between a dispute about moral matters and a dispute about factual ones. Hence, from an objectivist view, there exists no reason in principle to object to behavioral studies of moral attitudes.

A subjectivist view, which is sometimes associated with nonnaturalism, intuitionism, or noncognitivism, argues that moral statements are nonobjective opinions or intuitionist views. More specifically, a moral theory is subjectivist if it argues that moral judgments are neither true nor false or if it argues that moral judgments, regardless of their truth value, are primarily reflections of the psychology of individual observer's desires, feelings, biases, and so on.

Accordingly, the subjectivist view suggests that moral standards are more a matter of individual taste than objective duties or features of a moral world. If so, then moral disputes cannot be settled by empirical methods. However, subjectivism does not necessarily exclude the possibility of moral discourse. People do, in fact, talk to one another about moral issues, and words such as *good* and *bad* must have some intersubjective meaning. Accordingly, a subjectivist might accept the possibility of describing moral attitudes, suitably relativized to particular social contexts, even if moral disputes involving those attitudes could not be settled. In ethics, the existence of social, virtue-centered moralities, such as Confucianism, are evidence for the possibility of shared community meanings with respect to moral talk. In short, subjectivism does not preclude the possibility of survey descriptions of contending moral attitudes, and this is the major point we wish to establish here.

The Wittgensteinian view rejects the idea that language has a literal meaning outside of its use. No literal meaning is conceded to exist. Meaning is use. Accordingly, a unified semantic account of language meaning is impossible. More broadly, Wittgensteinians argue that the search for general explanations is not appropriate to philosophical inquiry. This view seemingly rules out all empirical approaches to the study of ethical attitudes, and, indeed, Wittgenstein's highly particularistic view is embraced by some contemporary ethicists. Stated simply, "Ethics cannot be put into words" (Wittgenstein 1961, 6.421).

We might include with the Wittgensteinians all other views that emphasize a highly decentralized, private nature of moral meanings. Here is found deconstructionism, whose proponents tend to dismantle all moral principles in the belief that texts have no fixed meaning. The view also might embrace various mystical traditions, which argue that transcendental moral ideas must be understood through nonlinguistic and nonempirical means. Any real understanding of ethics must be empathic, and such knowledge cannot be studied scientifically. Among foreign policy scholars, Charles Kegley describes the contours of such a view:

> It is likely that the analysis of foreign policy opinion is bound up with a general (and unexplained) theory of state-society relations, a theory that stresses the role of the individual as a register of opinion and sovereign source of public will. . . . Such a theory may be contrasted with a social theory of cognition, which holds that human understandings . . . are socially or culturally (not individually) constituted through a ceaseless dialogue within the community as a whole. From the latter point of view, expressions of "opinion" are not taken to be registers of some set of psychological dispositions fixed within the individual mind. They are instead understood as passing contributions to an open-ended dialogue in which people within a political culture simultaneously appeal to socially recognized interpretive themes (mutually comprehensible ways of seeing and regarding the world), articulate understandings in performing their socially established roles as citizens, and contribute to the dialogue by which these themes and understandings are affirmed or transformed. (1986, 450–51)

This brief account of the various possible interpretations of word meaning allows us to identify a number of important points regarding efforts to use behavioral techniques to study ethical belief systems. First, there is no clear consensus among philosophers about how moral language should be understood. Without such a consensus, one can raise epistemological doubts about almost all social science research. Second, some key philosophical perspectives, such as the objectivist and at least some subjectivist outlooks, are compatible with the basic assumptions of behavioralism. Only the Wittgensteinian view is clearly incompatible with a survey research approach that neither insists on probing highly idiosyncratic attitudes nor requires the study of a radically alien discourse group.

Metaethics

However, such philosophy of language considerations only establish a generalized possibility for behavioral studies of these attitudes. One might argue plausibly that moral discourse is more elusive than ordinary talk. To explore this issue, we turn to metaethics. At least four relevant, and not necessarily mutually exclusive, metaethical positions can be distinguished here. Naturalism sees ethical statements as having meanings and truth values that can be established empirically. Nonnaturalism views ethical statements as having truth values but holds that ethical meanings cannot be defined in any logical or empirical manner. Intuitionism argues that moral discussions depend on at least one primitive term, such as *good,* which stands for an objective moral reality that cannot be confirmed empirically but must be intuited. Noncognitivism views ethical statements as simply not having a truth value; their meanings cannot be defined logically or empirically. Instead, ethical statements serve functions like expressing a speaker's general feelings or declaring principles.

This overview again reinforces the notion that it is possible to study ethical belief systems empirically. Any school of thought, such as naturalism, that argues for objective moral judgments must believe that they can be interpersonally validated. Furthermore, many philosophical schools of ethics hold that it is at least possible to talk in some meaningful manner about one's ethical beliefs. In this sense, most metaethical outlooks are not Wittgensteinian in tone, since they would not rule out the empirical study of moral attitudes. Second, many philosophers believe that the nature of moral utterances, moral meaning, and moral reasoning remain problematical. The Wittgensteinian view and related outlooks might raise doubts about capturing ethical attitudes with behavioral methods, but these are only doubts. At this stage in our understanding of the role that moral belief systems may play in public policy, we should seize every opportunity to shed light upon normative attitudes and beliefs and to probe the limits of empirical methods in this endeavor.

Philosophically, a behavioral research design is consistent with either the objectivist or moderate subjectivist outlooks. With respect to the notion of truth, survey research embraces a reality-grounded semantic conception. Truth is thought to be derived from correspondence relations between language and descriptive states of the world. If challenged as to why such a conception of truth should be presupposed, supporters of this position would argue that empirical research requires a reality-based view, and there seems to be no other plausible noncorrespondence alternative. Of course, the assumption that truth is empirically approachable does not imply that it is easily attainable.

Complexities in Deriving Ethical Belief Systems

A discussion of some of the complexities of applied ethics in foreign policy decision making should be useful at this point. Of particular interest is the just war doctrine, which offers one of the more complicated sets of normative prescriptions in foreign policy. Its essence lies in one seemingly simple principle. The golden rule holds that one should follow the policies you wish others to adopt or, more traditionally stated, Do unto others as you would have them do unto you. Beginning with this premise, just war thinkers reason that military action is an acceptable policy option only when waged against the guilty to protect the innocent. From this viewpoint, killing in a just war is regrettable, but it is acceptable because one is taking the life of the guilty as a last resort to protect the life of the innocent. Such killing is to be distinguished from murder, which is the immoral act of taking the life of an innocent, that is, one who is not threatening other innocents. As applied to international politics, it is considered moral for a government to fight a defensive war in case of attack by a murderous state. However, just war doctrine insists that there are certain moral limits that the defending state must not violate.

While it might seem that the derivation of just war precepts should be relatively straightforward, their application may involve complex theoretical, strategic and empirical factors. Indeed, a contemporary debate rages over whether the just war precepts are solid enough to offer any guidance in real-world decision making (Yoder 1984; Secrest, Brunk, and Tamashiro 1991b). How do we decide when another state has crossed the line and war becomes a moral alternative? How can we tell when all options short of war have been exhausted? On logical grounds, it seems that many disparate positions are possible. In short, as in much of the philosophical literature, a thesis that appears to be simple can mask many complexities. If the reasoning complexities are great, then they will overwhelm the systematic components to decision making and few statistical covariances will exist in people's attitude structures.

In general, adoption of a coherent ethical framework raises philosophical, theoretical, empirical, and semantic issues. It is a philosophical issue in that deriving a coherent position involves understanding the ethical content and moral logic that underlies the framework. It is a theoretical issue in that one must consider policy-making patterns and conventions and the strategic properties of the nation-state system. It is an empirical issue in that this derivation must be applied to distinct technological contexts and political issues, which in turn requires determining specific factual matters. And it is a semantic issue in that this derivation rests crucially on fine distinctions of word meaning.

For example, justifying the application of just war precepts demands some background ethical theory, and some of the ethical theories that might be called upon to defend just war principles are controversial. Just war thinking focuses on the principles of discriminate means and proportionality in war conduct. Two different ethical theories might be summoned as warrants for these principles. The ethical theory that stands behind discriminate means says that some actions, such as purposely targeting civilians in war, are inadmissible under any circumstances. Another theory, sometimes referred to as consequentialist, argues that no actions are morally inadmissible a priori, and all policies must be judged in terms of their consequences. A seemingly unattractive action may be morally acceptable if it has good consequences.

Consequentialist thinking underlies the proportionality directive of just war logic. A consequentialist would argue that one determines what is right in terms of what is good, and what is right is what yields good consequences. In contrast, the opposite ethical approach holds that one determines what is right independently of the good. Some actions are right or wrong because of their nature, not because of their consequences. Two experts working from opposing moral theories might both accept the more fundamental principle of the golden rule while rejecting just war doctrine, because just war thinking legitimizes certain background ethical theories that are objectionable. Conversely, two people might both accept the just war doctrine on the basis of different background ethical theories.

A third matter that could split experts over the just war derivation concerns ethical presuppositions. Just war precepts presuppose that war can be a purposeful political and moral activity. True, just war thinking dictates that war should be a measure of last resort, but by specifying the rules for waging war, just war thinking legitimizes it as an instrument that may be used to adjudicate certain value conflicts. On the other hand, some argue that the golden rule teaches self-abnegation and absolute love and that the biblical injunction "Love thine enemy" is the proper way to understand the golden rule (see. e.g., Gordis 1964, 9–11). Accordingly, how faithfully just war precepts preserve the spirit of the golden rule can be debated. Just war may promote temperance while the golden rule directs abstinence.

The force of these philosophical themes is that experts might decide on technical grounds to accept the golden rule and still split over the appropriateness of just war thinking. Or they may all embrace the just war doctrine, but not for the same reasons. The ethical entailments linking the golden rule to just war can be unclear for experts and nonexperts alike, but the inferential uncertainties extend further because, even if philosophical disputes do not arise, splits can emerge from theoretical differences. It is possible to accept the golden rule, accept the validity of just war precepts on ethical grounds, and yet reject just war precepts on the basis of nonethical theoretical beliefs about the international system.

For example, suppose that one recognizes the golden rule on moral grounds and accepts nuclear deterrence on theoretical grounds, and suppose that one believes it is theoretically impossible to fight a nuclear war and remain faithful to just war precepts. Under these conditions, one could agree with the golden rule, together with a deterrence policy intended as a bluff, while at the same time doubting the efficacy of just war constraints governing the waging of nuclear war. Indeed, this is not far from the position described in the French bishops' pastoral letter as an ethic of distress ("French Bishops' Statement" 1983). In their view, implementing French deterrence policy would be condemned by the Second Vatican Council as a crime against God and man; yet the bishops argued that this logic cannot be pressed too far. While it is immoral to use these weapons, the threat to use them still is needed to ward off nuclear blackmail, since a dispute between superpowers can quickly become a game of chicken, where the first nation to declare that it will not use nuclear weapons loses credibility. Therefore, it is possible to support the golden rule while rejecting just war implementation on theoretical, rather than ethical, grounds.

Another example of such theory generating irony springs from Graham Allison's (1971) bureaucratic politics model, which argues that the foreign policies of a modern state are the product of complex and often unpredictable behavior. Under such circumstances, the leadership of a government might act purposefully, but because of command and control problems or high-level bargaining tangles, its final position may be unpredictable and unintended in its application. In such a situation it is possible to reject just war rules as unsound, since one's country cannot hope to abide by them.

Finally, if one holds philosophical, theoretical, and empirical issues in abeyance, it is still possible to have disputes on semantic grounds. The intuitions embodied by just war precepts may be self-evident, but the meanings of the terms used to convey those intuitions are not. In turn, this variation in word meanings can call up different understandings, empirical bases, theoretical outlooks, and philosophical concerns. For example, the golden rule calls on people to treat others as they might wish to be treated, but the status of these others is unclear. Should *others* be operationalized as other individuals, or can the term refer to collectivities such as other governments? Is it conceivable for someone to accept the golden rule at the individual level while rejecting just war precepts at the nation-state level in a manner akin to Reinhold Niebuhr's distinction between moral man and immoral society?

As yet another example of semantic complexity, we note that one of the just war precepts directs that the state must have a just intent in waging a war, but it is not obvious what constitutes the state in this context. Are sovereign states presumed to have some sort of collective intention? If a collective mentalism is not implied, are the state's intentions to be identified with its leaders and officials? If so, must unanimity exist among officials before a state can be said to have an intention? If not, then which officials' intentions are to be taken as those of the state? Clearly, this is ambiguous, and it is not trivial hairsplitting. The meaning we assign to the word *state* will indicate what sort of verifiability criteria should be applied in determining whether the state has good intentions. If the state is taken to mean its leader, then we might seek psychological evidence. If the state is defined as a bureaucratic entity, then we might look at policy-making processes for telltale standard operating procedures. If the state is defined as a unitary rational actor, then external government behavior would become our primary focus.

Given this semantic flexibility, it is not hard to imagine experts disagreeing over the acceptability of just war precepts because of divergent semantic understandings. In fact, the practical applicability of just war standards to modern warfare has become an area of debate among contemporary experts. Some of them question whether its traditional criteria can offer decision makers any substantive guidance and whether the doctrine can really act as a restraint on the conduct of nation-states. The difficulties in applying just war precepts are illustrated by three quite different assessments of the Gulf War by just war theorists. One concluded that the U.S. had waged a virtually perfect war by just war standards. Another reviewed each precept and cited some violations but refrained from drawing any general conclusions regarding the war's overall justness. A third strongly condemned the United States, stressing its violation of the proportionality requirements because he assumed there had been extensive Iraqi casualties. In general, the three assessments differed in both their understandings and their applications of the doctrine's proportionality requirements (*La Civiltà Cattòlica* 1992; Walzer 1992; Weigel 1992).

Are There a Manageable Number of Moral Belief Systems?

Such issues would seem to make the investigation of moral attitudes problematic. Perhaps this is why the study of normative belief systems in international relations has remained largely in the philosophical realm where fine distinctions of meaning, rather than empirical generalities, dominate scholarly exchanges. Despite this, some researchers speculate that the practical decision-making landscape of nonphilosophers is not filled with the minute distinctions that animate academic discussions. As yet, this hypothesis has not been adequately tested for conflict beliefs, but if the supposition is true, it would make mapping attitudes feasible, particularly if certain beliefs are deductively related.

Why might only a relatively few belief systems dominate among nonethicists? This might occur if observing particular rules provides their followers with individual or group survival benefits. Among social choice theorists, James Buchanan and Gordon Tullock first argued, in *The Calculus of Consent* (1962), that certain types of rule systems have utility-maximizing benefits for governments, but their work was overlooked by most political scientists, who ignored social choice models during the 1960s and 1970s, when they were unpopular with the political left. In game theory situations, certain normative strategies, such as tit-for-tat, also have been found to be more successful in computer simulations than alternative competing strategies (Axelrod 1984).

Historical case studies also support a strategic explanation for the adoption of normative positions. John Roemer (1985), for example, examining the situation in Russia before the 1917 revolution, argued that the ideologies adopted by Lenin and the czar were strategies designed to maximize their different goals. Similarly, the actions of Mahatma Gandhi can be seen as a means to force the British colonial government of India to adopt his political program (Chatterjee 1974). It is not difficult to imagine real-world situations in which all the traditional approaches toward warfare would have some utility to their followers. While adopting the precepts of pacifism would rarely assure survival in the modern world, pacifism's tenets were useful to some people in medieval times, when those who demonstrated extreme religious faith were treated with deference. In modern times, nonviolence also has proven a useful strategy in certain limited situations.

If these speculations about the usefulness of certain normative rules are correct, then the frequency of adoption of various belief systems regarding warfare should differ among elite groups according to the goals and functions of each group. Beliefs promoting a group's collective goals should have more value to their members than beliefs that are opposed to a group's goals or only marginally related to them.

Another source of the possible tractability of moral belief systems rests in consistency in reasoning. This requirement was used by Thomas Aquinas and later medieval philosophers to justify their advocacy of just war doctrine. Various empirical studies in political science have found that as individuals become more knowledgeable in a policy area, their attitude structure also becomes more coherent (see, e.g., Kuklinski, Metlay, and Kay 1982).[8] Even some politicians have been noted to become more consistent the longer they stay in office. This probably is because systematic reasoning is easier to defend than a series of ad hoc explanations for each successive action (Asher and Weisberg 1978). House Speaker Tip O'Neil often told newly elected freshmen, "Tell your constituents the truth the first time, and then you won't have to remember what you said."

Even though many people use systematic reasoning to organize their beliefs, this is no guarantee that everyone will come to a consensus about public policy. The most significant contemporary philosopher who has addressed this matter is John Rawls (1971), who believes that societies can discover a fair set of rules once their members are willing to divorce themselves from their real-world positions. But this argument has been increasingly challenged by empirical researchers who find that individuals inherently favor different sorts of rule systems (e.g., Reynolds and Shelly 1985; Bayer 1990; Ricoeur 1990; Bond and Park 1991). Rather than reflecting a consensus on reasonable governmental policy and on the nature of justice itself, preferred rule systems seem to reflect fundamentally different personal sensibilities. If Rawls's critics are correct, then no fair set of rules can ever achieve universal approval. Instead, consensus occurs only when all the commonly adopted rule systems agree about the nature of proper conduct.

Nevertheless, the well-informed elite may recognize that sometimes there are only a few easily defensible moral belief systems and that a manageable number of policy prescriptions flow from them. Most individuals will be drawn to one of these few platonic positions. Which moral belief system individuals adopt may emerge from a matching process whereby people try to find the ethical position that best accords with their fundamental reality and normative beliefs. Seen in this light, a major goal of government officials becomes better understanding the different moral belief systems of their citizens and avoiding as far as possible those situations where commonly held belief systems pull people in opposite directions regarding policy.

SUMMATION

What can we conclude from this short survey? After decades of approaching politics from a rational self-interest perspective that has denigrated the role of traditional ethics, scholars are increasingly returning to a belief that normative concerns do make a difference in some people's attitudes and can make a difference in public policy decisions. While there are formidable problems facing a quantitative study of ethical attitudes, having examined the philosophical assumptions of survey research, we can see no reason why such a methodology cannot be used to examine moral belief systems.

The insights of empirical data analysis in testing moral conjectures should be theoretically rewarding as long as careful interpretation is used to clarify the issues under study. Unfortunately, up to this point the technical mastery of statistical matters has likely exceeded our interpretive understanding of the ethical realm. Accordingly, the temptation to use purely data-driven, atheoretical methods has been great, but such uninformed analyses are unlikely to be very useful, because alone they cannot penetrate the interpretive complexities of applied ethics. Instead, atheoretical methods blindly employed are apt to generate superficial and misleading findings. It is less clear whether the complexities of applied ethics are so great that they will overwhelm any systematic components in the attitudes of U.S. elites. That issue will have to be decided empirically.

FOUR

Research Design

Scholars have tried to infer the fundamental sources of public policy attitudes in a variety of ways. Among quantitative political scientists, a common approach is to examine responses to closed-ended survey items. Attitudes are said to be constrained if people who feel a certain way about one policy tend to have a predictable direction of response toward another policy. This sort of attitude constraint approach is usually applied to survey items measured at the same level of complexity.

In contrast to the straightforward methodology of simple opinion surveys, social psychologists often use open-ended questions in trying to infer the structure of human thinking. While social psychologists have generated important conjectures about moral reasoning using this methodology, it has a peculiar type of failing all its own. Respondent comments are open to an even greater degree of interpretive laxity than is true of attitude constraint studies based on Likert-type survey data. This is because it is particularly difficult to shield open-ended comments from being viewed from the wrong perspective, and researchers' interpretations of how people reason may be more a reflection of their own biases than the actual way their subjects think.

Previous research into the nature of political reasoning suggests that a combination of approaches might be particularly useful in investigating conflict belief systems. The first consists of posing a series of Likert items, which ask people how much they agree or disagree with statements embodying various precepts of the traditional schools of thought. The second approach consists of open-ended questions based on short scenarios designed to elicit in-depth comments about the rationale for one's attitudes regarding particular conflict situations. Our work builds upon the best aspects of both approaches. While our statistical analyses are based on Likert items, our substantive interpretations of the quantitative data are supplemented by numerous open-ended comments by the elites who participated in our study.

LIKERT SURVEY ITEMS

The use of Likert items is the most reasonable approach for statistically examining ethical belief systems. Of course, all empirical methods have distinctive strengths and weaknesses, and a Likert-type survey is no exception. One criticism that might be raised about such inquiries is their brevity. Can moral queries be captured in such reduced form? To establish this possibility, we note that moral attitudes are often condensed into proverbs in the traditional literature and these serve the purpose of moral heuristics. Such proverbs represent the distilled wisdom of long human experience and are indicators of attitudes that find application in particular situations.[1] There is no reason in principle that survey research would not be useful for monitoring such attitudinal indicators.

The just war doctrine is one of the more intricate teachings on war, but it consists of a series of moral rules expressed in the form of maxims. Thomas Aquinas, one of the doctrine's leading developers, held that its underlying principles could be understood and even discovered by ordinary folk through the application of reasoning. Likewise, the fundamental argument of the reason of state doctrine is that moral considerations are irrelevant in war decisions, and this concept also is easy to embody in Likert items. An example from our survey that probes support for the reason of state approach reads: "We should go to war whenever it is to our advantage." The basic positions of the legalism and the retaliatory ethic doctrines are equally straightforward and clear; for example: "If a foreign enemy stops observing moral principles, we should also stop observing moral principles."

Rule-based approaches have displayed surprising power in complex reasoning environments. Examples include expert systems in artificial intelligence and computer simulations of morally distinctive competitors in game theory contexts (Axelrod 1984; Tamashiro and Brunk 1985). Indeed, some authorities argue that such maxims are to be preferred in such a context because they focus people's moral judgments in applied situations (Nye 1986, 97–100).

There is another important methodological issue here. In principle, can summary survey items span the range of important moral perspectives? Three points should be raised. First, concerning comparativeness, our subsequent statistical analysis will show that there is enough shared meaning among the traditional schools to sustain a careful, comparative, survey-based inquiry. Second, concerning whether all key moral perspectives are accessible using Likert items, of course it is possible that some sources of moral knowledge are beyond our empirical methods. While the problem of inductive inference is never completely settled, theorists understand that their best moral speculations may be an incomplete or biased subset of a larger moral reality. Still, this potential for incompleteness has not discouraged ongoing inquiry. Just as useful mathematics gets done within the confines of Goedel's Incompleteness Theorem, so too does useful social science continue within the limits of its own conditions of inductive incompleteness.

Third, with respect to whether Likert items preserve moral meanings and do justice to moral subtleties, no research design can completely preserve meaning in such a translational sense. It is difficult to establish synonymy in such research, and it is impossible to separate that part of a word reflecting its meaning from that part reflecting background information. Despite this fundamental indeterminacy in the use of language, it is possible to distinguish good applications of survey methods from poor ones. More to the point, we believe the essence of the various traditional moral schools of thought toward warfare can be captured without lapsing into a series of crude caricatures.

The results of a pilot survey administered to pretest potential survey items indicated that it was impossible for most respondents to distinguish among many of the minor variations and subtleties found in the philosophical and religious literatures about conflict. Accordingly, we tried to strike a balance by constructing characterizations detailed enough to preserve the distinctive features of each traditional school, yet simple enough so as not to exhaust our respondents or artificially press people beyond their normal discriminatory inclinations.

In contrast to Likert items, open-ended interviews have well-known and peculiar failings of their own. Regarding ethical belief systems, this is best illustrated by an example of how a researcher's preconceptions might influence interpretations of such data. Suppose that a respondent is a moral perfectionist and acts according to the fundamental principle that one should always promote the physical well-being of others. Next, suppose that our respondent muses in the context of an open-ended interview that in some contexts it is all right to lie to children — to frighten them away from using drugs, for example — but that in other contexts it is wrong to lie. Particularly if the respondent is unaware of these underlying principled appraisals, we might mistakenly believe the answers came from a metaethical relativist who believes that no way exists to identify a correct moral code.

In other words, even disregarding potential researcher bias, an open-ended interview may not unfold at the proper level of generality for correct interpretation. If so, it becomes difficult to identify apparent attitude switching as an outcome of a fixed underlying principle expressed under different circumstances. Philosophers call this descriptive relativism, as contrasted to metaethical relativism. In conducting our research, we discovered that it was common for individuals to be unaware of their own position relative to the precepts of traditional ethical doctrines. Normative scholars of the ethics of warfare might be particularly blind to seeing this problem since they are so immersed in the subtleties of their field.

If we try to safeguard an open-ended interview procedure against the danger of wrong interpretations, we have to introduce fine distinctions that usually are not held by the technically untrained — descriptive relativism versus metaethical relativism, for example. This path is open to great peril, since our pilot survey showed that most respondents are unable to make such technical distinctions. As noted by many critics of this approach, as a technique, open-ended interviews may produce results that are mostly an artifact of the externally imposed distinctions of researchers rather than the attitudes, however untutored, actually held by their subjects.

Some of the evidence analyzed by social psychologists probably suffers from this problem. While their work is valuable in explaining how moral development progresses in children, when classifying adults by their level of cognitive development some social psychologists have been baffled by why seemingly sophisticated people morally "regress" to a lower stage of reasoning when dealing with certain sorts of problems. Such an apparent anomaly likely occurs because the wrong distinctions are imposed on the open-ended questions these researchers use in formulating their theories.

An apparent example of this is Lawrence Kohlberg's (1980) belief that political liberalism reflects of the highest level of cognitive development.

He reached this conclusion after finding that only cognitively advanced individuals could incorporate empathy for others into their thought processes. But does this mean that all political conservatives are cognitively immature, or that conservative political logic represents a "regression" to a lower level of reasoning? To conservative scholars, this contention is implausible, if not patently offensive. Why it is implausible will become clear as we examine the effect of risk assessment on the structure of moral belief systems. The risk involved in following altruistic beliefs in real-world situations was a factor of evaluation that Kohlberg did not explore, and it could not readily be revealed by examining the sorts of data he collected using an open-ended research design.

The problem of researcher bias is even more obvious when we examine the applied public policy literature. Ideological biases are often the major determinant of one's conclusions, and quantitative techniques are not a panacea for the problem (Brunk 1989). With regard to certain hotly debated issues, such as the efficacy of the death penalty, it is often possible to predict how researchers will interpret their statistical evidence by knowing their political ideology. Since most social choice theorists view all behavior as a single-minded quest for one's self-interest, this has led them to conservative policy prescriptions. Leftists can be similarly myopic, seeing economic or conspiratorial elements in many government actions which they think are taken to defend the economic position of a privileged elite.

In selecting a Likert format as a major tool, we judged that imposing ethical queries of great complexity would not harmonize with our principal goal of determining the fundamental building blocks of conflict belief systems. In designing our survey, we tried to appropriately abstract from the diversities of human experience to explore general attitude profiles. To reduce researcher bias, we refrained from stipulating meanings for the normative terms used, and in a cover letter we directed respondents to impute their own meanings to basic terms. Whether we decided wisely should be determined by the plausibility and usefulness of our findings.

DEVELOPING A SURVEY

Initially, it was unclear to us whether nonscholars could distinguish among all the perspectives about conflict found in the traditional literature. A number of academics argue that the most important issues in moral analysis for philosophers are not of similar importance to nonscholars (e.g.,

Donagan 1977; Hare 1981; Kohlberg 1981). Because of this speculation, we suspected that some of the doctrines on conflict described in chapter 2 might be too far removed from everyday life for even well-educated elites to distinguish among them. To determine if this was the case, we conducted a trial run of a longer form of the survey. In it we included more than a hundred Likert items designed to tap the various frameworks. Respondents were asked to indicate whether they "strongly agreed," "agreed," were "uncertain," "disagreed," or "strongly disagreed" with each statement. The pilot study was administered to academics, military officers, our students, and others, who were asked to provide detailed comments on the items.

For an ethical school to be included in the final version of the questionnaire, we demanded that a consistent response pattern be observable among the pretest subjects. Responses to the individual items that tapped each ethical doctrine had to be correlated with each other in an interpretable manner. Failure to observe such a pattern indicated that our respondents did not have a cognitive structure that was related to the principles of a particular doctrine. Because this criterion was not met by the items that represented the ethics of utilitarianism and fatalism, these doctrines were dropped from the final questionnaire since the intricacies of these two schools of thought seem to be too esoteric for most Americans to distinguish.

In the cases of moral perfectionism and moral nonperfectionism, those who strongly supported the statements that tapped one of these two approaches tended to strongly oppose the statements that tapped the other. Consequently, the two ethics form the opposite ends of the same cognitive dimension. Moral perfectionists answered in a manner that put them at one end of the dimension, while moral nonperfectionists answered in a way that put them at the opposite end of the dimension. Therefore, the same set of items can be used to measure support for both schools of thought.

A common complaint of the pilot respondents was that our survey instrument was much too long. To ensure maximum response rates from busy elites, survey length became a major constraint.[2] Taking advantage of the fact that the principles of many traditional doctrines overlap, we were able to shorten our instrument by reducing the number of items that explicitly tapped each doctrine to three inquiries. The only exception was the just war doctrine. A more or less standard list of seven specific items catalog the conditions that determine whether a war is just. By these means, we were able to keep the survey to a reasonable length and elicited responses from many high-ranking American elites who might otherwise have refused to respond.

The thirty-four items included in all five versions of the final survey instrument possess three attributes. First, they are theoretically meaningful. Second, they attempt to tap separate aspects of a particular framework. Third, they are correlated in the correct direction with other questions tapping the same framework in the pilot study. To prevent the problem of response set, whereby an individual may get into the habit of answering an entire series of questions in either the affirmative or the negative, we randomly worded questions negatively or positively whenever possible.[3] The items then were randomly sorted and did not appear in the order they are presented in table 4.1, but did appear in identical sequence on all five versions of questionnaire. Besides providing the exact item wordings, this table also provides the item number and name of the particular principle of a framework that is being tapped by each inquiry.

THE ELITE GROUPS

Previous studies have found that elite profession is a predictor of foreign policy attitudes. However, a common complaint about many of them is that their elite populations were so poorly defined that what groups were being surveyed was often unclear. We solved this problem by using well-defined populations that clearly represent specific elite groups rather than the general public. Our five subject groups were chosen in an attempt to maximize the differences in norm acceptance caused by institutional roles and to provide a broad cross section of government and nongovernment elite opinion. The samples consist of members of Congress, diplomats, journalists, military officers, and the parish priests and hierarchy of the American Catholic Church. By choosing such a varied selection of individuals, we attempted to maximize variation in responses among groups and took advantage of the best attributes of a cross-sectional, correlational research design. This means that we should be able to better separate the influences of fundamental moral sensibilities, political ideology, and elite position in determining attitudes toward conflict.

Each of the five versions of the questionnaire began with the same baseline set of thirty-four items. Since the foreign policy attitudes of military veterans have been found to be more coherent than those of non-veterans (e.g., Kirkpatrick and Regens 1977), we reasoned that many military officers probably had career experiences that crystallized their

Table 4.1 **Survey Items**

Golden Rule
1. **Golden Rule Principle:** Our government should treat other countries in the same way that we want to be treated.
2. **Spying:** If we do not want other nations to spy on us, we should not spy on them.
3. **Treaties:** If we want other countries to keep their treaty promises, we should keep our treaty promises.

Just War
4. **Competent Authority:** A war must be legally authorized before it can be considered to be moral.
5. **Discriminate Means:** Efforts to avoid killing civilians are necessary for a war to be moral.
6. **Just Cause:** A war must be an act of self-defense in order for it to be moral.
7. **Just Intent:** A moral war must seek only to defeat the enemy's military and not to totally destroy his society.
8. **Last Resort:** It is not moral to fight a war until all peaceful alternatives have been tried first.
9. **Probability of Success:** It is not moral to fight a war that one has no chance of winning.
10. **Proportionality:** The amount of war damage and casualties to both sides is important in deciding whether a war is moral.

Legalism
11. **Legalism Principle:** If there is a conflict between one's personal moral beliefs and our country's law, one should obey the law.
12. **Surprise Attack:** If legally ordered by our government, it is all right to launch an attack against another country.
13. **War Crimes:** If the only way to avoid defeat in a battle is to commit a "war crime," then we should do so.

Moral Crusade
14. **Duty to Punish:** When at war, we have a moral duty to punish and totally destroy the enemy.
15. **Forced Conversion:** It is all right to use military force to convert others to our beliefs.
16. **Isolationism:** There are moral values so important that we should not deal with those who disagree with these values.

Moral Perfectionism
17. **Absolute Principles:** Moral principles are absolute and do not depend on the situation.
18. **Context:** Our country's decision to go to war should be based only on universal moral principles and not on the particular context facing our nation.
19. **Military Planning:** Our military planners should not rule out any type of future military actions because of moral principles.[a]

Nuclear Pacifism
20. **MAD (Mutually Assured Destruction) Deterrence:** It is morally acceptable to threaten the use of nuclear weapons against enemy cities as a way to prevent nuclear attacks against our cities.[a]
21. **MAD Retaliation:** Destroying enemy cities with nuclear weapons is immoral even if our cities are attacked with nuclear weapons first.
22. **Nuclear War:** It is better to accept defeat than participate in a nuclear war.

Table 4.1   *Continued*

Pacifism
23. **Nonresistance:** Morality requires that a nation should not resist if attacked by a foreign country.
24. **Nonviolent Resistance:** If one must choose either nonviolent resistance or participating in a war, nonviolent resistance is the only moral choice.
25. **Prohibition on Killing:** It is always wrong to kill another person, even in war.

Reason of State
26. **All that Matters Is Victory:** The only thing that matters in war is victory.
27. **National Advantage:** We should go to war whenever it is to our advantage.
28. **National Interest:** National interest, rather than morality, should determine our foreign policy.

Retaliatory Ethic
29. **Harsh Response:** Harsh and unrestrained military actions are justified against an enemy who launches an unprovoked attack on our nation.
30. **Negative Reciprocity:** If a foreign enemy stops observing moral principles, we should also stop observing moral principles.
31. **Revenge:** Revenge against an enemy's civilians is morally acceptable if that nation has attacked our civilians.

Supreme Emergency
32. **Evil Justifies Ignoring Morality:** Sometimes our enemies are so evil that it may be necessary to ignore moral concerns in order to win a war.
33. **Preventive War:** It is all right to attack an enemy first, before he becomes strong enough to defeat us.
34. **Supreme Emergency Principle:** If an enemy's goal is the total destruction of our nation, morality should still influence our actions in times of war.[a]

Note: Items were randomly sorted and did not appear in this order in the survey, but were in the same order in each version of the questionnaire. The ethics of *moral perfectionism* and *moral nonperfectionism* are measured as opposite ends of the same scale.

a. Disagreement indicates support for the framework being probed. Coefficients computed using this item need sign reversals for proper interpretation.

thinking about morality and warfare. It seemed likely that their experiences — 54 percent of military respondents had been in combat — would have caused many of them to ponder the ethics and morality of warfare, but clearly few of these military officers can be considered to be technically skilled moralists. Feeling that it would be easier to interpret the attitude structure of such a relatively cognitively coherent population, we used retired officers as the first subjects in our research in 1986 (Tamashiro, Secrest, and Brunk 1989; Brunk, Secrest, and Tamashiro, 1990). On the basis of their open-ended comments, in subsequent versions of the questionnaire we added additional items designed to measure in greater detail the interesting theoretical issues that emerged from our initial analysis.

The orientations of the five groups regarding international conflict should be quite varied. The clergy can be assumed to be well versed in just war theory, since the just war doctrine is official church policy and was used by the American Catholic bishops in their examination of nuclear weapons issues (Castelli 1983). The Catholic clergy constitute one living version of the skilled moralists described by Thomas Aquinas and other medieval theologians in their derivations of just war doctrine, but while they have studied the moral issues involved in war, unlike the military officers in our study they are not skilled in the practice of war.

The diplomats also are professionals in various aspects of international affairs, but they are not as skilled in the moral issues of war as clerics, nor are they as skilled in the practice of warfare as military officers. Some theories of norm acceptance predict that these foreign service officers should have relatively coherent attitudes toward international conflict since they possess the most information about international affairs, but other theories predict just the opposite. Accordingly, since warfare issues were not particularly relevant to American diplomacy during the closing days of the cold war, the ethical aspects of conflict should not have been incorporated into the professional belief systems of most diplomats. Furthermore, the recently developed hierarchical approach to explaining belief systems suggests that technical information is largely irrelevant to attitude coherence. Those who use a few general organizing principles in structuring their attitudes do not become so bogged down with the details, exceptions to rules, and special cases often cited by the diplomats in our study.

Congress is the most studied of American institutions. Most contemporary students of its behavior have adopted a self-interest perspective and assumed that the drive for reelection is the ultimate political goal that shapes a member's decision calculus. But unlike the other elites examined here, members of Congress represent distinct geographical constituencies, and the truism that all politics is local may so completely structure congressional decision making that many legislative scholars argue that the general good is never considered by Congress members and private interests always predominate. Congress, however, also is given the ultimate constitutional power to declare war, and this is an area where individual interests would seem to have very limited influence. So the institution's special war-making responsibilities may have caused many members of Congress to incorporate systematic beliefs about international conflict into their modal belief system.

Our final subject group consists of journalists. Because the fourth estate is relied upon to inform Americans about the implications of foreign policy, it may have a distinctive modal position on warfare that reflects its institutional biases. However, there is no consensus in the scholarly literature about the nature of such biases. It may be that journalists' attitudes largely reflect the dominant political ideology, whims in public opinion, or current government rhetoric. Regarding foreign policy, this would mean that journalists routinely ratify most foreign policy decisions or, at the very least, accept the interpretive slant offered by American leaders. An alternative thesis is that journalists unthinkingly savage national policy in an unreflective fashion (see, e.g., Robinson 1976). A third, intermediate, position is that the media mirror government positions when there is little dissension, but freely adopt a wide variety of stances when a consensus does not exist.

Taken together, these five elite groups should be expected to have very different institutional perspectives on the issues of morality and war that may be reflected in their belief systems. We chose our exact samples from national mailing lists. The questionnaire was sent to 1,000 retired members of a major organization of military officers, of whom 620 responded. The survey of diplomats was conducted by sending letters to both the chief of mission and the public affairs officer at each foreign diplomatic post. These letters described our project and asked for encouragement of voluntary participation. Varied numbers of questionnaires were sent for distribution to willing foreign service officers, according to the post size. We received 511 completed questionnaires, but have no way of knowing how many were distributed. In 1987, the survey was mailed to all 382 members of the American Catholic hierarchy, of whom 84 returned the instrument. It also was sent to a random sample of the 18,000 priests assigned to U.S. parishes. Of the 1,518 questionnaires mailed in this manner, 382 parish priests returned the instrument.

Our sample of editorial-page editors of daily newspapers was drawn at random from a list provided by the Editor and Publisher Company. It was sent to 1,586 individuals, of whom 371 returned completed forms. In 1988, we sent a version of the questionnaire to the mailing addresses of all retired members of Congress who are listed in the *Directory of the United States Association of Former Members of Congress*. Each of the 583 members of this organization was sent a personal letter requesting participation in our study. Undoubtedly, a number of the letters never reached their intended destination and many were screened out by secretaries. A major problem with conducting elite research is that responses may not be coming from the desired population. Instead of studying members of Congress, one really may have collected data on their secretaries' opinions.

Table 4.2 **Political Ideology, by Elite Group** (in percent)

	Liberal	*Moderate*	*Conservative*	*Group Average*[a]
Diplomats	30	56	14	28
Catholic priests	25	48	27	32
Journalists	19	63	19	33
Members of Congress	25	48	27	34
Military officers	3	41	56	51

Note: Totals may not equal 100 percent because of rounding.

　　a. The average ideology of a group is based on rescaling responses so that liberal = 0, moderate = 50, and conservative = 100.

Our solution to this problem was to include an item at the end of the survey asking if it had been filled out by a member of Congress or a staff person. Over 45 percent of the questionnaires were returned, but because 95 of the congressional surveys were answered by staff members, only 169 were usable.

Respondents' Characteristics

We also gathered data on a wide variety of potentially important demographic and attitudinal characteristics in hopes of obtaining a better understanding of the sources of elite policy attitudes. While many characteristics have been found to be weakly related to foreign policy attitudes by past researchers, political ideology is one of the few important variables known to be correlated with conflict beliefs.[4] Because of this, an item that appeared on all five versions of the survey reads, "What is your political viewpoint?" The possible responses were "liberal," "moderate," and "conservative." Table 4.2 presents the percentage of individuals in each of the five groups who defined themselves as adherents of one of these political positions. With the exception of the military, there was not much ideological difference among the groups. The retired military officers in our study tended to be markedly more conservative than the other U.S. elites. Only 3 percent of the military officers claimed to be liberals, while this figure ranged from 19 to 30 percent among the other groups.

　　Another characteristic of potential theoretical relevance that has substantial variability among respondents is the size of one's hometown. Commentators on the American scene often argue that people from rural areas and small towns are inherently more moral than are their cousins from big cities. According to a game theory perspective, this is because altruistic behavior can thrive in the small closed populations that define small town America, but altruism is only infrequently reinforced in large cities where repeated social interactions are rare.[5] There was a substantial difference among the elite groups in the value of this hometown variable. On average, the respondents from the smallest towns were journalists, which reflects the random geographical sampling of newspaper editors.

There was also substantial variation in rank and career specialization among the elites. Among the Catholic clergy, 18 percent of respondents were members of the hierarchy. Among the military, 3 percent were junior officers (rank O1 to O3), 86 percent midlevel officers (O4 to O6), and 12 percent senior officers (O7 to O10). Among the diplomats, 20 percent were junior level, 52 percent midlevel, and 29 percent senior level. The difference in average rank between the military respondents and the diplomats probably reflects their age differences, since we surveyed mostly retired military officers, but all the foreign service officers were on station. The average age of the diplomats was 41 years, while it was 57 years for the military officers. There also was a broad mix of specialties. Among the foreign service officers, for example, 15 percent were administrative, 12 percent consular, 17 percent economic, 38 percent political, 13 percent USIA, and 6 percent other categories. Similar variability exists on a wide range of other demographic variables.

Finally, we asked a number of questions designed to measure the elite characteristics that we thought would be the most salient or interesting for our investigation. Given the recent attention paid to religion and politics, members of Congress were asked a series of questions about religious fundamentalism and the role that religion should play in politics. The clerics were asked whether they belonged to a religious order, if they were well informed about church teachings on war, and whether they had a strong interest in world affairs. Among other things, diplomats were asked whether they believed people are basically good or evil. Military officers were asked a series of items about their combat experience and career history. Newspaper editors were asked what general influences were the most important in developing their views on morality and war. When appropriate for our discussion, we will refer to such data in later chapters.

FIVE

American Endorsement of Normative Criteria

The broad principles that should govern our international conduct are not obscure. They flow out of the practice by the nations of the simple things Christ taught. — John Foster Dulles

The traditional literature outlines a series of prescriptions for dealing with conflict issues. Because of the large number of policy remedies that can flow from the different solutions that are advocated by the various frameworks, it would be useful at this juncture to determine if any of their basic precepts are supported by contemporary U.S. elites. We approach this issue in three steps. First, we examine the percentage of all respondents who agree and disagree with their precepts. This provides a very broad overview. Second, we determine the average level of support for the traditional frameworks by each group to see if any systematic differences exist among elites. Finally, we examine in more detail elite support for specific principles of war justification and war conduct.

To produce estimates of support for the frameworks, we took the average level of support for all the items representing their tenets as listed in table 4.1, above. For purposes of this analysis, the responses of "strongly agree" and "agree" have been collapsed into one category, as have "strongly disagree" and "disagree."[1] This initial evidence is based on the total number of respondents. Of the 2,152 elites who participated in the survey portion of our study, there were 620 military officers, 511 foreign service officers, 481 clergy, 371 journalists, and 169 members of Congress.[2]

DOCTRINAL CONSENSUS AND DISUNITY

Elite divisions are more salient than consensus in our survey results. The nature of these divisions across the different doctrines reveals some interesting variations. The acceptance of attitudinal norms often is measured by asking people the sorts of questions used to construct table 5.1. While there is no consensus in the literature about the percentage of individuals who must accept a proposition for it to be considered part of a group's norm structure, the most commonly used standard is 90 percent agreement or disagreement, although some writers have lowered this to 80 percent. None of the traditional frameworks is accepted at the 90 percent level by U.S. elites, and only pacifism and moral crusading are rejected by 80 percent or more of the respondents.

This initial evidence seemingly indicates a lack of any strong consensus on norms about international conflict among U.S. officials and opinion leaders, which may explain why policy disputes arise frequently when a war drags on without resolution. After an initial rally-round-the-flag stage, the passage of time allows people to see that they disagree over the justification for conflict or how a conflict should be waged and, more important, to realize they disagree at a fundamental level. Nevertheless, this apparent surface disunity among Americans invites further investigation into the nature of support for the traditional viewpoints.

The Golden Rule

Among all the approaches to conflict, the golden rule precepts are given the greatest support. There is an average of 70 percent support for the golden rule items, only 27 percent disagreement, and 3 percent are uncertain. Our respondents overwhelmingly agreed with the two items that read, "Our government should treat other countries in the same way that we want to be treated" and "If we want other countries to keep their treaty promises, we should keep our treaty promises." The only major bone of contention regarding the application of the golden rule in foreign policy concerns spying. A substantial majority disagree with the proposition, "If we do not want other nations to spy on us, we should not spy on them."

Moral Perfectionism and Nonperfectionism

A closer examination of table 5.1 shows that at a fundamental level U.S. elites are split about the reasonableness of perfectionist moral reasoning. While an average of 57 percent support elements of nonperfectionist reasoning, 35 percent believe that perfectionist logic is the only defensible

Table 5.1 **Support and Opposition for the Doctrines** (in percent)

	Support	Opposition
Golden rule	70	27
Moral nonperfectionism	57	35
Just war	50	43
Supreme emergency	48	43
Moral perfectionism	35	57
Legalism	35	51
Retaliatory ethic	27	65
Reason of state	24	70
Nuclear pacifism	22	68
Pacifism	11	85
Moral crusade	8	87

Note: Figures give the average level of support among all respondents across each precept of a doctrine. Support is defined as "strongly agree" or "agree." Opposition is defined as "strongly disagree" or "disagree." Responses to appropriate items are reversed (see table 4.1, note). *Moral perfectionism* and *moral nonperfectionism* are measured as opposite ends of the same scale. Totals may not equal 100 percent because of rounding and because individuals could choose "uncertain" as a response.

approach when deciding matters of foreign policy. Since this is such an important philosophical distinction, it would seem that in this decision-making criterion may lie a fundamental source of attitude and policy divisions. American decision makers and opinion elites do not agree on this basic principle of reasoning regarding conflict issues. As a result, they are not likely to agree as well on a series of related issues or the doctrines that embody their principles: What are the proper rules of the game in the international arena? What constitutes a serious violation of the rules? What should be done about such violations?

Just War

The potential policy divisions among Americans become more evident as we move to their evaluations of just war logic. While just war's principles receive the third highest level of support, with 50 percent approval, they also are opposed, on average, by 43 percent of respondents. Consequently, the application of just war logic to conflict situations seems a likely area for future policy disputes. This disagreement on the basic rules of the game in international affairs becomes even more evident when we examine support for just war's norms of war justification and norms of war conduct.

Supreme Emergency

This approach argues that commonly observed constraints on war should be obeyed unless a state's national existence is imperiled by an evil enemy.

Since one stream of the supreme emergency doctrine evolved from the just war tradition and has a similar derivation from just war thought, it is not surprising that Americans are as split regarding the reasonableness of supreme emergency reasoning as over the broader matter of just war logic. While 48 percent of elites allow for the possibility of suspending moral constraints under extreme circumstances, 43 percent reflect a more perfectionist type of reasoning and are opposed to the possible suspension of widely accepted rules of war under any circumstances.

Supreme emergency reasoning is also evident in a number of the comments expressed by U.S. elites. As one example, in answering whether a person could commit a war crime to prevent certain military defeat, a captain argued that it "depends on how serious is the result of the loss of one battle." Another military officer responded in a similar manner: "Depends on the enemy. . . . If he intends to subjugate us, yes. But not just any enemy."

Legalism

The legalist doctrine is intricately woven into military life because of the practical necessity for soldiers to obey the legitimate orders of their superiors. Regarding legalist theory, the ethical problem facing contemporary military personnel is the potential that some orders may not be legitimate because they involve actions that are illegal according to their nation's own laws or are war crimes prohibited by international convention. Although in the past U.S. troops have committed serious atrocities in such conflicts as the Philippine Insurrection, the potential for this type of behavior by American forces was not widely publicized until the massacres of Vietnamese civilians. The military services responded to the moral problems presented by My Lai by making a serious effort to clarify for their personnel the differences between valid and invalid orders, but despite these efforts, subsequent studies often found that the general requirement of unquestioned obedience to orders obfuscates the possibility that illegal orders may be issued. As a result, a substantial minority of enlisted personnel continued to reject even the theoretical possibility that illegal orders could be issued by an American officer, and during the 1970s it appears that about one in four U.S. soldiers would have been willing to engage in war crimes if so ordered (Bachman, Blair, and Segal 1977; Cockerham and Cohen 1980).

Some of the officers we contacted had resolved this dilemma by dismissing the possibility that American soldiers could ever be given illegal orders. Such an argument was well expressed by an admiral who was involved in the early stages of our research. At the level of broad military policy, he argued, all issues involving illegal orders and war crimes are, in practice, irrelevant for U.S. personnel: "In spite of the Nuremberg trials, you cannot allow military men to decide what legal laws they will obey and not obey. If our civilian government is doing its job, all laws, ipso facto, are moral laws, or they would not have become laws in the first place."

What is seen in the data regarding the application of legalist principles appears to be disarray rather than consensus. On average, the component principles of legalism are supported by 35 percent of American elites but are rejected by an average of 51 percent. This sharp division of opinions about legalism has led some U.S. elites to a particularly cynical position. As one midlevel officer who had served in Vietnam put it, "What is a war crime? The usual definition for me is a loser. Anything a loser does is a war crime." Another officer who had served in World War II and Korea argued that soldiers may have no practical choice about the commission of war crimes. Like the admiral quoted above, he felt that the moral issue here is moot: "Morality in war is a tough problem. The Nuremberg trials set a precedent that leads to an inevitable conflict between morality and discipline in which the losing service man is in danger of being labeled a war criminal when his only alternative at the time was to be executed for disobedience."

On the other side of the debate over the application of legalist principles are those who strongly oppose any reflex action that calls for obeying orders without thought. For such people, any unthinking acquiescence to their government's policy positions is immoral. A cleric commented, "A person's individual moral conscience, a well-informed one, far outweighs a country's laws. Integrity of the human conscience should not be violated." Given such opposition to unthinking obedience to secular authority, it should come as no surprise that the attitudes of military and religious leaders are quite different toward certain foreign policy problems.

Retaliatory Ethic

We operationalized the retaliatory ethic using survey items that measure willingness to countenance revenge, negative reciprocity, and a harsh response. This approach, sometimes called tit-for-tat, has proven very successful when pitted against alternative strategies in computer simulations (Axelrod 1984). The retaliatory ethic also is a matter of some dispute among Americans. On average, the retaliatory ethic is supported by only 27 percent of U.S. elites and is opposed by 65 percent.

In reflecting this ethic and responding to the item that reads, "Our government should treat other countries in the same way that we want to be treated," a captain noted that he agreed with the idea but "only so long as they reciprocate." In a similar vein, a newspaper editor offered a disapproving comment on what he saw as the natural outcome of the retaliatory ethic in becoming a Gresham's law of morality: "In the end, there is no morality in war. The British terror-bombed German civilians. The Americans shot surrendered Japanese. . . . In war, the lowest common denominator predominates. Bad morality drives out good. After it's over, the winners decide who was moral."

Reason of State

The items tapping reason of state thinking were crafted to measure the amoral version of this doctrine and deal with issues of national advantage and national interest. The comments of one foreign service officer reflected an implicit approval of the reason of state approach because of the impracticality he perceived in applying any moral standard to the day-to-day problems of international affairs:

> It seems to me that a fundamental political problem in a country like the U.S., where moral values are generally deemed important but where no established ideology, moral code, religious orthodoxy, etcetera, exists, is the effort of those who do find their policy preferences in morality to impose an ethical value judgment on others, something alien to the U.S. system. It is precisely because U.S. ideals reject imposition of particular ethical systems on the populace as a whole that attempts to impose a morally based policy, whether by the right, Ollie North, the conservative social agenda, or by the left, as exemplified by the modification of the Carter Administration's excessive emphasis on human rights, or the nuclear freeze movement, generally fail.

Surprisingly, given its overwhelming importance in the international relations literature, the amoral reason of state approach lacks substantial support from U.S. elites. An average of only 24 percent agree with the reason of state items we posed, and these have an average disapproval rate of 70 percent. Nevertheless, a closer examination of other responses by the U.S. elites indicates that two types of reason of state logic can be discerned in their attitudes. The first is the commonly recognized amoral variety or Machiavellianism, which is captured by the three reason of state survey items. But there is also a moral or ethnocentric variety of reason of state, which is captured by other inquiries in our survey. It was reflected in many comments, particularly by military officers. A senior officer said regarding the distinction between morality and national interests, "They should be linked to one another." A captain commented, "I cannot conceive of our national interests not being moral." Still another officer argued, "I believe that morality is one of the bases, as well as goals, of our nation. Therefore, our foreign policy is a reflection of our morality, and our national interest is of a moral character."

A version of the moral reason of state approach was also embedded in the comments of some members of Congress. A generalization as it may apply to Western democracies — and a theme recently given prominence in the scholarly literature — was expressed by one of them: "Wars among democratic, constitutional, nonsocialist governments rarely, if ever occur. So when we really consider war we are talking about nasty governments as enemies, and this makes a difference." Another member of Congress elaborated on the general theme of a characteristic American morality: "The people of the United States are sovereign. They have all of the power. Generally speaking, the people have made the right decisions; and I have confidence that when our citizens are given the facts, they will make the right decision for the country and the world." A final comment by a foreign service officer is useful in reinforcing the perception that many U.S. elites support a morally based or ethnocentric reason of state approach. "Morality is an essential part of U.S. foreign policy, and thus intimately embodied in U.S. national interest. Thus in some extreme circumstances, moral equals that which achieves the national interest."

Pacifism

There is an average of only 11 percent support for the pacifist items among Americans and an overwhelming 85 percent disapproval toward this doctrine's separate principles. The essence of this opposition to pacifism was succinctly stated by a member of Congress: "To preserve peace, a potential enemy must be afraid of you and not know exactly what our national response will be." The strategic problems presented by adopting a governmental version of pacifism were stressed by another member of Congress:

> As one who tried to be a Christian, all war is, I think, immoral, but evil is in the world and to fight it wars have seemed necessary for survival. In my time Hitler represented the greatest evil, with Stalin a close second. If Hitler had obtained the atomic bomb before we did, I don't believe the civilized world would have survived. Our only hope is the prevention of war, and that depends, I think, on military strength until that day when all people lay down their swords and spears.

The real-world problem that must be considered by decision makers is that a nation can be successful and practice pacifism only if all other nations have adopted a like policy. As a national strategy, it can be defeated by any foreign leader who is willing to use military force.

Nuclear Pacifism

The nuclear pacifism viewpoint also is rejected by most U.S. elites, but it has more support than does universal pacifism. While on average 22 percent of elites approve of the component principles of nuclear pacifism, an average of 68 percent disapproval is evident, as well. In rejecting the U.S. policy of nuclear deterrence during the cold war, a cleric commented, "The theory of deterrence is childish and morally lacking—groundless. Nuclear attacks will be prevented only through dialogue, common understanding between nations of our unique spiritual and moral and philosophical views. We must work at this end and stop childish games of roulette."

Moral Crusade

Given the often heard criticism that the United States has engaged in a series of moral crusades to support capitalism and ideological principles around the world, our last general finding about American elite support for specific conflict doctrines is the most surprising. Among contemporary American decision makers and opinion leaders, the lowest level of support is given to moral crusading principles. There is an average of only 8 percent support for its individual tenets and 87 percent disapproval.

ARE DIFFERENT DOCTRINES MODALLY SUPPORTED BY ELITE GROUPS?

Overall, Americans seem to favor an ethical approach to war that is nonperfectionist. They reject both the perfectionist extremes of pacifism and the moral crusade and reject the amoral reason of state approach, as well, but behind these generalities may lie serious divisions.

Table 5.2 shows the level of support by each group for the various frameworks. In this canvassing of opinions, two groups seem to stand apart from the other three. The clerics provide the highest level of support for the golden rule, just war doctrine, moral perfectionism, pacifism, and nuclear pacifism. They exhibit the least support for moral nonperfectionist reasoning, supreme emergency and legalist arguments, the retaliatory ethic, and reason of state and moral crusading outlooks. Almost mirror opposite positions are held by American military officers. The military

Table 5.2 **Support for the Doctrines, by Elite Group** (in percent)

	Members of Congress	Diplomats	Journalists	Military Officers	Priests
Golden rule	72	64	73	63	81
Moral nonperfectionism	62	62	56	75	25
Just war	51	45	45	36	65
Supreme emergency	39	28	25	44	8
Moral perfectionism	27	29	26	19	68
Legalism	46	29	28	61	8
Retaliatory ethic	35	25	27	44	5
Reason of state	31	24	20	41	3
Nuclear pacifism	16	15	22	5	55
Pacifism	11	9	13	6	17
Moral crusade	10	6	7	11	4

Note: Figures refer to the average level of support among respondents in each group across the precepts of a doctrine.

gives the greatest level of support to moral nonperfectionism, supreme emergency reasoning, legalism, the retaliatory ethic, and the reason of state doctrine. Military officers also offer the greatest level of support for moral crusading, but even among the military the support for this approach to decision making is only 11 percent, which is just marginally higher than the average of all other U.S. elites.

Between the positions of the military officers and the Catholic clerics are the three secular groups: members of Congress, the diplomatic community, and journalists. While there are statistically significant differences in the evaluations of the traditional frameworks by these three groups, the differences tend to be smaller than those between the seculars and the military and between the seculars and the clerics. Consequently, we can conclude that in some important way the beliefs of Americans vary according to their positions in society. Given this evidence, it appears that norms of proper decision-making behavior toward international conflict problems are somehow integrated into the cognitive patterns of certain elites. This observation merits a deeper examination of how elite positions in society are related to their attitudes toward the two major components of the doctrines: justifications for war and constraints on war conduct.

JUSTIFICATIONS FOR WAR

American attitudes regarding war justifications and war conduct can also be examined in terms of elite group norms. These issues are at the heart of the just war doctrine, whose application is hotly disputed. While we already have discussed the general tenets of the major conflict doctrines, it is useful to elaborate as well on their justifications for initiating conflict. Disagreement about what causes can justify going to war mark the key differences among the doctrines of just war, pacifism, moral crusade, and reason of state.

Justifications for Conflict

Over the past two thousand years, there has been a continual evolution of the just cause requirement in just war doctrine. On the one hand, it has been firmly established that certain causes can justify war, and this has required the rejection of pacifism by just war theorists. On the other hand, just war thinking has evolved in the opposite direction from the moral crusade and reason of state doctrines toward particularistic interpretations of the just cause requirement, which has narrowed the list of potential causes that can justify a resort to war. By the twentieth century, evolution of the just war component of international law led to the idea that only national defense against a major armed attack could justify war.

A number of causes were rejected through this winnowing process. One was the use of war to export religious or secular beliefs as justified by the moral crusading and holy war doctrines. Another was the military advancement of reasons of state and national interests, other than those of national survival when threatened by armed attack. Certain causes were also eliminated. These can be found in the writings of early just war thinkers who allowed military responses to nonmilitary actions of other states or to military actions that did not threaten substantial harm. In the latter category, the last resort principle was important as a *jus ad bellum* requirement when controversies short of actual warfare developed between states. Today, the narrowing of the just cause principle to response to an armed attack has almost nullified the last resort requirement. Nevertheless, exceptions to this generalization occur in attempts to morally justify preemptive and preventive wars. We include the last resort requirement here because it is a key indicator of attitudinal restraint on the issue of resort to war.

Turning again to the survey items, five of these are particularly relevant in determining the norm structure of justifications for warfare. Item 6 is the just cause provision of just war doctrine: "A war must be an act of self-defense in order for it to be moral." Item 8 regards just war's last resort requirement: "It is not moral to fight a war until all peaceful alternatives have been tried first." Item 15 regards the moral crusading and holy

Table 5.3 **Agreement with Justifications for War, by Elite Group** (in percent)

Survey Item and Principle	Members of Congress	Diplomats	Journalists	Military Officers	Priests
8. Last resort	81	71	79	58	94
6. Just cause	45	42	43	28	77
15. Forced conversion	4	6	2	8	2
23. Nonresistance	4	2	4	2	4
27. National advantage	1	2	1	3	1

Note: Norms are defined as positions accepted or rejected by at least 90 percent of group respondents. Thus all values greater than or equal to 90, and all values less than or equal to 10, represent norms.

war justification of forced conversion: "It is all right to use military force to convert others to our beliefs." Item 23 speaks to the pacifist policy of nonresistance: "Morality requires that a nation should not resist if attacked by a foreign country." Item 27 is the national advantage issue from the amoral reason of state doctrine: "We should go to war whenever it is to our advantage."

The data in table 5.3 indicate that a level of consensus exists among elites regarding some of these warfare justifications. Three of the five items are so overwhelmingly rejected by Americans that their rejections constitute attitudinal norms for all five groups. Americans soundly reject engaging in war simply to promote our national advantage and engaging in war to force others to adopt U.S. beliefs. Similarly, all five groups reject the pacifist position that nations should not resist when attacked by others.

There also is substantial agreement among the five groups regarding the last resort principle: one should exhaust all other measures before resorting to warfare. A recent example of the importance of this principle concerns the Gulf War. Before U.S. forces entered Kuwait, spokespersons for the countries allied against Iraq devoted considerable effort to crystallizing public opinion by arguing they had attempted to meet all the *ad bellum* just war criteria before entering into the conflict. Shortly before the push into Kuwait, one of the few issues that remained in dispute was whether the last resort criterion had been met or whether the allies should have given Iraq more opportunities for peaceful withdrawal.

As is often the case with many of the just war criteria, this was a judgment call, and particular just war elites could debate the issue. Any strict implementation of the just war doctrine can have serious strategic disadvantages. To buy time and forestall an attack, an enemy such as Iraq could manipulate the just war rules by continually pretending to be about to withdraw from an occupied state. During the interim period, the society and infrastructure of the conquered state could be so systematically destroyed that little might remain to be liberated. Given this circumstance, many just war scholars would conclude that a war to remedy the conquest would accomplish so little that it would no longer be just.

The last resort criterion is an attitudinal norm only for the clerics. Not unexpectedly, the most opposition to this criterion comes from the military, but even 58 percent of them support the last resort standard. Sandwiched between the attitudes of the clergy and the military are the attitudes of the three secular groups, with 71 to 81 percent of the diplomats, members of Congress, and the media supporting the last resort principle.

All in all, there is a remarkable level of consensus among American elites on the justifications for war. The major matter likely to provoke controversy is the just cause issue. The only substantial disagreement evident over basic principles is whether a war need be an act of self-defense for it to be moral. As is becoming the repeatedly observed pattern in our data, the clerics and the military often sharply disagree over U.S. policy. Clerics show the most support for the just cause criterion, at 77 percent, while military officers agree with it the least and provide only 28 percent average support.

CENTRAL AMERICAN WAR SCENARIOS

While a consensus exists among U.S. elites on most of the theoretical justifications for warfare except the just cause requirement, this requirement is not a trivial matter. It is at the heart of most propaganda efforts at the beginning of wars. Thus, these differences in norm structure demand more investigation, and for this purpose we developed a series of scenario questions to measure in greater detail the legitimacy U.S. elites ascribe to various conflict justifications. However, the finding of these initial normative differences among elites occurred during the analysis of data from the first waves of our survey, and while this discovery allowed us to craft a series of additional items to examine these differences in greater detail, we are limited to examining variations in their support by those who responded to the supplementary items in the later waves of the survey. This is because they were asked only of the diplomats, journalists, and the clergy.

Since some elements of just war thinking are disputed by Americans, its precepts provide a useful organizing structure for discussions of war justifications. The controversy over just war principles relevant to U.S. actions in Central America was particularly heated during the Reagan administration, which often took a moral crusading position in its public pronouncements (Kornbluh 1987; Krauthammer 1985, 1986). The Soviet Union was called an "evil empire" and potential enemies were branded as being so evil or U.S. goals so just that any actions employed to punish and destroy the enemy were reasonable. Since Cuban and Nicaraguan aggression posed a "clear threat" to Latin America and the southern United States, the actions of the Reagan administration were morally required. To quote the president in reflecting such a viewpoint, his policies were "morally . . . the only right thing to do" (see Reagan 1984).

The American justifications for hostile actions against perceived enemies in Central America were addressed by the World Court in *Nicaragua v. United States* (1986). The court ruled customary international law regarding Nicaragua's supplying arms to El Salvadorian rebels was intervention rather than armed attack, and while Nicaragua had violated international law, its violations were not serious enough to justify the U.S. responses in the name of collective defense. In mining Nicaraguan harbors and attacking its oil installations the United States had violated the obligation not to use force against another state. American arming and training of the contras also were ruled illegal by the court (Henken et al. 1987, 708–36).

Although contemporary just war theorists consider national defense to armed attack to be the main justification for the resort to war, they differ on whether there are exceptions to this emphasis on defensive war. The Reagan administration cited a series of categories of justification to support its 1983 military intervention in Grenada and its policies toward Nicaragua. A number of these categories may have been important in evaluating just cause in terms of the Nicaragua controversy.[3] They include preventive war, preemptive war, humanitarian intervention, and military intervention to protect the right of national self-determination. Using many of these just war justifications, we developed a series of scenarios regarding potential Nicaraguan actions and asked U.S. elites whether they thought any of them could justify the use of American military force against that nation.

Preventive War

A preventive war is a conflict waged against a nation believed likely to conduct military aggression. In the usual scenario, the military balance of power is thought to be shifting toward a potential aggressor who could become more powerful in the foreseeable future than a potential victim state. Consequently, attacking the potential aggressor before it can strike is really a defensive act. The reasoning is that principles of morality should allow potential victims to defend themselves by destroying their enemies before their enemies can gain a military advantage and harm the innocent.

The moral arguments against this type of war rest on the last resort principle of just war theory, which holds that all methods short of armed conflict should be tried before force is used. Those who argue against preventive war feel that it is an early resort to conflict that excludes lesser means. Preventive war justifications also are easily manipulated by jingoistic and paranoid leaders who see all nations as potential aggressors who must be destroyed. In Immanuel Kant's words, "There is no state whose leader does not wish to secure permanent peace in conquering all the universe."

A further complication exists regarding preventive war, since any nation pursuing the moral goal of self-defense may honestly err in estimating the intent of another state. As a result, launching a preventive war becomes choosing the certain evil of war over the uncertain evil of future aggression.

Preemptive War

A just fear of imminent danger, though there be no blow given, is a lawful cause of war. — Francis Bacon

A preemptive war also involves the innocent nation striking first, but only when a clear and present danger exists. Such would be the case if another country's army was moving toward our border with an obvious intent to launch an attack. The moral justification for preemptive war is that a state should not have to wait for an actual attack to be able to defend itself. Instead, a country should have the advantage of striking first so that it can defeat an obvious aggressor. Just war theorists are sympathetic toward this line of reasoning, although they place great importance on correctly interpreting other's intentions.

Humanitarian Intervention

Two of the fundamental principles of international law are the rights of states to sovereignty and the corollary duty of nonintervention in the internal affairs of other states, but important exceptions to these principles occur when a state uses its right to freedom from outside interference to conduct genocidal activities against its own citizens or to attack foreign residents. If the international community does not act collectively to prevent these abuses, then a foreign state may take military action to protect the innocent in another country. This is termed humanitarian intervention. In such cases, the motivation of the intervening state should not be its own self-interest, and the intervening state's actions should accord with the last resort requirement, which means that no other effective alternatives short of war are immediately available.

National Self-Determination

The morality of the use of force to protect another state's national self-determination is a matter of controversy among contemporary ethicists. Examples of this justification include Reagan's policy of aiding the "freedom fighters" in Central America who were attempting to overthrow Marxist governments and helping Islamic resistance fighters to defeat Soviet military intervention in Afghanistan (see Johnson 1988). The heart of this debate concerns the proper interpretation of the right of national self-determination.

The more common interpretation embodied in international law holds that a country has a right to determine its political system and domestic affairs without outside interference. A protector state may use military force to intervene only if there has been a prior military intervention by a third party. According to this principle, military action to protect national self-determination must be counterinterventionist. By this interpretation, U.S. aid to the *mujahidin* in Afghanistan was justifiable because of prior Soviet intervention, but U.S. support for the contras in Nicaragua violated that country's right to self-determination, as the Sandinistas had gained power without the help of any military intervention by outside forces.

American Attitudes

To measure support for these various justifications concerning the resort to force, we asked U.S. elites a series of questions that began: "Please check all the situations below that you feel are serious enough to justify the U.S. going to war with Nicaragua." The wordings of the specific scenarios are presented in table 5.4, as are the support percentages for the three groups who were asked to address these issues. The category of war described in each scenario is given as well.

The heart of a just war analysis is that military force generally should be used to defend against armed attack. In evaluating elite attitudes, let us begin with item 45, which embodies the defensive war justification with aspects of a preemptive war. A large majority of all three groups can justify the use of military force if it seems likely that a country is about to engage in aggression against the United States. Despite the generally high

Table 5.4 **Agreement with Justifications for a Hypothetical War with Nicaragua, by Elite Group** (in percent)

Survey Item	Diplomats	Journalists	Priests
Would support a war with Nicaragua:			
40. If Nicaragua sets up a communist government (protect the right of self-determination)	4	4	5
41. If Nicaragua starts a military buildup that overshadows its neighboring states (preventive war)	8	7	8
42. If Nicaragua sends aid (arms, advisers, etc.) to communist movements in neighboring countries (intervention or indirect aggression)	14	17	13
43. If Nicaragua invites Soviet military military bases to be set up within its borders (preventive war)	35	41	26
44. If Nicaragua invades a neighboring country (defensive war)	63	46	36
45. If there is clear evidence that Nicaragua is going to join an attack on the United States (defensive and preemptive war)	83	80	65

Note: The introduction to the Nicaragua scenarios reads, "Please check all the situations below that you feel are serious enough to justify the United States going to war with Nicaragua." Items did not appear in this order on the questionnaire. Norms are defined as positions accepted or rejected by 90 percent of group respondents. A version of this table appears in Secrest, Brunk, and Tamashiro 1991b, 548.

level of support for this scenario, the Catholic clergy are 15 percent less supportive of using force in this circumstance than are the two secular groups. While the military were not included in this portion of our study, it seems reasonable to assume that their answers would be at the opposite end of the scale of attitudes from the clerics on such matters.

Moving to an examination of item 44, the three groups are all substantially less supportive of using military force to defend a foreign nation that was a victim of direct Nicaraguan aggression. The responses to item 42, a scenario in which Nicaragua aids communist revolutionaries in adjacent countries, are interesting as well. Such actions in international law usually are considered to be intervention or indirect aggression, rather than aggression in the sense of an armed attack that can justify a defensive military response (von Glahn 1981, 576–85). Only small minorities of the three groups supported this justification for the use of force.

Central to the Reagan administration's justification for its attacks on Grenada and its policies toward the Sandinistas was the preventive war argument. The president claimed that Grenada had become a "Soviet-Cuban colony being readied as a major military bastion to export terror and undermine democracy" by allowing the construction of facilities for Soviet forces (Secrest 1986, 238). The administration also contended that the Sandinista government had massed such an array of conventional forces that it had achieved military superiority in Central America, had allowed Nicaraguan territory to become a Soviet strategic military asset and was becoming a Soviet client (Shultz 1986).

Two of the scenarios that we posed involved the justifiability of preventive war. Item 41 posits "Nicaragua starts a military buildup that overshadows its neighboring states." American elites overwhelmingly rejected this justification for war, and their rejection was at the level of a norm for all three surveyed groups. The level of support for the justification presented in item 42, wherein Nicaragua aids communist movements in other countries, was only slightly greater. In the case of a potential Soviet military threat, all three groups show greater support for preventive military action, although this is still below majority support.

The final scenario involves military intervention to protect the right of national self-determination. Just war scholars generally consider self-determination to be violated when an outside power intervenes to control another state's affairs. Accordingly, the existence of a communist government does not necessarily represent the absence of self-determination. A contrasting position was taken by Charles Krauthammer (1986). In supporting the Reagan Doctrine, he equated self-determination with electoral democracy.[4] If one accepts this position, then aid to the Nicaraguan "freedom fighters" was fully supportive of the self-determination principle. However, the responses to item 40 indicate that the three surveyed groups opposed the Krauthammer position, and their opposition was at the level of a norm for all three groups.

CONDUCT OF WAR

You may be obligated to wage war, but you are not obligated to use poisoned arrows. — Baltasar Gracian y Morales

Norms of elite conduct often are thought to crystallize when professionally derived rules are useful in furthering a group's goals. If the institutional goals of a group are strongly related to the problems encountered in international conflict, there is an expectation the group will develop a series of norms about proper war conduct. On the other hand, if a group's institutional purpose is less directly related to problems concerning conflict and settling international disputes, agreement is unlikely. Such a lack of consensus can occur in two circumstances. Either conflicting positions about proper conduct are held by different group members because of conflicting principles, or the attitudes of most individuals have not yet jelled into structured sets of beliefs because norms on these matters are largely irrelevant to the group's concerns.

The development of professional conflict norms is best illustrated by examining the case of military officers. Given the institutional interests of the elites whose attitudes we surveyed, the military should be the most concerned with the lives of their own group rather than those of the enemy. Since members of the military may be routinely involved in combat, their time frame for evaluating the consequences of hostile actions is likely to be quite short. A major worry will be the possibility of death in battle. This concern is likely to be so strong that it may override considerations for the long-run consequences of their actions for the international system. Conversely, a concern for one's personal well-being and that of one's comrades can also produce altruistic heuristics. This is how cooperation developed between opposing European armies during the trench warfare of World War I (Axelrod 1984). Both sides discovered that if they did not shell their enemy's food wagons, their opponents would let them eat in comparative peace.

The rules of the game likely to be held as norms among military officers are those that best support the advancement of their group goals. The collective outlook of military officers causes them to support many aspects of legalism, since legalist principles are highly supportive of their mission. For anyone living in the uncertain environment of the battlefield, failure to obey a legitimate order may be a suicidal act and endanger one's comrades. It is reasonable, as well, to suspect that military officers will show more support for war conduct norms that stress short-run consequences, less support for just war constraints that restrict their potential actions, and no support at all for pacifist sentiments.

These hypothesized military norms can be contrasted with those expected from the leaders of most U.S. religious denominations, whose institutional goals include improving the long-run good of humanity. Most contemporary Western theologians argue that we should value all life rather than only the lives of our restricted in-group. Although the leaders of pacifist churches believe that all life is sacred and that no one's life

Table 5.5 **Support for War Conduct Constraints, by Elite Group** (in percent)

	Members of Congress	Diplomats	Journalists	Military Officers	Priests
7. Just intent	81	71	79	70	95
5. Discriminate means	73	76	75	57	95
29. Harsh response	67	50	58	77	12
32. Evil justifies ignoring morality	52	34	38	57	8
26. All that matters is victory	42	22	27	59	6
10. Proportionality	24	29	22	10	64
33. Supreme emergency	35	15	19	31	4
31. Revenge	24	20	16	36	3
13. War crimes	24	13	17	30	3
14. Duty to punish	14	5	7	17	0

Note: Response percentages for item 32 are reversed to achieve consistency. For other items, agreement with the principle of a school is indicated by support. Norms are defined as positions accepted or rejected by 90 percent of group respondents.

should be taken, even in retaliation for murder, most contemporary American religious leaders have examined warfare issues from a strategic, long-run perspective. Consequently, they have concluded that it may be necessary to take the lives of military aggressors to save the lives of innocents. Since the pacifist position rarely is survival-maximizing, most Western religious leaders have adopted some version of the just war tradition.

On matters of war conduct, we expected that the attitudes of other U.S. elites would fall between the relative extreme positions of the military and religious leaders. While some of these individuals may have developed coherent beliefs about warfare, there is comparatively little in their institutional settings that would draw them to any particular set of international conflict norms.

Secular Elite Attitudes

The average levels of support given for the ten items concerning war conduct are presented in table 5.5. Because of the comparative complexity of interpreting such a large table, we also have presented the findings visually using z scores in figure 5.1. Here, each group's support for an item has been standardized by comparing it to the level of support given to all ten items by members of the five groups. A general pattern is again evident. The three secular civilian groups respond quite similarly. Most obviously, the positions of the journalists almost perfectly reflect the average

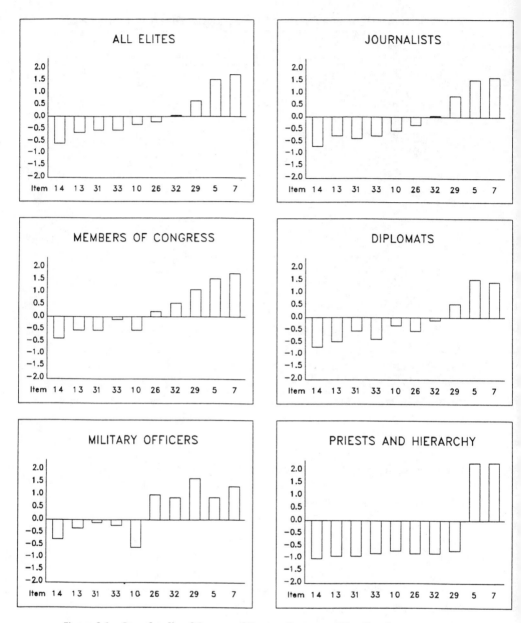

Figure 5.1 **Standardized Scores of Survey Items on War Conduct**

level of U.S. elite opinion on war conduct issues. Standing apart from the centrist elites are the military officers, whose attitudes are skewed in one direction, and the clerics, whose attitude pattern is skewed in a radically different way.

While the responses of the three secular civilian groups do not show clear and strong support for any particular approach, it is useful to discuss their responses in terms of potential norms. In the case of the just war doctrine, the two items of discriminate means and just intent protective of enemy civilians receive strong support, but only the just intent item can be called a norm for any group except the clerics, using even a weak definition of 80 percent support to determine norm acceptance. The proportionality item is strongly opposed by all the U.S. groups except the clergy. There is majority support for the harsh response items by all the secular groups, but the potential for harsh military response is soundly rejected by the Catholic priests. Regarding other items, the only point of general agreement among the secular civilian elites concerns the unacceptability of moral crusading, as represented by rejection of the principle that people have a duty to punish the enemy. In fact, rejection of moral crusading is the only norm of war conduct that is held by all five elite groups.

Although not a particularly strong pattern, the secular civilians also support waging war in a restrained way against enemy civilians (items 14 and 31) but not against enemy military forces (item 29). To some extent, the secular elites also support lifting morally based constraints in particular situations (items 32 and 33). They appear to be making a distinction between the legitimacy of attacking an enemy's military forces and that of attacking its civilians. This is evident in elite support for the discriminate means and just intent items, coupled with their rejection of the revenge motive and the proportionality requirement. The major situational factors that the secular elites accept as justifications for abandoning war constraints against an enemy's military are unprovoked attack and an imminent supreme emergency.

The pattern of responses of the secular elites consequently reflects a sliding scale of morality (see Walzer 1977, 228–32). The more one perceives justice in a war's cause or the greater the perceived injustice of a bad outcome, the greater the justification for abandoning commonly accepted constraints during war. United States secular elites consider "harsh and unrestrained military actions" as justified in the case of suffering an unprovoked attack (item 29), and they favor "ignoring moral concerns" to avoid defeat by evil enemies (item 32). The supreme emergencies posited in items 32 and 33 differ slightly. The emergency that is imminent receives over 40 percent agreement, while the nonimminent emergency receives only 20 percent support.

In exhibiting a sliding scale of moral judgment, the secular civilian elites appear to be using reasoning that stresses deductively derived principles but also adheres to a type of teleological logic that regards the circumstances of a situation and the consequences of actions as important factors in evaluating foreign policy. Such people are willing to take into account a concern for others in an enemy state, but they are not willing to bind themselves to universal rules that are independent of situational context.

More specifically, for these elites the perceived legitimacy of certain war actions and justifications also reflect the predominance of reasoning that stresses situational factors over the key principle of discriminate means. However, the latter restraint may not be set aside primarily because of such reasoning per se. Virtually everyone believes that circumstances and consequences must be taken into account when one chooses a course of action in war. The abandonment of the discriminate means principle stems from such teleological reasoning but is combined with underlying values that are not conducive to its survival. One source of the discriminate means principle is a combination of values that support the right to life of universal innocents as a supreme goal. Suppose that this goal is held along with the competing values of a concern for national others as well as protecting vital national interests. When a war involves situational factors that seriously threaten national others or national interests, the least immoral alternative for many people will be to withdraw what turns out to be the gift, rather than the right, of discriminate means from enemy civilians.

Military Attitudes

The military officers are the least supportive of just war constraints on the conduct of warfare against both the civilian and military sectors of an enemy state. In fact, rejection of the doctrine of proportionality is a norm among the military. While a majority of the military respondents favor constraints on warfare against enemy civilians, they do so to a noticeably lesser degree than other secular groups on the items of discriminate means and revenge, although there is little difference on the just intent inquiry.

While military officers strongly oppose a moral crusading outlook, they still support it more strongly than all other U.S. elites. At least 30 percent of them agree with all the non–just war items that sanction unrestrained warfare directed against the enemy's military. Among the modal military positions are approval of reason of state and supreme emergency logic and strong approval of the harsh response item. When contrasted with the other secular groups, the military show more agreement with war conduct principles reflecting the nonideological, teleological-consequentialist goals of national survival and victory embodied in items 14, 26, 29, and 31. They also show more agreement with principles that take into account interrelated situational and circumstantial factors, such as the nature of the enemy and its actions, as in items 29 and 32. The military's strong opposition to the proportionality requirement further suggests a value orientation that may legitimize unrestrained warfare against an enemy's forces.

Clerical Attitudes

Unlike the dissension evident among members of the Catholic clergy on issues of justifications for war, clerical beliefs constitute a clear norm system regarding the conduct of war. On war conduct issues, their norm system is the embodiment of just war doctrine. While the most obvious pattern regarding the clergy's responses is their strong agreement with just war principles regarding war conduct, we should also stress that these just war principles are incompatible with all the other major doctrines. Agreement with just war constraints not only requires support for the three just war items regarding war conduct, but also calls for a rejection of the other items. This pattern is clearly evident among the clergy, who show the greatest level of collective coherence evident among these three groups on war conduct issues. The only minor exception to this general pattern is the almost 30 percent drop in clerical support for the proportionality item when compared to virtually unanimous support for the discriminate means and just intent items.

The differences between the clergy and the U.S. secular elites on the retaliatory ethic and the supreme emergency items also are important. In consistency with just war doctrine, the clergy do not consider the particular types of actions or the goals of an enemy as relevant to how wars should be fought. There is no sliding scale of moral judgment here. In contrast, the secular groups use teleological logic in considering the circumstantial and situational factors that play a major role in their policy attitudes.

CONFLICTING MOTIVATIONS?

Thus far in our discussion, four conclusions stand out as particularly important. First, there is no consensus in the United States on the correct prescriptions that should be followed for evaluating warfare issues. Sec-

Table 5.6 **Support for Universalist and In-Group Sensibilities, by Elite Group** (in percent)

	Members of Congress	Diplomats	Journalists	Military Officers	Priests
Universalist sensibilities					
1. Our government should treat other countries in the same way that we want to be treated.	89	84	92	85	89
3. If we want other countries to keep their treaty promises, we should keep our treaty promises.	97	96	98	96	99
In-group sensibilities					
23. Morality requires that a nation should not resist if attacked by a foreign country.	95	98	95	98	95
25. It is always wrong to kill another person, even in war.	79	79	74	89	75

Note: Support for universalist sensibilities is based on how many in each group "agree" or "strongly agree"; for in-group sensibility items, figures are for "disagree" and "strongly disagree."

ond, while there is general agreement about the validity of certain particular justifications for warfare, some of the just war principles are in dispute. Third, there is little agreement about proper conduct in waging war. Finally, in almost all respects the military and clergy stand apart in their evaluation criteria from the three secular groups whose attitudes we have probed.

Our closer inspection of elite group responses suggests a likely reason for these findings and suggests why the validity of just war teachings is so disputed. The empirical evidence indicates that people are motivated by two competing moral sensibilities when making judgments about the reasonableness of military conflict. One moral sensibility is based on the golden rule, emphasizing such virtues as empathy, restraint, generosity, mercy, and kindness. The other is an in-group morality that demands loyalty, team spirit, self-sacrifice, and the elevation of in-group goals over the needs of competing groups. In international relations, nationalism is the strongest manifestation of this second sensibility. There is much evidence to suggest this pattern. First, the data in table 5.6 indicate that all U.S. elites strongly support both universalistic and in-group sensibilities. Extensive comments by the decision makers and opinion leaders who participated in our study confirmed this pattern. It seems improbable that all five groups were confused and, moreover, confused in the same aggregate manner.

A common indication of a fundamental value conflict among survey respondents is agreement with items that match their values even when these items are incompatible. Our survey patterns seem to fit this interpretation, as does the traditional normative literature, which highlights the importance of the fundamental moral tension between golden rule sentiments and self-interest or group interests (e.g., Niebuhr 1932; Donagan 1977; Maxwell 1990). Virtually all people, including those who hold extreme moral positions, sometimes feel pressured by this value conflict. Its practical importance has been summarized by Jane Mansbridge: "It is hard for a polity simultaneously to legitimize self-interest and to persuade its citizens to make the common good their own. The task becomes harder when political scientists, economists, and psychologists insist that common interests are a myth and that appeals to such interests are either mystification or a waste of effort" (1990, x).

Two important observations should be made about the fundamental moral sensibilities that pit the generalizability of the golden rule against its more limited application. Striving for universal rules and group aggrandizement both have survival value. Golden rule sentiments promote cooperation and standards of fairness that make social organization possible. In-group sentiments give societies cohesion during war. Second, the morality of the golden rule and the morality of serving one's own group are sometimes in competition. The former encourages compassion; the latter promotes aggressiveness toward enemies. Therefore, a fundamental dilemma exists. The portion of this dualism given the greater attention tilts a person's attitudes about international conflict, and many other matters, in a characteristic direction. This moral dualism is at the heart of much of the traditional literature on warfare and is one key to deciphering the puzzle of the sources of attitudes about conflict issues, but it is not the only key.

SIX

Fundamental Structure

How can Americans simultaneously express support for such diverse ethical positions as the golden rule, legalism, and the supreme emergency? There are four possible explanations. First, U.S. elites may not have responded to our inquiries on the basis of any strongly held beliefs but merely provided what they thought were appropriate answers. The obvious response to the question "Are you a loyal American?" would be yes, but this could be uttered without any reflection about what it means to be a loyal American. Such a pattern of responses could be the product of many socializing agents, including the American educational system. Although students are asked to pledge allegiance to the flag each morning, there is little cognitive content to this ritual.

In the ethical training of children, the closest analogy to recitation of the pledge of allegiance is the teaching of the golden rule. Around the world, most children are taught some version of the golden rule. Therefore, it should not be too surprising that people offer extensive support for this most general of moral prescriptions. As another example of such a potentially reflexive reply, all military trainees are taught to obey orders, immediately and without conscious thought. By itself, this experience might explain the overall level of support for legalism principles among many U.S. elites.

A second possibility is that people respond to questions about norms of warfare in a largely unsystematic manner because they have no strong and well-developed opinions on the subject. This might happen if such issues are remote from most people's day-to-day agenda or if a person has not yet been able to work out a systematic approach to certain policy problems. Jimmy Carter is an apparent example of this possibility. He held unsystematic beliefs about many aspects of politics, and it was difficult to find coherence to much of his general attitude structure, although not necessarily to his attitudes about international conflict. Carter's speech writer noted the incoherence of many of his attitudes when he wrote:

> I came to think that Carter believes fifty things, but no one thing. He holds explicit, thorough positions on every issue under the sun, but he has no large view of the relations between them, no line indicating which goals will take precedence over which when the goals conflict. Spelling out these choices makes the difference between a position and a philosophy, but it is an act foreign to Carter's mind. (Fallows 1979, 42)

In reflecting an equally unstructured set of beliefs, an admiral recounted to us the varied policy positions he had taken during his career. These included advocating the execution of repeated drug offenders and thinking that we should pressure Israel to withdraw from the West Bank since their "40,000 Zionists were too noisy." He also recalled that he had urged the secretary of state to threaten a nuclear attack on the Soviet Union unless it removed Soviet troops from Eastern Europe. In reflecting on his past attitudes and policy prescriptions, he said, "I feel that my positions on what is moral are all mixed up and inconsistent."

A third possibility is that most people have a structure to their beliefs about conflict, but the issues involved in international relations are so complex and situationally dependent that there is little commonality of viewpoints. While all U.S. elites may be answering in an internally consistent manner, there may be so many different systematic approaches to conflict issues that a collective muddle is all that appears to any observer. This would be the result if the cognitive frameworks of U.S. elites resemble the moral hairsplitting that dominates the philosophical literature. All individuals may be rational, and all individuals may be moral by their own lights, but when their views are examined in the aggregate they may appear to be neither rational nor moral, just confused. This viewpoint is reflected by James Rosenau:

> Opinion makers by no means comprise a homogeneous or organized group. The formulation of precise categories for analytic purposes suggests an orderliness and organization of the opinion-making public which in fact does not exist. Rather, its members are almost infinitely varied in their . . . mode of

forming and circulating opinions . . . in their familiarity with foreign affairs, and in their attitudes toward issues of foreign policy . . . heterogeneity rather than uniformity characterizes the ideology of the opinion-making public. Each of its multitudinous segments has its own conception of what the aims and techniques of American foreign policy ought to be. There are few issues on which widespread or general agreement exists. . . . The impersonal and personal channels of communication are filled not with a few main currents of opinion, but with countless eddies, each swirling in its own undertow. (1961, 71–72)

A final possibility is that while the conflict views of Americans are moderately complex, they are best conceived in a reasonably well-ordered, multidimensional space. Such a space would be complicated enough to have eluded detection by traditional normative ethicists, most of whom could understand only the comparatively small portion of the space that they inhabit, but simple enough to provide future social science researchers and metaethicists with general guidance. In studies of international relations attitudes this conjecture finds guarded support from Charles Kegley: "It appears that foreign policy beliefs consist of several dimensions or components but we do not know yet what they are, how many there are, or what the relationships among them are" (1986, 456). Differences in foreign policy opinions are sometimes explained by empirical social scientists in terms of the two cognitive dimensions of cooperative internationalism and military internationalism, but this approach has been only partially successful (see, e.g., Bardes and Oldendick 1978; Wittkopf and Maggiotto 1983a; Holsti and Rosenau 1986; Wittkopf 1986). The usefulness of any multidimensional explanation must be judged by the insights it offers. When a particular cognitive space is proposed, does a knowledge of where individuals are located in that space tell us anything about their attitudes and their decision making?

If truly successful, such an approach should also be useful in resolving a number of the apparent paradoxes found in both the applied policy literature and in public opinion studies (see, e.g., Fleishman 1988). The continued existence of these anomalies can only serve to confuse us about the nature of our opponents' reasoning. While our enemies could be acting morally from their own perspective, if we do not understand their form of moral reasoning we will not recognize their actions as ethically motivated. The ubiquitous fallback position to explain actions that cannot be understood from our particular ethical viewpoint is the reason of state doctrine that dominates many contemporary international relations textbooks.

SOPHISTICATION OF ATTITUDES

Lawrence Kohlberg's theory of the stages of moral development provides an interesting framework for beginning a discussion of attitude sophistication. According to Kohlberg (1980, 1981), individuals are believed to progress through six sequential stages on the way to a final principled orientation based on universal ethical principles. These highest-order principles — like the golden rule — are abstract and appeal to comprehensiveness, universality and consistency. But not all people progress to this highest, privileged type of reasoning, which Kohlberg identified with a particular political ideology: liberalism. According to him, the pattern has been for states to become more liberal as they move toward greater fulfillment of the ideals of justice that take into account a universalist concern for others.

Those who denigrate political conservatism place American conservatives at least two steps below the ultimate status in Kohlberg's scheme of moral development. At stage four, there is a law and order orientation. Right conduct here involves doing one's duty, having respect for authority, and maintaining the social order for its own sake. Upon initial review, the classification of conservatives as ethically immature individuals seems to agree remarkably well with our description of modal U.S. military beliefs. Following Kohlberg's logic, most military officers must be cognitively immature, since their reasoning is dominated by in-group concerns. By this standard, diplomats, journalists, and members of Congress are also comparatively immature when compared to Catholic priests. The application of this argument to foreign policy seems to be implausible and rings of a bizarre sort of 1960s liberal academic ethnocentrism. Why? The Kohlberg thesis deals with levels of cognitive development and argues that universal concepts of justice can be utilized only by those at the highest level of moral development. What the thesis does not consider is the consequentialist possibility that universalist criteria may not apply in all situations, and therefore universalistic rules cannot be accepted by all decision makers as guiding principles in their particular policy realms.

A reasoned acceptance of universalism depends on one's strategic situation. This realization also explains the paradox of moral regression, noted by some social psychologists, whereby people occasionally appear to use a lower level of cognitive reasoning to solve particular types of problems. Instead of moral regression, such occurrences in public policy discussions probably reflect an accurate assessment that universalist criteria can be applied successfully in certain environments, but not in others.

If a politician or a military officer discounts the risks of the international system and this calculation is in error, his nation may be destroyed and the decision maker may be killed. Harold Hughes, former Iowa governor and a Democratic presidential candidate during the 1970s, renounced his political ambitions after such a personal revelation. Reflecting on the awesome responsibilities of the presidency, he realized late one night that he was unwilling in principle to engage in nuclear war. That, he felt, made him strategically unsuited to be commander-in-chief, and he withdrew altogether from political life.

Just war thinking can be adopted only by people who are willing to discount some of the risks found in the international system. This is perfectly reasonable for Catholic priests, who assume that their organization has an eternal life, but it is not as reasonable a perspective for a government official whose principal concern is the protection of the nation-state. It is quite possible to have a well-thought-out, reasoned, and highly developed moral view that takes into account the suffering caused to others by our military actions, but still see the world as such a risky place that prudence must dominate over a universalistic concern for foreign nationals since the golden rule cannot be implemented fully in international politics. This is not the moral regression of social psychologists — it is prudent behavior. Among thoughtful conservatives, including many of the military officers who participated in our study, the prudential approach to armed conflict is utility-maximizing because risk is seen as the dominant characteristic of international affairs.

Factor Analysis

One statistical technique that permits an examination of the underlying cognitive structure of attitudes is factor analysis. It allows us to see if any of the conjectures about the nature of beliefs are correct and permits an informed conclusion about which of these possibilities is the most accurate reflection of U.S. elite thinking on international conflict issues. Because our survey tapped support for the fundamental features of each doctrine of decision making in international relations, a factor analysis of responses also is useful in judging the amount of shared variance in attitudes among U.S. elites, which is not possible to determine by examining frequency counts. In turn, a close inspection of the nature of this shared variance reveals any underlying structure to conflict attitudes.

Finding a simple and coherent cognitive structure to such thinking would render it unlikely that we have measured only unsystematic responses or nonattitudes or that we have overinterpreted the statistical evidence. Ad hoc attitudes would not display the internal consistency demanded of a robust factor structure that can be interpreted in a reasonable manner. As a method of investigation, factor analysis has the substantial added advantage that the amount of variance explained by its dimensions provides a measure of the shared systematic components to American reasoning about conflict matters. The greater the level of explained variance, the greater the amount of shared structure to the evaluative criteria used by U.S. elites.

All five versions of our questionnaire posed a series of thirty-four items designed to tap agreement with the principles of the major schools. Each item deals with a particular aspect of a framework or doctrine. Factor analysis can sort these items into dimensions that indicate to what extent our survey findings are consistent with the positions advocated by the major doctrines. The dimensions extracted in factor analysis also probe interrelationships among the survey responses and can reveal the common themes of individual concern that motivate responses. Such themes may be even more fundamental than the descriptions of the doctrines found in the traditional literature. If such a coherent underlying structure exists for U.S. elite attitudes, it suggests that a core set of concerns motivates the views of people toward war. In turn, these concerns may serve as building blocks to construct a model of attitude formation and decision making.

A preliminary analysis indicated that six factors have eigenvalues of 1.00 or greater. While they explain 53 percent of the total variance in responses, three of them lack obvious interpretations, are only marginally greater than 1.00, and appear to result from chance associations rather than causal connections. Another common way to determine which factors are substantially important is to examine a scree plot, which presents the eigenvalue associated with each successively derived factor. When the slope traced by successive eigenvalues flattens out, we have identified the substantially important factors. The scree plots presented in figure 6.1 are from separate factor analyses of the five groups. They suggest that only half of the factors with eigenvalues greater than 1.00 are of substantive importance. Overall, the first three factors explain 42 percent of the variation in all elite responses. It is at least equally important to note that all five groups structure their beliefs toward international conflict in a similar fashion (see Tamashiro, Secrest, and Brunk 1993).

The interpretation of the level of explained variance in this analysis merits further discussion. A relatively high percentage of explained variance among responses would suggest a high degree of patterning to Amer-

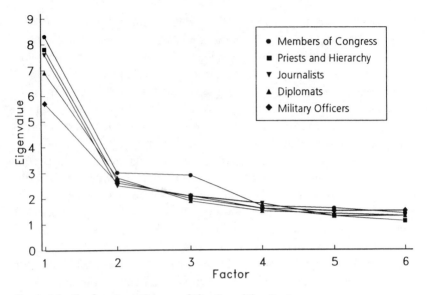

Figure 6.1 **Explanatory Power of the Cognitive Factors**

ican attitudes regarding decision making in times of conflict. This would mean that elite judgments are highly structured and that people's moral beliefs display a high level of resemblance. In contrast, a low percentage of explained variance would suggest that individual judgments are either unstructured or derived from a large number of different standards of evaluation. While that too would be an important empirical finding, it would mean that our work could go no further because further empirical analysis and theoretical generalization are fruitless. The actual level of statistically explained variance lies between these extremes, and so more investigation is in order.

What are the implications for understanding attitude formation and foreign policy decision making? First, it is clear that there is a general pattern to these policy views. Certain judgments occur together more frequently than others, but overall U.S. elite views are neither rigidly structured nor doctrinaire. In other words, and as we saw in the previous chapter, attitudes display patterns, although American elites differ on some of the fundamental bases of their decision-making approaches. But if these bases can be isolated, their identification should allow us to construct a general theory of deliberating on international conflict issues.

Another issue of importance concerns the diversity of reasoning within the elite groups. As we demonstrated in the last chapter, military officers and clerics express a high level of aggregate agreement about conflict issues in comparison to the attitudes of other U.S. elites. One possible interpretation of this evidence is that since military officers and religious leaders have more of an institutional interest in these matters, attitudes of individual officers and clerics are more coherently organized. An alternative explanation is that the individual attitudes of all U.S. elites are, on average, equally well organized, but at the aggregate level of analysis, the military officers and clerics appear to have more coherent attitude structures because the members of these two groups tend to hold similar beliefs about conflict, while members of Congress, diplomats, and journalists are split in their approaches to deciding such matters.

The potential for different levels of cognitive sophistication also was reflected in many respondent comments. Some elites argued that the problems posed by warfare are much too complex to be captured by survey items, a sentiment expressed by a number of diplomats and journalists. One foreign service officer commented, "I think that morality is situational. The idea that there's absolute right and wrong seems to be a traditional moral concept." A newspaper editor said simply, "There are no absolutes." Another argued, "I do not believe in the concepts of morality, ethics, or any other absolute system of appropriateness of behavior." The comment of a fellow journalist nicely summarizes this type of reasoning: "Your context is too simplistic. What may be moral—justifiable—in dealing with Hitler may be immoral—unnecessary or even counterproductive—in dealing with the Sandinistas."

We suspected that a belief in the importance of situational complexity in public policy might be a product of the convergence of at least two contemporary streams of thought. First, the modern American education system faces the nightmare of trying to deal with moral standards when it appears to many that all moral standards are culturally relative. This deprives people of a generally accepted framework for deducing specific rules of conduct. As almost anything is acceptable to someone, it has become unacceptable to impose any particular set of rules because all standards lack interpersonal moral validity. The result is an almost faddish and unstable public morality, somewhat similar to the moods of public opinion that reason of state theorists cite in their justification for excluding morality from foreign policy.

Second, a rule of thumb that has developed among many applied policy analysts is the complexity argument. When faced with problems that do not seem to have obvious solutions, rather than continuing the search for a fundamental structure, analysts often argue that such issues are so complex that they have no easy solutions. When the moral relativism and complexity arguments are coupled, there is a characteristic response. A high ranking military officer put it this way: "The issue of morality and warfare is highly complex. The very definition of morality is open to debate. The answer to almost every question is scenario dependent."

Just because some elites view most real-world situations as complex does not mean they act idiosyncratically. They may apply a series of similar simplifying heuristics when trying to resolve even the most complex policy problems. Most of the U.S. elites who objected to the idea that a survey could capture the intricacies of practical policy judgment apparently went on to answer our questions in a coherent manner. Some of these people may sincerely believe that the attributes of specific situations are of overriding importance, although most U.S. elites share certain core beliefs that fundamentally structure their thinking. If so, then the individuals who publicly resist adopting general rules may principally differ from their colleagues in their failure to realize that most people use just a few core values to structure their attitudes toward conflict.

As figure 6.1 shows, the amount of variance in item responses explained by the factors is comparable for the elite groups. In fact, all five groups show the same general pattern of individual factor coefficients (see Tamashiro, Secrest, and Brunk 1993). In the aggregate, all U.S. groups rely on a series of similar criteria when forming their attitudes toward decision making in foreign affairs. In other words, no one group of these opinion leaders appears to be much more sophisticated in its level of reasoning than the others.[1] No elite group's attitudes are structured in a significantly more complicated way than the policy attitudes of the other groups, and the evaluation criteria used are similar for all five groups. This further suggests that the appeal to situation ethics made by some elites might be an attempt to appear more sophisticated than other people, or it may be a rhetorical strategy they incorporate into their day-to-day conversations that allows them to dodge issues they do not want to address publicly.

The level of explained variance in our factor analysis also has substantial face validity for constructing a general theory of moral cognition. The literature on applied ethics stresses the importance of an ethical compass, but it is filled with many fine distinctions, special cases, and qualifications of general rules. Accordingly, we find that much of the variability in elite attitudes can be explained by reference to a series of simple judgmental criteria, but the landscape of conflict is not so easily managed. Beyond the application of these criteria, we move into the bailiwick of fine distinctions, special cases, and qualifications of general rules. So after we discover a systematic pattern to these policy attitudes, there still remains substantial flexibility in applying problem-solving heuristics to such matters.

COGNITIVE DIMENSIONS

The first three factors derived from our statistical analysis are substantively meaningful, allow for a theoretically rich interpretation of attitude formation, and shed light on a number of paradoxes in the literature about decision making. The factors tap largely distinct aspects of the cognitive framework, thus strengthening our suspicion that an empirically based categorization of ethical beliefs is possible. Such a classification should be able to encompass a substantial amount of the variability found in the tenets of the traditional frameworks but will not be so complex a cognitive mapping that it is impossible to make speculations about the disputes likely to arise over the future use of military force.

Since factor analysis is a technique that tries to impose structure on empirically observed data, a number of statistically derived factors may be only a result of the random error variability that exists in any collection of data. When one attempts to determine the cognitive structure of people's beliefs toward conflict, the burden of proof for a particular interpretation lies in whether a factor solution can be justified and, in this case, whether its separate dimensions can subsequently be used to reconstruct the tenets of the traditional schools of thought through deductive reasoning. If these goals can be reached, then we have made a very strong prima facie case that the empirically derived factors have been interpreted correctly, and they should offer deep insights into the policy-making process.

A detailed substantive interpretation of this three-factor solution is necessary to define the generic classificatory concepts connected with the findings. Table 6.1 displays the weights for each item on the three factors. A high positive or high negative loading tells us that an item should be used as a guide to interpreting a dimension's substantive meaning. The three dimensions we have identified deal with risk aversion, the legitimacy of force, and constraints on warfare. The following discussion explores why our interpretations of these factors are reasonable. Tables 6.2 through 6.4 are used in justifying these interpretations. Our analyses are based on consistency in predicting the sign of the correlation between each item and

Table 6.1 **Factor Coefficients**

Survey Item and Principle	Factor 1: Risk Sensitivity	Factor 2: Legitimacy of Force	Factor 3: Constraints on Warfare
32. Supreme emergency	.73	−.13	−.14
30. Retaliatory ethic	.71	.05	−.20
26. Reason of state	.71	−.19	−.06
34. Supreme emergency	−.70	−.01	.12
29. Retaliatory ethic	.69	−.27	−.12
13. Legalism	.65	−.13	−.17
28. Reason of state	.63	−.31	−.23
19. Moral perfectionism	.63	−.26	−.21
14. Moral crusade	.62	.03	−.23
11. Legalism	.62	−.31	−.10
31. Retaliatory ethic	.54	−.15	−.31
12. Legalism	.46	−.42	−.28
17. Moral perfectionism	−.32	.14	.15
10. Just war	−.30	.30	.13
24. Pacifism	−.10	.66	.15
22. Nuclear pacifism	−.39	.64	.17
2. Golden rule	−.21	.61	.19
23. Pacifism	−.01	.60	−.07
21. Nuclear pacifism	−.48	.56	.18
25. Pacifism	−.12	.55	.04
20. Nuclear pacifism	.41	−.54	−.10
9. Just war	−.06	.52	.25
18. Moral perfectionism	−.34	.51	.25
16. Moral crusade	.15	.22	−.10
1. Golden rule	−.09	.04	.63
3. Golden rule	−.12	−.04	.63
8. Just war	−.15	.31	.60
7. Just war	−.24	.10	.60
6. Just war	−.15	.31	.54
15. Moral crusade	.32	−.02	−.52
27. Reason of state	.37	.13	−.48
5. Just war	−.32	.21	.46
4. Just war	.01	.29	.39
33. Supreme emergency	.36	−.26	−.38
Eigenvalue	10.15	2.34	1.83
Percent variance explained	29.86	6.89	5.39

its principal factor according to our interpretation of that factor's meaning. Later, we examine the implications of these findings for modeling the processes of decision making and attitude formation.

Risk Aversion

Table 6.2 summarizes the essence of each item that correlates at 0.40 or greater with factor one, risk aversion. The correlations in this table are presented by their rank order, beginning with the greatest correlation on the highest loading factor. Assume that positive values on this dimension should be taken to represent an aversion to risk. On the basis of this proposed interpretation, we made predictions of the expected signs of the fourteen items most strongly correlated with the factor.[2] These expectations are also presented in table 6.2. Reasonable predictions can be made for all the items except 14, which comes from the moral crusading doctrine. It has no obvious relationship to risk sensitivity, unless one assumes that punishment will deter future aggression, and its correlation may be spurious. Correct predictions can be made for all the other items, and these predictions are consistent with the interpretation of factor one as sensitivity to risk.

U.S. elites appear to respond to four types of uncertainties as reflected in this dimension. The first is the risk of military defeat, which is well captured by items 13 and 19. A risk-averse individual is relatively unwilling to constrain military planning in the service of moral principles. Accordingly, risk-averse elites would be predisposed toward worst-case analyses when deciding on a proper course of action and accepting expedient measures to guard against worst case possibilities. Furthermore, the evidence shows that risk-averse elites are more willing to consider the possibility of committing a war crime to prevent military defeat.

The second type of uncertainty concerns the intentions of other countries in the international system. Items 11 and 28 represent this type of risk. Risk-averse individuals tend to believe that national interest, rather than universalist morality, should guide foreign policy. Furthermore, risk-averse elites tend to believe one should follow the law rather than conscience. In the world's uncertain environment, failure to obey legitimate military orders risks mismanagement and destruction.

The third type of uncertainty concerns the nature of the enemy. If the enemy is victorious, we will find ourselves at his mercy, and his postwar behavior may be brutal and intolerant. If we fear such a possibility and we are not constrained by other moral factors, then we should do everything possible to avoid military defeat. Three items bear on this issue. Item 13

Table 6.2 **Interpretation of Risk Sensitivity**

Essence of Survey Item	Expected Response[a]	Consistency of Response	Factor Weight
32. We can ignore morality to win a war.	Positive	Consistent	.73
30. If an enemy is immoral, we can be immoral.	Positive	Consistent	.71
26. All that matters is victory.	Positive	Consistent	.71
34. Morality applies in wars to the death.	Negative	Consistent	−.70
29. Harsh actions are justified if attacked.	Positive	Consistent	.69
13. If necessary, we can commit war crimes.	Positive	Consistent	.65
28. National interest should determine policy.	Positive	Consistent	.63
19. Morality should not override planning.	Positive	Consistent	.63
14. We have a duty to punish the enemy.[b]	—	—	.62
11. Obey the law, not your conscience.	Positive	Consistent	.62
31. Revenge is acceptable if attacked.	Positive	Consistent	.54
21. Using nuclear bombs on cities is immoral.	Negative	Consistent	−.48
12. Surprise attacks are acceptable.	Positive	Consistent	.46
20. Threatening use of nuclear bombs is moral.	Positive	Consistent	.41

Note: All items correlated at 0.40 or greater with the factor are presented in descending order of magnitude.

a. Under "expected response," "positive" does not automatically mean "agree," and "negative" does not automatically mean "disagree." Positive and negative refer to the expected signs of the factor loadings for each item, which are a function of both the direction of item wording and how responses were coded. We took each issue into account in determining consistency of response.

b. Prediction cannot be made because item 14 comes from the moral crusading school.

allows for the commission of war crimes to prevent defeat, while items 32 and 34 allow us to relax moral constraints if an enemy is very evil or if an enemy is bent on the total destruction of our society.

The final type of uncertainty deals with the bonds of mutual restraint that sometimes develop between enemies. Informal agreements often emerge that prohibit certain behaviors such as bombing food wagons during the trench warfare of World War I or the use of poison gas during

Table 6.3 **Interpretation of Legitimacy of Force**

Essence of Survey Item	Expected Response	Consistency of Response	Factor Weight
24. Nonviolence is the only moral choice.	Positive	Consistent	.66
22. Defeat is preferable to nuclear war.	Positive	Consistent	.64
23. We should not resist if attacked.	Positive	Consistent	.60
2. We should not spy on others.	Positive	Consistent	.61
21. Using nuclear bombs on cities is immoral.	Positive	Consistent	.56
25. It is always wrong to kill.	Positive	Consistent	.55
20. We can threaten to use nuclear weapons.	Negative	Consistent	−.54
9. A war is immoral if you cannot win.	Positive	Consistent	.52
18. Going to war should be a moral decision.	Positive	Consistent	.51
12. Surprise attacks are legitimate.	Negative	Consistent	−.42

Note: All items correlated at 0.40 or greater with the factor are presented in descending order of magnitude. See table 6.2, note, regarding interpretations.

World War II, but these prohibitions tend to be fragile. To some extent, all the retaliatory ethic items tap this type of risk. Accordingly, one must be ready to retaliate and punish enemy violations of tacit agreements.

Legitimacy of Force

The second dimension measures the legitimacy that individuals ascribe to the planning and use of military force.[3] In general, this dimension may be interpreted as the source of the ethical and practical warrants used to justify the use of military force. Again, this interpretation can be validated through a consistency analysis. The relevant evidence is presented in table 6.3. Of the ten items correlated at 0.40 or greater with this dimension, all can be interpreted as measuring legitimacy of the use of force or planning for the use of force. The direction of each factor coefficient is correctly predicted by this interpretation.

At least two major types of force legitimacy are captured here. The first is that force is at least minimally legitimate in some instances. This is addressed by the pacifism items, which are rejected by most Americans. Universal pacifists are at one extreme on this cognitive dimension, while the strong opponents of pacifism appear at the other. The second type of legitimacy concerns the use of nuclear weapons. The premise of contemporary nuclear pacifism is that since nuclear war can serve no useful purpose or reasons of state, it must be condemned. The more one supports the legitimacy of the use of nuclear force, the more one tends to disagree with the nuclear pacifism position.

Constraints on War

The third dimension measures the belief that special moral responsibilities must accompany one's willingness to engage in war. Table 6.4 presents a similar consistency analysis of this interpretation. The sign of each of the eight items that correlate with this dimension at 0.40 or greater can be correctly predicted using such an interpretation. The universalistic principle most strongly associated with this dimension is represented by items 1 and 3, which are taken from the golden rule framework.

This moral responsibilities dimension embodies the principles reflected in the idea of a just war. All the just war items are positively correlated with this dimension, and five of the seven are related at 0.40 or greater.[4] However, the interpretation of attitudes toward constraints on war is more general than only the specific principles that make up the just war doctrine. All three items dealing with the golden rule correlate positively with this dimension as well. This finding is consistent with the thesis that just war principles will be derived by thoughtful individuals who believe in the golden rule and accept a few other simple premises — in particular, the belief that force can be used to protect the innocent from harm, as embodied in the second dimension (Secrest, Brunk, and Tamashiro 1991a).

Although this is not immediately apparent from the statistical analysis, a person who agrees with the basis of this third dimension is likely to disagree with the ethical principles advocated by certain other traditional schools of thought. In particular, supporters of constraints on warfare will tend to oppose statements 14 and particularly 15, which are taken from the moral crusading school. These items argue that force can be used to convert others to our beliefs or to punish them as infidels or heretics. Second, supporters of these war constraints also oppose the position of supreme emergency advocates that surprise attacks may be authorized against an enemy, which is embodied in item 33. Third, supporters of responsible war constraints reject the reason of state argument that we should go to war whenever it is to our national advantage, as reflected in item 27. Finally, it also seems reasonable to find that the American sup-

Table 6.4 **Interpretation of Constraints on War**

Essence of Survey Item	Expected Response	Consistency of Response	Factor Weight
1. We should treat others like ourselves.	Positive	Consistent	.63
3. We should keep our treaty promises.	Positive	Consistent	.63
8. War should be the very last resort.	Positive	Consistent	.60
7. We should not destroy the enemy's society.	Positive	Consistent	.60
6. A war must be for self-defense.	Positive	Consistent	.54
15. We can use force to convert others to our beliefs.	Negative	Consistent	−.52
27. We should go to war whenever it is to our advantage.	Negative	Consistent	−.48
5. We should try not to kill civilians.	Positive	Consistent	.46

Note: All the items correlated at 0.40 or greater with the factor are presented in descending order of magnitude. See note to table 6.2 regarding interpretations.

porters of war constraints reject the notion of revenge against noncombatants in other nations.

ELITE EVALUATION OF THE FRAMEWORKS

The substantive interpretation of the relation among these three dimensions can be illustrated visually by plotting the traditional frameworks in the three-dimensional cognitive space of U.S. elites. This is done in figure 6.2 and indicates how Americans view the frameworks. The factor weights of all the items used to tap support for a framework's precepts are averaged to obtain its plotted position in the cognitive space (see table 4.1, above). Not only does this approach allow for a discussion of each framework in a succinct manner, but it illustrates, as well, the extent to which U.S. elites view the various traditional schools of thought in international relations to be similar or distinct positions. The closer two frameworks are in the cognitive space, the more they are viewed alike by Americans. The farther away two schools are located, the more they are viewed as separate sets of decision-making criteria.

Let us first examine the location of these doctrines relative to the legitimacy of force dimension. Elites locate pacifism, whose items have

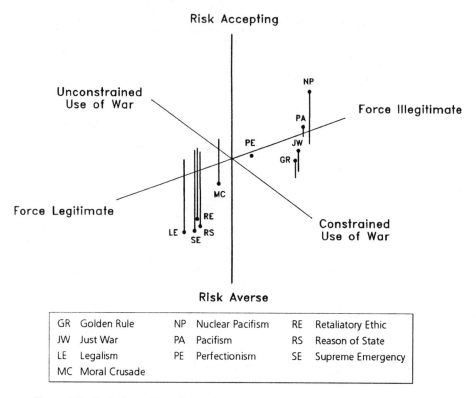

Figure 6.2 **Location of Traditional Frameworks in the Cognitive Space**

an average loading of 0.60, toward one end of their cognitive evaluation space.[5] Located very close to pacifism is nuclear pacifism, which has 0.58 as its average loading. The distinctive extreme position of these moral doctrines so far away from any other set of decision-making rules is associated with their consistent rejection by U.S. elites.

Located farthest from the pacifism doctrines on this dimension are legalism (−0.29), which sees constraints on the use of force as irrelevant to an individual's decision calculus; the supreme emergency doctrine (−0.13), which is willing to suspend all constraints on war conduct if the nation is imperiled; reason of state (−.12), which sees the pursuit of national interest as overriding moral concerns; and the retaliatory ethic (−.12), which demands an eye-for-an-eye response to enemy actions. These last three doctrines all contend that the use of force is legitimate in many circumstances. Lying intermediate between pacifism and the relatively unrestrained doctrines is just war (0.29). The followers of the just war doctrine admit to the consequentialist possibility that the use of force may be necessary in international politics, but they are concerned that military force be applied in a constrained manner.

Concerning the factor that measures constraints on war entry and war conduct, our interpretation of this dimension again is supported through a plotting of the traditional frameworks. The pacifism and nuclear pacifism doctrines do not load significantly on this dimension, since their precepts are not relevant to the waging of war. Elites view the much more detailed just war doctrine as requiring the constrained use of force, and its value is 0.42 on this dimension. Because all the other traditional doctrines are viewed as not requiring as much restraint, they are located at the other end of this dimension. These include the moral crusading doctrine (-0.28), supreme emergency (-0.21), reason of state (-0.26), retaliatory ethic (-0.25), and legalism (-0.18).

The most interesting pattern concerning the cognitive space of U.S. elites emerges with regard to the risk sensitivity dimension. A traditional doctrine that supports a moral perfectionist interpretation of constraints on war conduct and views military force as illegitimate is seen by Americans as involving risk. Geometrically, this is suggested in figure 6.2 by the risk-averse doctrines of supreme emergency, legalism, reason of state, and the retaliatory ethic all being located in the lower force-is-legitimate/unconstrained-use-of-warfare octant. As one moves toward the upper force-is-not-legitimate/constrained-use-of-warfare octant, the morally restrictive doctrines of just war and pacifism increase in their plotted amplitude, shifting upward toward the risk-accepting end of the dimension. In short, the more restrictive the precepts of a doctrine, the more it is viewed by Americans as risky. Anyone who is particularly sensitive to the risks that exist in the international arena would view such doctrines as decision-making frameworks to be avoided.

TENTATIVE CONCLUSIONS

This analysis reveals an interesting and somewhat surprising structure to the attitudes of U.S. policy elites and opinion leaders. The best way to summarize our findings so far is to address a series of questions. First, do any of the traditional doctrines found in the religious, philosophical, and international relations literatures have any relevance for contemporary Americans? The answer is a definite yes, but the diversity we find in their views means that an important qualification is in order. The core set of moral concerns that govern U.S. attitudes toward war is not dominated by any single traditional doctrine.

Golden rule sensibilities and the principles that flow from them are given substantial support, but such universal idealism conflicts with a risk aversion that may be necessary to safeguard one's country. People may sincerely believe in the golden rule but feel that it cannot be implemented because it is not practical in the threatening arena of international politics. This value conflict is partly resolved in the traditional literature by the relativist flavor of the golden rule. Morally allowable actions are determined by one's particular ethical code, and most coherent ethical codes are consistent with some interpretation of the golden rule. Therefore, Americans generally see the directives of the golden rule as consistent with most of their public policy judgments.

Equally important, the dimensions derived from our factor analysis do not uniquely identify individual doctrines. Instead, they reveal that the cognitive map of Americans is built on even more fundamental core beliefs, suppositions, or sensibilities. These fundamental sensibilities can be combined in a variety of ways to produce the doctrines of the major schools of thought about international conflict. Our empirical evidence thus goes further than past inquiries by identifying a limited set of commonly shared precepts that are used by real-world U.S. elites to structure their views toward conflict issues.

At this juncture, we also can offer an assessment of the ethical focus Americans use when evaluating decisions involving the use of force. Many different criteria are proposed in the philosophical literature to decide whether an action is right or moral, including the overall nature of a situation, people's motives, and a consideration of their suffering and sacrifices. In practice, these alternatives seem relatively unimportant. Instead, American elites focus on the nature of actions and their consequences when making decisions about the use of deadly force. Perhaps most surprising, we find that the most important criterion for the moral evaluation of conflict issues by real-world elites is not a traditional ethical principle at all. Instead, it is one's willingness to tolerate risk. Consequently, people who are risk-averse are likely to adopt belief systems quite different from those of risk-accepting people.

SEVEN

Characteristic
Belief Systems

The three belief systems introduced in this chapter express the modal tendencies most likely to be embraced by U.S. elites. We call them *strict just war, better safe than sorry,* and *ambivalence.* While many typologies can be created using logical inference and imagination, the construction of our frameworks results from extensive empirical analysis, and they are consistent with the statistical evidence. In the chapters that follow, we will develop a model of attitude formation that ties together our various findings, allowing us to predict the modal positions likely to be adopted by American elites, and to offer explanations for a series of apparent attitude and policy-making paradoxes.

The belief systems described here reflect how people actually view the precepts of the traditional doctrines and incorporate them into their orientations toward conflict. All three characteristic belief systems view war as tragic and regrettable, but the real-world followers of these belief systems diverge on how to make the trade-off between the goals of group survival and the demands of applying moral rules in a universal way to all people.

In describing the three belief systems in categorical terms, we do not wish to imply that all people embrace one of them in its pure form. Indeed, the evidence suggests that many people do not. Life is a process of adapting to often changing circumstances. At any stage in their life cycle, and because of their official position, many people will not have been able to find an all-purpose heuristic perspective on conflict. Instead, they may be muddling through in their attempts to reconcile conflicting moral and professional demands. What we characterize in this chapter are the ideal types of reasoning that flow from the logic of the traditional frameworks and our statistical analysis and how the differences in these belief systems are viewed by Americans.

PACIFISM AND MORAL CRUSADING AS REAL-WORLD ALTERNATIVES

To move toward a deeper understanding of belief systems, we should first discuss two important traditional doctrines that have little support among contemporary U.S. elites. These are pacifism and moral crusading. The precepts of pacifism fit nicely into the cognitive space we have described, and while the philosophy of pacifism is important for understanding the structure of elite views, few Americans support its principles.

The survey included three general pacifism items and three nuclear pacifism items. A universal pacifist should be expected to support all six, and a pacifism scale can be constructed from them to measure whether a respondent is a practicing pacifist. No American elite who participated in our study supported more than four of these six items. While pacifism has great theoretical importance in the intellectual history of conflict beliefs — since it is the extreme case of rejection of force — the number of universal pacifists holding leadership positions in American society approaches zero.

A second doctrine that merits some initial discussion is the moral crusade. Our evidence here is at first counterintuitive. Despite the commonly ascribed historical importance of moral crusading as an explanation for much of American history, this doctrine received as little support from contemporary U.S. elites as pacifism. An average of only 8 percent support was given to each of the individual tenets of moral crusading, and only three individuals agreed with all the moral crusading items in the survey. Furthermore, there was a striking lack of open-ended comments from our respondents that could be interpreted as moral crusading. The position closest to a moral crusading viewpoint, occasionally expressed, was that the United States can legitimately provide weapons to citizens of a foreign country that has suffered the evil of an indigenous communist regime. As one military officer put it,

> While I don't feel it is appropriate or moral to convert with the barrel of a gun, I feel very strongly that as free people we are obligated to assist resistance to imposition of totalitarian regimes. Wherever someone picks up a gun to

force someone to submit to a Marxist or fascist regime, he is constructively committing an act of aggression against me as a free person and has thereby made himself my enemy. With the internationalist duty perceived by Marxists to support Marxist revolutions throughout the world, whether free people have a similar internationalist duty to resist imposition of totalitarian regimes is a very appropriate question.

Since the contemporary leaders of American society so soundly reject the fundamental assumptions of a moral crusading point of view, another explanation for its historical ubiquity must be advanced. Our review of the traditional writings on war suggests that crusading beliefs often become common after prolonged conflict. That a person like General William Tecumseh Sherman, quoted earlier, would express crusading sentiments after seeing the destruction of the American Civil War is understandable, but such feelings also are embodied in the writings of an American president known for his sophistication and education. Commenting about the English and their actions in the War of 1812, Thomas Jefferson writes, "We concur in considering [the English] government as totally without morality, insolent beyond bearing, inflated with vanity ambition, aiming at the exclusive domination of the [world], lost in corruption, of deep-rooted hatred toward us, hostile to liberty wherever it endeavors to show its head, and the eternal disturber of the peace of the world" (1848, 519).

Why should crusading sentiments be common after a prolonged conflict? At the beginning of a war, most moral adversaries appear to be willing, in principle, to give their opponents time to recant. If our enemies quickly realize the virtue of our cause and the wrongness of their beliefs, they can receive the gift of forgiveness promised by traditional religious teachings. But if our enemies are not soon defeated and cause us serious harm, a period of frustration ensues. As it becomes increasingly obvious that such a situation is likely to continue for a long time without a dramatic change, any means to punish and destroy our enemies begins to appear to some people to be legitimate, if not morally required. In contemporary times this has led to numerous excesses, including the paramilitary organizations of Northern Ireland, "ethnic cleansing" in Bosnia, and the assassination of an Israeli prime minister. But since the United States has not had a costly and prolonged military conflict since Vietnam, the psychology of moral crusading has almost totally died out, and today few U.S. elites have such sentiments. This has made it increasingly difficult for Americans to understand what motivates those who advocate holy war. Most contemporary Americans tend to dismiss the followers of Islamic *jihads,* and most recently the violent segment of the militia movement, as mentally ill or uneducated religious fanatics whose intellectual beliefs are not worth serious study.

STRICT JUST WAR

The first set of principles that can be identified as composing a distinctive belief system among contemporary American elites is based on just war thinking. The strict just war belief system encompasses only the just war doctrine and not the varied precepts of the broader just war tradition. It is located in the upper right front octant of figure 6.2, above. As can be seen in that figure, elites view it as a distinctive position. The only other framework located close to just war in their cognitive space is the golden rule. The main principles motivating the strict just war belief system are that all human life is sacred and that all war requires a moral justification. It affirms and defends the rights of the enemy, while all the alternative moral frameworks, except the practically nonexistent pacifist option, do not.

Table 5.1, above, shows that 50 percent of U.S. elites, on average, support individual just war precepts. But not nearly so many support the strict just war belief system. There are two strong presumptions of strict just war theory. First, as a general principle, war is not justified. This is embodied in its relationship to factor two, legitimacy of force. The second presumption is that force is not a good way of handling disputes and that violence only begets violence, which is reflected in factor three, constraints on warfare.

Only if there is strong evidence that international conflict may be necessary will strict just war elites proceed further to investigate whether there are compelling reasons for overriding their beginning presumption against war. The advocates of war always face the burden of proving their case. For strict just war believers, the primary purpose of these restrictions is to minimize violence. Their country's success in war is less important to them than following a constraining set of moral rules. Notions of realism and military necessity are morally irrelevant. In general, war is framed not in terms of political calculations and considerations of effectiveness but according to its utilitarian capacity to maximize the long-run good of humanity. Victory is always secondary to moral concerns. The followers of strict just war, unlike all the other approaches except pacifism, are willing to contemplate ending a conflict or even national surrender for moral reasons. Accordingly, this view tends to impose constraints on declaring and waging war.

The major moral criteria of strict just war are those of the just war perspective. Why should war be conducted? War can only be waged for defense. When should war be conducted? War should be a last resort when sanctioned by a legitimate authority and only when the good achieved by the war outweighs its evils. How should war be conducted? A nation's conduct during a war must protect the rights of innocent parties among the enemy. All these criteria must be satisfied before a war is deemed acceptable. While supreme emergency arguments play some part in the broader just war tradition, they are held to be inadmissible by those adhering to the strict just war belief system. Indeed, supreme emergency arguments are an important component of another real-world belief system.

A world in which most nations follow strict just war constraints would have many advantages. Precisely defining and following the terms and conditions for war would reduce processing costs for responsible national leadership. Nevertheless, there are clear cases when strict just war is not a utility-maximizing position, which explains, in part, why the belief system has not been universally adopted. When would this approach be particularly counterproductive? One circumstance is when defensive war appears to be impractical. An example of this perception occurred in Europe before World War I, when a cult of the offensive was widely accepted. This doctrine argued that offensive war had great technological and strategic advantages over defensive war. If a war is likely in such a situation, then a country should move first. To do otherwise and adhere to just war constraints would risk suicidal defeat. Similarly, the code of the samurai approved of deception and surprise attacks, and following just war principles in medieval Japan would have threatened the survival of one's group.

BETTER SAFE THAN SORRY

The better safe than sorry belief system was first described in our research on military attitudes (Brunk, Secrest, and Tamashiro 1990). It occupies an area in the back, lower left octant of the elite's cognitive space and indicates how a number of traditional positions on war are collectively viewed by Americans. In figure 6.2, the better safe than sorry belief system is at the nexus of legalism, reason of state, the retaliatory ethic, and supreme emergency thinking. These doctrines are located so close to each other in the cognitive space of Americans that obviously they find little of practical importance to differentiate them. People tend to view the tenets of these four traditional views similarly. Collectively, these doctrines and the better safe than sorry belief system itself are defined best by their aversion to risk and, secondarily, by the views that force is legitimate and that it can be used in a comparatively unrestrained way.

The nexus of beliefs that define better safe than sorry does not have a direct analogy to any position developed by philosophers or theologians toward war. Instead, it is an empirically observed decision-making framework that has not been extensively discussed in the scholarly literature. It is a strongly defensive position that has developed from the reflections of people coping with real-life problems rather than philosophers contemplating ivory-tower issues.

This risk-averse outlook appears to have developed in the same practical way that others have observed when describing the evolution of cooperation. As with cooperation, adopting the better safe than sorry perspective has survival benefits in particular situations. If the principal motivation of military personnel is to avoid court-martial for disobeying orders, they will rarely engage the enemy, and when they do so, they will minimize the risks to themselves. As a consequence, the overall casualty rate in their army will increase, while enemy losses will decline (Jencks 1979). If, instead, soldiers promote the general good of their group, they will engage in combat more readily, which increases the survival chances of their group and consequently improves the overall chances of their own survival.

In the cognitive space of U.S. elites, the better safe than sorry belief system inhabits nearly the opposite position of strict just war. Under this view, the priority is in-group security. Given the realities of war, better safe than sorry types think that it is doubtful anyone can impose enduring, voluntary constraints on conflict. Instead, the side that adopts unilateral constraints as permanent rules only decreases its chances of victory and survival. In many ways, better safe than sorry is the most interesting of the real-world belief systems since it indicates that certain beliefs about states of affairs — that the world is a very risky place, for example — have a very important prior impact on human values.

National Security

The demand for reciprocity on national security matters is very strong among those who follow better safe than sorry logic. This reciprocity among adversaries is assumed to be violated whenever a nation's security is perceived to be threatened. In this sense, the appropriateness of war follows from threats to in-group security when these threats cannot be deflected by peaceful means. In this way, the better safe than sorry view links provocability and reciprocity. Briefly, the message to outsiders is this: While we do not wish to act aggressively toward others, we also expect others not to act aggressively toward us. This demand for reciprocity is felt very strongly, and when violated it provides the sense that our in-group security is threatened, which can justify a strong military response.

An example of better safe than sorry reasoning can be seen in the American response to the Cuban missile crisis. While the Soviet actions that precipitated the crisis seemed to some to be analogous to the United States' basing nuclear missiles in Turkey, others viewed the similar placement of Soviet missiles in Cuba as violating a tacit agreement that neither superpower would place further nuclear capabilities in the other's sphere of influence. The U.S. response cannot be understood from a strict just war perspective. It can be explained only from the better safe than sorry view, whereby any serious threat to national security should be violently opposed and it is moral to do so. Only after our in-group security is safeguarded can we turn our attention to any other moral considerations, such as those prescribed by the just war tradition.

Strict reciprocity is not required under the better safe than sorry view. Better safe than sorry individuals can justify some actions as legitimate when taken by their own country but will see the same actions as threatening when taken by other countries. As we now know, the Soviets did not want to engage American forces but felt threatened by the U.S. response to their forces in Cuba. The Soviets had at least nine tactical nuclear weapons on the island, and their on-site commanders had been given authorization for their defensive use in the case of a U.S. invasion.

Better safe than sorry types can overturn the usual constraints on the use of military force when national security is believed to be at major risk if they are followed. This interpretation also is useful in explaining some recent U.S. actions, including the Reagan administration's policies in Central America and the Caribbean. In the better safe than sorry belief system, the highest priority is given to in-group security. While just war justifications are desirable if a war must be waged, they are not necessary for embarking upon military action. Flexibility of response is much more important than establishing all-encompassing, morally defined restrictions on our national policy. Indeed, given the realities of achieving national survival in times of international tensions, better safe than sorry adherents think that it is doubtful one can ever impose such enduring constraints. An enemy can manipulate a nation that attempts to do so by making it seem as though all the just war criteria have not yet been met until it is too late to militarily defeat him. Iraq seems to have attempted to do this prior to the Gulf War.

National interest, national authority, and military necessity weigh heavily in the better safe than sorry view. Accordingly, the benefit of the doubt always is given to one's government. As long as the legal authorities are perceived as pursuing group security in a way consistent with a nation's traditional cultural and legal norms, followers of better safe than sorry thinking will support their government's war policies. For better safe than sorry elites, the burden of proof always rests on those who advocate military constraints, because constraints could jeopardize the chances of victory and national survival. The better safe than sorry view holds that specific moral restrictions on the waging of war are acceptable only after our in-group security has been safeguarded.

However, the better safe than sorry outlook is clearly different from an amoral reason of state approach. For those who adhere to the better safe than sorry position, war is never an exemplary activity. As our evidence shows, most contemporary elites reject the tenets of moral crusading, which endorses war as a moral virtue. Better safe than sorry followers also reject the Machiavellian view that war is just another policy instrument that may be used to acquire political advantage. While they do not want to act unjustly in an aggressive, military sense, better safe than sorry elites also demand that others do not act aggressively toward them. At best, war is seen as a necessary evil to safeguard group defense.

Risk

For followers of the better safe than sorry perspective, war remains regrettable, but a lesser evil than risking the safety of one's group. The key evaluative element for better safe than sorry elites is risk. They believe that the international system is so dangerous that following predetermined rules in all circumstances invites disaster. An essential idea of this view is that conflict is an uncertain activity. This is why one must act so prudently. Since the risk aversion dimension we have discovered is an empirically derived concept rather than one deduced from a series of abstract premises, it is important to delve more deeply into its substance.

Many writers suggest that the critical factor in explaining attitudes toward foreign policy during the cold war was whether one believed that the Soviet Union's principal goal was to gain world hegemony or to protect itself, just as the United States wanted an equal measure of national security. After a brief cooperative period during World War II, U.S. public opinion was structured by how one viewed such Soviet actions as the 1948 Czechoslovakian coup and the 1948–1949 Berlin blockade. While these actions were resented, Americans also took into account the possible consequences of a military response. For example, the proportion of people who advocated using the atomic bomb against the Soviets declined when the USSR got the bomb as well (Gaddis 1987; Shapiro and Page 1988). While such events shaped U.S. assessments of the Soviet threat and what could be done about it, they did not affect all people's attitudes in equal measure.

On the one hand, public opinion tends to be united when America's enemies engage in threatening activities from both a strict just war and a better safe than sorry perspective. Such was the case with the Pearl Harbor attack that brought the country together to defeat Japan. On the other hand, opinions tend to be fragmented when the actions of a foreign nation are threatening according to the evaluative criteria of only one belief system. Consequently, public opposition to military actions in such places as Grenada and Panama probably would have increased if those conflicts had become more prolonged and costly, since the security threats to American interests there were obscure. These observations also provide insights into the debate over the Vietnam War and why some people unexpectedly oppose military conscription when their country is fighting what their belief system tells them is an immoral conflict. In the words of Muhammad Ali, speaking of the draft:

Keep asking me no matter how long —
On the war in Vietnam I sing this song —
I ain't got no quarrel with the Viet Cong.

The concept of prudence is central to the better safe than sorry belief system and perhaps best distinguishes it from strict just war. It is a concept that permeates all the classic reason of state writings. Recognizing this, in the pretest of our survey we included many items that dealt with prudence, but it did not emerge as a defining characteristic of the classical reason of state doctrine in the pretest. Consequently, we did not explicitly include prudence in any of the reason of state items in the first wave of our survey tapping military attitudes. Nevertheless, prudence emerged anyway as the most important metalevel principle organizing the cognitive space of Americans toward conflict.

Even though prudence is central to risk aversion, it is not consistently defined in the traditional literature. Instead, it is referred to variously as caution, moderation, defensiveness, and stability seeking. Thomas Hobbes refers to prudence as conditioned, unarticulated, and often nonrational expectations arising from regularities in one's experiences. Others refer to it as practical morality, a striving for morally desirable ends that are politically possible or realistic (Thompson 1983, 25). From this perspective, prudence is concerned with interpreting and applying the principles of morality in particular situations and with making instrumental calculations, not with balancing or trading off moral principles against other values. In this view, "Morality is one thing, prudence another" (Mapel 1990, 433). Machiavelli calls prudence an adaptiveness that may border on expediency and the ability to use deception and decisive force when needed without regard for moral scruples. Hans Morgenthau refers to prudence as consequentialist thinking, predictive power, and the "weighing of the consequences of alternative political actions" (1967, 10). For some other realists, prudence is seen as a procedural policy-making process, but prudence of this sort lacks an explicit substantive value content.

Even though prudence as vigilance and defensiveness was not used explicitly to define the reason of state school in the first wave of our survey, it emerged in the empirical analysis anyway. Prudence as risk aversion is a global ordering feature that cannot be identified uniquely with any school of international relations. Prudence is not associated only with the reason of state tradition; as a statistical concept, it embraces aspects of many different schools. It is a salient feature that does not define any particular doctrine, but embodies the principles of the many doctrines that are related to the risk sensitivity dimension.

Clarifying the Better Safe than Sorry Belief System

Since prudence is such a universal decision-making criterion, in the research subsequent to our initial survey of military attitudes we attempted to determine whether better safe than sorry is purely a military outlook or has broader applicability. We thought that it would be most useful to the military, since experimental studies in game theory have shown that cooperative behavior can be greatly increased in groups that have a strong sense of identity (see, e.g., Dawes, van de Kraft, and Orbell 1988). We were particularly surprised when military attitudes were found to have the lowest level of variance explained by the risk sensitivity dimension of all groups (see fig. 6.1). While aversion to risk is important to members of the military, and the better safe than sorry framework may dominate military thought, as an organizing principle of belief constraint, aversion to risk is more important in explaining differences in attitudes among members of all the other elite groups than it is for the U.S. military.[1]

While just war thinking has been discussed extensively, better safe than sorry as a coherent belief system largely has gone unnoticed in a literature that has not recognized this particular collection of beliefs as a distinct framework. Since it is not directly analogous to any of the historical positions developed by philosophers, theologians, or political theorists, it deserves more attention here. One commentator called a similar viewpoint "parity plus damage-limiting" or more simply "live and let live" (Dyson 1984, 273). This outlook has two basic principles. First, if given a choice between saving our own people and hurting the enemy, we should save our own people. Second, we always should retain the potential to hurt our enemies as much as they can hurt us. Such a strategy also is called the brass rule, and it provides a framework that is both defensive and risk-averse, the fundamental features of the better safe than sorry approach.

The prudence of better safe than sorry encapsulates a strategic perspective of the international system. This game theory conception can be contrasted with the view of Lawrence Kohlberg (1980), who argues that at the highest stage of moral reasoning people are political liberals who always take the views of others into consideration and do not act just to maximize their own egoistically ends. But Kohlberg's approach is unable to explain why some people "regress" to a lower stage of cognitive development and fail to adopt a liberal policy option in all real-world situations.

The key to understanding this paradox is to realize that the better safe than sorry belief system also represents a higher level of cognitive theorizing than does simple egoistic behavior. It takes into consideration consequentialist possibilities, as does strict just war thought, but better safe than sorry adherents see the world as such a dangerous place that it is often impossible to act in any other way than self-defense. In such a Hobbesian world, the implementation of Kohlberg's liberalism is viewed by better safe than sorry adherents as unrealistic because others will not reciprocate our actions. Instead, they will turn our goodwill against us, attempting to destroy us and take our possessions. However, if reciprocity is deemed to be possible, better safe than sorry elites will be inclined to act in Kohlberg's liberal manner and show concern for others. Consequently, a deep-seated conflict over political ideology emerges. During the cold war, people who expressed liberal attitudes domestically might have been forced to adopt a better safe than sorry view when confronting international communism because they believed no rules could be applied effectively in the international system.

To refine the ethical contours of better safe than sorry, we added a series of additional inquiries on subsequent versions of the survey instru-

Table 7.1 **Wording of Supplemental Better Safe Than Sorry Items**

Who Is the In-Group

35. **Protect Our Troops:** In a war, if forced to make a choice between protecting our own people or winning a military battle, we should protect our people.

Potential for Military Response

36. **Equality of Forces:** For military purposes, we should maintain an ability to damage our enemies as badly as they can damage us.

37. **Superiority of Forces:** If our enemies are too weak to hurt us now or in the future, then it is not necessary to have military forces capable of destroying them.

Potential for Suspending Morality

38. **Secret Weapon:** In a war, if the enemy develops a new, powerful secret weapon, it may be necessary to ignore moral concerns in order to counter the weapon.

39. **Possibility of Defeat:** It is better to act morally in war and be defeated than to act immorally and win.

ment. These items were designed to clarify a number of issues: Who is the in-group for better safe than sorry proponents? How much does this belief system reflect a philosophy of maintaining a restrained ability to hurt an enemy? How does the better safe than sorry belief system encompass the supreme emergency doctrine of suspending moral concerns toward others during extreme situations? The additional items we developed are presented in table 7.1 and were posed to the diplomats, journalists, and clerics who participated in the final waves of our survey.

By examining the correlations between the five supplementary items and the original risk sensitivity factor, we can more fully define what is measured by risk sensitivity and this aspect of the better safe than sorry belief system. The first of these additional items concerns whether a specific military in-group is defined by the dimension. Item 35 presents a contrast of the sort posed by Dyson (1984). If given a choice between protecting our own people, which is of immediate advantage to the armed forces, and winning a military battle, which is to the long-term advantage of our own people most broadly defined, do better safe than sorry individuals automatically define *us* as the nation's military forces? The responses to this item are only weakly correlated (−0.18) with the risk factor, which means that the military is not an exclusively defined in-group that is the only concern of better safe than sorry elites.

The next two items deal with the potential for military response against a hostile state. Item 36 contends that we should follow Teddy Roosevelt's admonition to carry a big stick by always having sufficient force to damage our enemies as much as they can damage us. This item is correlated with the risk dimension at 0.38, providing weak evidence that keeping a substantial reserve of forces to counter the actions of a powerful potential enemy is associated with the factor. Item 37 deals with maintaining forces superior to those of potential enemies who now are militarily weak. A negative response on this item indicates risk aversion. It is correlated in the correct direction for a risk sensitivity interpretation, but this is a weaker relationship, having only a −0.28 correlation. Taken together, the responses to these two items indicate that risk-averse individuals who lean toward the better safe than sorry framework are indeed prudent, but this prudence is a measured and calculated response. As the perceived risk from a potential enemy declines, so too does the concern of prudent, better safe than sorry elites. This interpretation seems to capture what is essential to the risk factor and the better safe than sorry belief system: it is a calculated response to actual or perceived threats.

The essence of risk aversion, and the defining characteristic of the better safe than sorry framework, is most evident in an examination of two more items. In these scenarios, the level of risk to the United States suddenly and dramatically increases. Item 38 deals with the possibility that an enemy has discovered a new and powerful secret weapon. In such a case, should we ignore moral concerns to counteract the weapon's potential? This scenario is similar to what prompted Israel to bomb an Iraqi nuclear installation ten years before the rest of the world realized that Iraq was trying to develop nuclear weapons. By the mid-1990s the same option was being discussed in the United States as a response to similar actions by North Korea. The item is correlated with the risk dimension at 0.66, which is a much stronger relation than the previous inquiries. So too is the issue of whether "it is better to act morally in a war and be defeated than to act immorally and win." The correlation of item 39 with the prudence factor is −0.64. Both items thus reflect a prudent, supreme emergency logic.[2]

Applicability

The better safe than sorry belief system has a number of interesting features. It is an empirically observed framework that responds to real-life problems. It has survival benefits for its followers, who see the international system as a very risky place. It has evolved, particularly among the military, out of years of experience, and its precepts are taught heuristically to new recruits.

The two real-world belief systems we have described so far have an important impact on people's attitudes, but they also have different utility for various groups. Better safe than sorry has numerous advantages for military officers, who may face the possibility of day-to-day battle. It may have advantages as well for structuring the attitudes of other elites, such as members of Congress, who have to deal with certain aspects of international conflicts. It offers much less utility to journalists and religious leaders, who are not involved in making these decisions and have no direct responsibility if a policy goes awry.

AMBIVALENCE

For those who take an ambivalent view, the highest priority is in-group security, but moral considerations are also important. In reflecting this approach, a military officer commented, "I think war is basically immoral, but part of human nature. The U.S. should take the high moral road in international relations, but when attacked you have to win. We are not good losers."

The ambivalent view has three distinguishing traits. First, it assigns to moral constraints a more important role than better safe than sorry does. In order of priority, a series of moral concerns justify the acceptance of some risk to in-group safety. How should war be conducted? One should strive to protect innocents. When should a war be conducted? One should exhaust all options before choosing war, which is the last resort criterion of just war doctrine. Why should war be conducted? War should be waged only for defensive purposes. The ambivalent view rejects wars of aggrandizement. War should be used only for defensive reasons and only after diplomatic efforts have failed.

Second, among ambivalents, in-group security is a higher priority than morality. Nevertheless, moral concerns are important enough to justify the acceptance of some risk to the in-group. This sentiment does not depend on enemy reciprocity. In the cognitive space of U.S. elites, the ambivalent view lies between better safe than sorry and strict just war.

Third, the ambivalent view depends on situational assessments of risk. Because of this, the position tends to produce unstable attitudes and can lead to quick opinion changes and radical policy shifts. An important aspect of this orientation is that the attitudes of ambivalents are apt to be unstable, since they depend on changing perceived circumstances.

What factors do ambivalents examine when making decisions? Threats to national stability and organizational values would almost certainly count, in the abstract, as major sources of risk to most observers, but forecasting and monitoring such risks with respect to war is a complex affair that encompasses many questions. Is there some acceptable way of avoiding war? Will the war be long or short? Is the war being won? At what cost? Can constraints on conduct be imposed without risking defeat? Is the enemy showing reciprocal restraint? Answers to these questions would be useful for estimating risk. Accordingly, the degree of ingroup risk that is tolerable to protect innocents is often unclear. People can be powerfully crosspressured by their moral desires and their military objectives. Just when information is necessary to know whether a balancing act between one's ideals and one's group interests is possible, it may not be available.

The result is often a wavering policy. Contradictory attitudes dominate, and there is no intellectual coherence. Indeed, it might be more accurate to label the ambivalent view as a collection of moral inclinations and conditional permissions to act on these inclinations, rather than a coherent belief system. In some respects, the ambivalent view may be conceived as a continuum of contingent possibilities. Some situations might allow momentarily principled policy positions with little difficulty. Other situations may render adoption of a principled moral stand unlikely if one wishes to continue in a position of legal authority. Consequently, ambivalents often compromise the important moral principles they would like to follow in an attempt to achieve other valued goals. Compromise, rather than conviction, is characteristic of ambivalents. Hence, the practical and psychological distances from ambivalence to either the strict just war or better safe than sorry positions can range from very near to very far.

Faced with the difficulty of weighing in-group risk against a desire to protect the innocent, one's sense of ambivalence mounts, and a variety of contingent outcomes are possible. One might try risk balancing by simultaneously seeking military security while retaining the use of force, but unfavorable situational factors can make this reconciliation impossible, shifting attitudes toward risk aversion and better safe than sorry conclusions. Other possibilities include various forms of delay, vacillation, or muddling through. In any case, given the large number of contingencies one faces in international politics, a general theory of moral judgment is not possible for ambivalents. Leo Tolstoy described such a situation as faced by a military commander who

> is always in the midst of a series of shifting events and so he never can at any moment consider the whole import of an event that is occurring. Moment by moment the event is imperceptibly shaping itself, and at every moment of this continuous, uninterrupted shaping of events the commander in chief is in the

midst of a most complex play of intrigues, worries, contingencies, authorities, projects, counsels, threats, and deceptions and is continually obligated to innumerable questions addressed to him, which constantly conflict with one another. (1942, 921–22)

The ambivalent view falls midway between the strict just war and better safe than sorry belief systems, and is located toward the center of the elite cognitive space. As with better safe than sorry, the highest priority for these balancers is in-group security. While moral considerations seem to be at least as important as national interest in judging the nature of conflict, ambivalents can have great difficulty in deciding which of these goals should take precedence in particular situations. Many of them may not have fully recognized the depth of the real-world ethical conflicts they face. They may not realize that it is sometimes impossible to uphold their cherished moral principles and still achieve the short-run goals of their in-group.

In terms of figure 6.2, one would expect many ambivalents to fall in the broad region located between the strict just war and better safe than sorry belief systems. This ambivalent region would probably not extend to the far end of either the force legitimacy or constraints on war dimensions, because of a general reluctance among many ambivalents to embrace extreme outlooks on these matters. However, ambivalents might tend to drift toward the risk-averse end of the risk dimension, thus reflecting the ambivalent's high regard for in-group security.

A key moral justification for military conflict is that war is to be a last resort. Of equal importance in the ambivalent view is the desire to protect all innocents. Some risks to in-group security may be acceptable to secure protection for innocents. Such a moral sentiment does not depend on enemy reciprocity. Less crucial than the last resort and protection of innocents criteria is that a war be defensive. There appears to be no other major moral sentiments under the ambivalent view.

In describing the contours of the cold war international system, J. David Singer sees a situation with a number of similarities to the ambivalent view:

Premises of unbridled sovereignty clearly remain in the saddle, and when allegedly "vital interests" are at stake, it is difficult to observe much evidence of adherence to the more constraining principles embodied in either the "positive" law—as expressed in the Charter of the United Nations, the statute of the International Court of Justice and the hundreds of conventions and treaties now on the books—or the "natural" law found in the more scholarly literature. . . . While this impression would not be difficult to substantiate, for instance with respect to superpower behavior, it is also worth noting that when less vital commercial, cultural and technical interests are involved, conformity to legal constraints is remarkably frequent. (1986, 14)

The features of an ambivalent view were often evident among our respondents, particularly diplomats, who argued that the world is a complicated place where general rules cannot be applied in all situations. We can now understand why ambivalent diplomats would want to shield other decision makers — whom they believe are ambivalents, as well — from the vacillations of public opinion. Unlike the strict just war types, ambivalents are highly susceptible to sudden opinion shifts. Since the public does not pay a great deal of attention to day-to-day foreign affairs, when an international crisis does occur there is a rapid crystallization of attitudes against a threatening enemy, but this evaporates as the crisis fades from view. If U.S. elites are ambivalents who are willing to take the public's mood into consideration when formulating foreign policy, then national policy may vacillate with the mood of the day. Such public mood shifts could endanger stability in foreign policy, a frequently valued goal of diplomats.

Our characterization of the ambivalent view also suggests a solution to an interesting attitude paradox. It is sometimes noted, with general puzzlement, that occasionally there is more animosity between people whose policy positions are apparently similar than between people whose policy preferences are far apart. The key feature to be noted in solving this paradox is that the ambivalent belief system produces unstable positions that can change without warning. In other words, ambivalents cannot be trusted. They may not be deliberately deceptive nor act to benefit themselves without regard to others, but no matter how sincerely and forcefully they state their policy positions, they can change them in an impetuous fashion.[3] No one can really trust these ambivalents, not even those of their own political persuasion, but there is no necessary malevolence here. Ambivalents are unable to hold coherent and stable positions because their beliefs are not well structured or they are crosspressured by the desire to achieve noble goals that are in conflict.

In contrast to ambivalents, there are consistent people in politics who can be trusted by everyone. While one may strongly disagree with the policies of such an honorable adversary, these more ideological politicians can be trusted not to make sudden unpredictable policy shifts. Ronald Reagan was such a person. He was well liked by most of those who opposed him politically, and since his philosophy about government had been deduced from a few core beliefs about politics, he could be trusted not to make many sudden and unpredictable policy shifts that would take people by surprise.[4]

RELATIONSHIPS AMONG BELIEF SYSTEMS

When examining the adoption of belief systems by U.S. elites, it is useful to refer to the modal schools of traditional thought that are most relevant to prudence and conflict constraints. Better safe than sorry puts relatively few constraints on warfare, while pacifism — which has very few support-ers — requires total constraint. Pacifism is an extreme position of non-violence. Strict just war followers, on the other hand, neither advocate the extreme nonviolence of the pacifists nor engage in what they see as the excessive violence of the better safe than sorry framework. Between those who embrace better safe than sorry and strict just war positions are am-bivalents, who want both to be moral and to win, but often have difficulty in reconciling the conflicts between these goals. An example is Lyndon Johnson, who was never reconciled to the fact of the large number of American casualties in the Vietnam War. He commented about his agony in saying:

> If [I] had "lost" Vietnam . . . there would be Robert Kennedy out in front leading the fight against me, telling everybody that I had betrayed John Ken-nedy's commitment to South Vietnam. That I had let a democracy fall into the hands of the Communists. That I was a coward. An unmanly man. A man without a spine. Oh, I could see it coming all right. Every night when I fell asleep I would see myself tied to the ground in the middle of a long, open space. In the distance I could hear the voices of thousands of people. They were all shouting and running toward me: "Coward! Traitor! Weakling!" (Quoted in Wintle 1989, 431)

To clarify the relation among the various belief systems as inferred from our data, we should reconceptualize matters. Since the risk sen-sitivity dimension is virtually uncorrelated with the force legitimacy and constraints on war dimensions, we will set aside risk considerations mo-mentarily and consider a two-dimensional space that consists of these other factors of evaluation. Such dimensional labeling allows us to iden-tify certain special regions that are related to policy beliefs. Since dimen-sional coordinates extracted in factor analysis are not organized on a ratio

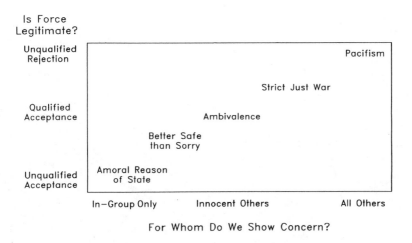

Figure 7.1 **Relationship of Just War Constraints to Belief Systems**

scale, we cannot identify precise locations, but the gross contours and relative positions of the belief systems presented in figure 7.1 are empirically justified.

In the lower left region, characterized by in-group concern and unqualified acceptance of force, is the classic amoral reason of state position. In the upper right region, characterized by universalism and rejection of force, we find the pacifist position. We should again stress that neither universal pacifists nor those who advocate the unqualified use of force appear prominently among U.S. elites, but we identify these positions anyway for purposes of elucidation. Closer to the center region, and representing varying degrees of practical concern for the innocent and a qualified acceptance of force, we find a region of mixed possibilities, including strict just war, ambivalence, and some elements of better safe than sorry once in-group safety has been secured. These are distinctive viewpoints reflecting real-world responses to the problems presented by conflict in the international system.

If our reconceptualization of these matters is correct, then we should be able to empirically classify U.S. elites as proponents of strict just war and better safe than sorry without much overlap in the classification. Operationally, we did so on the basis of how they responded to the seven just war items and the seven items most strongly correlated with the better safe than sorry framework (that is, the top seven items in table 6.2, above). To allow for interesting comparisons, we created approximately equal-

Table 7.2 **Belief System Supporters**

		Strict Just War	
		Not a Strong Supporter	*Strong Supporter*
	Not a Strong Supporter	1,472 (72.6%) Ambivalent (neither)	269 (13.3%) Strict just war
Better Safe Than Sorry			
	Strong Supporter	275 (13.6%) Better safe than sorry	11 (0.5%) Both

size groups of strong supporters of these two frameworks.[5] The evidence is presented in table 7.2, where we see that 13.3 percent of elites are strong just war advocates and 13.6 percent of them are strong better safe than sorry supporters. There is only a 0.5 percent overlap of individuals who support both frameworks. The ability to divide elites so neatly into these theoretically meaningful classifications once again is prima facie evidence of the reasonableness of our approach.

Before proceeding to another issue, we should briefly comment on the small number of individuals who were classified as strong supporters of both strict just war and better safe than sorry. As real-world actors, they hold an interesting position that is reflected in parts of the normative literature. According to the supreme emergency doctrine as derived from just war doctrine, it is possible to have an overlap in support for the better safe than sorry and strict just war belief systems, because a person could advocate just war constraints until they are overridden by supreme emergency logic. Empirically, this is reflected by the eleven elites who are strong supporters of both belief systems.[6] These people face a serious value conflict. On the one hand, they are strongly pulled toward protecting innocent parties in foreign nations. On the other hand, at some point they are willing to forego that responsibility to ensure the safety of their in-group. As we will see, this value conflict is particularly characteristic of one U.S. elite group.

NICARAGUA WAR SCENARIOS

If our model is sound, then the classification of U.S. elites as adherents of strict just war, better safe than sorry, or ambivalence should allow us to predict their likely policy positions on specific international conflict scenarios. We already have examined the potential for U.S. military action against the Sandinistas, but let us do so again in the context of these belief systems. The evidence is presented in table 7.3. An examination of American responses to item 45 indicates that 95 percent of the better safe than sorry elites would support a war against Nicaragua if that country intended to join in an imminent attack on the United States, but only 67 percent of the elites who support empirically defined strict just war would support such a conflict. Similarly, item 44 examines support for a war to defend a foreign nation that was a victim of direct Nicaraguan aggression. This justification for conflict receives 66 percent support from proponents of the empirically defined better safe than sorry position, but only 36 percent support from those who support strict just war.

Also interesting are responses to item 42, regarding a scenario whereby Nicaragua provides aid to communist revolutionaries in adjacent countries. Such actions in international law are usually considered to be intervention or indirect aggression rather than aggression in the sense of an armed attack that can justify a defensive military response. A large percentage of supporters of all three belief systems agreed with this distinction. Only 11 percent of those who strongly agree with most of the general principles of the just war belief system support such military action, but 32 percent of the better safe than sorry elites do so.

Two of the scenarios involved the justifiability of preventive war. In item 41, Nicaragua starts a military buildup that overshadows its neighboring states. All U.S. elites overwhelmingly reject such war. Only 21 percent of better safe than sorry advocates and 5 percent of strict just war followers consider such Nicaraguan actions as a justification for military conflict.

The most dramatic difference in support for the scenarios between adherents to better safe than sorry and strict just war is evident concerning Soviet bases. In item 43, Nicaragua invites Soviet military bases to be set up within its borders. Only 27 percent of those classified as likely supporters of the strict just war position believe that such Nicaraguan-Soviet actions provide a justification for war, but 65 percent of the better safe than sorry individuals see this as cause for war. The scenario involving

Table 7.3 **Support for a Hypothetical War with Nicaragua, by Belief System** (in percent)

Survey Item	Better Safe Than Sorry	Ambivalent	Strict Just War
Would support a war with Nicaragua:			
40. If Nicaragua sets up a communist government	13	4	5
41. If Nicaragua starts a military buildup that overshadows its neighboring states	21	7	5
42. If Nicaragua sends aid (arms, advisers, etc.) to communist revolutionary movements in neighboring countries	32	14	11
43. If Nicaragua invites Soviet military bases to be set up within its borders	65	33	27
44. If Nicaragua invades a neighboring country	66	52	36
45. If there is clear evidence that Nicaragua is going to join an attack on the United States	95	77	67
Average	49	31	25

Soviet bases has parallels to the Cuban missile crisis and shows how certain situations can produce intense disagreement.

Again, we have demonstrated one of the major distinctions between the foreign policy prescriptions advocated by followers of the real-world belief systems. As interpreted by just war scholars, most of the actions in these Nicaraguan scenarios are not a legitimate cause for conflict. The opinions of just war adherents on these scenarios stand in dramatic contrast to decision making based on the notion of prudence. Better safe than sorry elites see all major violations of national security as justification for military operations, while strict just war followers are far more reluctant to use force.

The scenario expressed in item 40 involves military intervention to protect the right of national self-determination. Just war scholars consider national self-determination to be violated if an outside power intervenes to control another state's affairs. Accordingly, the existence of a communist system does not necessarily represent the absence of self-determination, as was argued by the Reagan Doctrine. Both better safe than sorry and strict just war adherents agree with the standard interpretation of the self-determination principle. Only 13 percent of better safe than sorry adherents and 5 percent of just war advocates see this as a sufficient justification for war.

The overall pattern of responses to the Nicaraguan scenarios seen in table 7.3 is quite interesting. Not only do those who follow just war constraints find themselves in disagreement with the Reagan administration during the 1980s, but the same is true for the better safe than sorry elites who are far more willing to use military force in international affairs. In its public utterances, the Reagan administration often took a moral crusading position in attempting to galvanize public opinion by arguing that our enemies were so evil and U.S. goals were so just that any actions necessary to destroy our enemies were justified. To quote the president in reflecting that viewpoint, his actions were "morally . . . the only right thing to do" (Reagan 1984). However, the fundamental way in which most U.S. elites make decisions about foreign policy would have brought them into conflict with the president if he pushed the matter.

MIDDLE EAST WAR SCENARIOS

Before the Gulf War was any more than a theoretical possibility, we also posed a series of questions to U.S. elites about potential military actions in the Middle East. The purpose of these inquiries was not to determine what justifications for war they thought were acceptable but to investigate whether it was reasonable to abandon international moral constraints. While this issue should only be relevant to certain sorts of elites, a number of different schools of thought can be called upon to justify the decision. Legalism argues that the morality of individuals has no place in war, and the only duty for an individual is to obey legitimate orders. Amoral reason of state logic argues that nations should do whatever is to their own advantage, and moral concerns are irrelevant. Moral crusaders insist that sometimes our enemies are so evil or our causes so just that any action may be taken to destroy an enemy or punish it into submission. Finally, supreme emergency reasoning argues that the constraints of just war thinking must be followed unless the survival and core values of our nation are at risk. In such a case, the normal rules of morality can be suspended. While some just war scholars would adhere to supreme emergency logic, this position on the ethics of conflict is hotly disputed (see, e.g., Walzer 1977).

Table 7.4 presents the survey responses to a series of scenarios that

Table 7.4 **Support for Suspending Moral Constraints Toward Iran, by Belief System** (in percent)

Survey Item	Better Safe Than Sorry	Ambivalent	Strict Just War
Would support suspending moral contraints toward Iran:			
46. If Iran imposes an economically damaging embargo on the United States	30	5	4
47. If Iran invades a country friendly to the United States	46	15	10
48. If Iran is about to get nuclear weapons	63	22	10
49. If Iran begins attacking U.S. shipping	70	26	20
50. If Iran begins organizing terrorist attacks against Americans	80	34	18
51. If Iran begins military attacks on the U.S. homeland	94	54	34
Average	56	22	14

requested: "Check all the situations below that you feel are serious enough to justify the United States' suspending moral constraints when dealing with Iran." As in the Nicaragua scenarios, the greatest level of support is expressed for the situation when the United States is about to be attacked, but the overall support here is significantly lower than in the first set of scenarios.

Some 80 percent of better safe than sorry elites see terrorism as a sufficient justification for the United States to abandon its usually observed moral constraints, while only 18 percent of adherents to strict just war share this opinion. This is probably because terrorism is viewed by better safe than sorry elites as an illegitimate activity that should be met with eye-for-an-eye justice, while the just war doctrine forbids such retaliation. Even fewer U.S. elites support abandoning moral constraints in the scenario regarding Iran's imminent acquisition of nuclear weapons (item 48), which was one of a number of justifications for military action against Iraq during the Gulf War. Again, on close inspection we observe major differences in specific attitudes exist that are related to a person's belief system.

Overall, the general pattern of response to the Iran scenarios is somewhat different from that for the Nicaragua scenarios. The legitimacy ascribed to using military force (see Nicaragua data in table 7.3) is a function of the seriousness of a threat, but the justification for suspending moral constraints (see Iran data in table 7.4) depends on the perceived legitimacy of an enemy's action, given current norms of proper behavior in the international system. This interpretation can be seen in the larger percentage of elites who justify the use of force if Nicaragua invaded a neighboring country (item 44) compared with the percentage that see this as a legitimate justification for ignoring moral constraints when dealing with Iran (item 47).

The levels of support expressed for abandoning moral constraints if Iran is about to get nuclear weapons, if Iran attacks U.S. shipping, and if Iran engages in terrorism against American citizens can be interpreted similarly. Again, the issue these scenarios seem to capture is one of legitimacy more than military threat. So many countries have acquired nuclear weapons that doing so is a legitimate, if threatening, action, but both terrorism and direct attacks on our shipping are viewed as illegitimate actions that demand something other than a normal restrained response.

Individuals who follow the two extreme real-world belief systems always disagree over the amount of moral concern that should accompany one's dealings with an adversary. In most of the scenarios we have examined, the better safe than sorry elites are willing to suspend moral constraints to protect U.S. security, and their suspension of moral concerns occurs substantially before the advent of a supreme emergency. The strict just war belief system allows for suspension of moral constraints only if just war doctrine itself is considered a suspension of the moral constraints embodied in pacifism. Beyond this, the seven just war principles have a deontological character.

It is increasingly apparent that belief systems regarding conflict actually do have a relationship to real-world attitudes about the use of force. Specific attitudes vary according to situational contexts, and these belief systems explain why people disagree over the use of force and why certain policies, such as the Reagan Doctrine, never gained broad support. In the case of the administration's Central American policy of the late 1980s, knowing how an individual views matters of risk aversion and the general legitimacy of military force helps to explain specific attitudes toward potential conflict in that region.

EIGHT

Nuclear Deterrence

If I had only known I would have become a watchmaker.
—Albert Einstein

Using the cognitive space we have developed, it is possible to infer the likely policy positions of U.S. elites about the appropriate use of conventional force. This can be done through an examination of the salient characteristics of particular conflict situations and by knowing whether individuals are proponents of strict just war or the better safe than sorry position. Our approach is also useful for predicting when disputes over conventional warfare should be most acrimonious. When these inferences match our commonsense understanding of political reality, they provide more evidence for the reasonableness of this approach to studying foreign policy attitudes. The cognitive space of warfare beliefs is a reasonably simple tool that explains both general and specific attitudes toward conventional conflict, but before developing an explicit model of attitude formation that explains how people come to adopt their belief systems, we need to examine another important issue. Is the cognitive space of warfare beliefs related to contemporary disputes over nuclear weapons policy?

Many writers contend that the traditional moral criteria for evaluating war have broken down with the development of nuclear weapons. Ironically, others argue that the development of nuclear weapons has universalized moral sensibilities. Since people see nuclear war as a quantum leap beyond conventional war, this likely feeds an urge to contemplate basic moral values, heightening ethical consciousness (Blight 1990). Accordingly, the awesomeness of nuclear weapons intensifies the inclination to moral reasoning by national decision makers.

The problems of nuclear war are a relatively new addition to the philosophical landscape of conflict. Almost as soon as many leading normative thinkers had come to a consensus about the just war tradition, along came nuclear weapons (Acton 1991). While our belief system framework adequately describes attitude formation toward conventional warfare, this may not be the case for nuclear weapons policy. Instead, the destructive capability of nuclear war may have rendered meaningless the usual concerns over just war principles and destroyed the cognitive structure that our model has identified. The basic question posed in this chapter is whether the same framework that describes decision making for traditional warfare issues can also be used to evaluate attitudes toward nuclear deterrence.

MUTUAL ASSURED DESTRUCTION

For forty years the international system was structured by intense rivalry between the United States and the Soviet Union. Neither side much trusted the other. The Soviets were obsessed with military security after the terrible losses they suffered during World War II. So, too, was the United States, because of the threat it perceived from the Soviet Union; moreover, the surprise attack at Pearl Harbor had heightened American military insecurities. Many Americans saw communism as an ideological threat that sought to destroy the world's capitalist states without regard for moral or legal constraints. The rhetoric of communist leaders often validated Western fears and reinforced the need for supreme emergency reasoning in the face of this threat. Dmitri Zacharevichi Manuilsky stated in an address to the Lenin School of Political Warfare:

> War to the hilt between communism and capitalism is inevitable. Today, of course, we are not strong enough to attack. Our time will come in twenty or thirty years. To win, we shall need the element of surprise. . . . The capitalist countries . . . will leap at another chance to be friends. As soon as their guard is down, we shall smash them with our clenched fists. (Quoted in Wintle 1989, 254)

In the words of Mao Tse-tung:

> Can one guess how great will be the toll of human casualties in a future war? Possibly it would be a third of the 2,700 million inhabitants of the entire world. . . . But even half would not be so bad. . . . If half of humanity were destroyed, the other half would remain but imperialism would be destroyed

entirely and there would be only Socialism in all the world. (Quoted in Wintle 1989, 356)

The temptation to respond to the communist menace with military aggression was overshadowed by the existence of nuclear weapons (Gaddis 1987). Over time, a growing number of policy makers, strategists, and religious thinkers came to view the atomic bomb as having irrevocably changed the nature of great-power war and the relationship of war to foreign policy (Jervis 1989). Until Hiroshima, just war scholars thought that war, while at times massive and genocidal, could be limited through the application of certain rules. Nuclear weapons cast this assumption into doubt and there was a rethinking of the usefulness of war itself. In the words of Konrad Lorenz, "A few decades ago one could . . . still accept . . . 'My Country right or wrong' as a proper expression of patriotism; today this standpoint can be regarded as lacking in moral responsibility." And for Andrei Sakharov, "A thermonuclear war cannot be considered a continuation of politics by other means. It would be a means to universal suicide."

The debate over nuclear weapons caused some thinkers who had allowed for the possibility of traditional war to consider rejecting war as no longer a viable option in the modern age. The old rules did not seem to apply in a world that could see the extinction of civilization. Others saw nuclear warfare issues as largely technical problems, but problems that were no doubt equally insurmountable. Given a government's bureaucratic control problems, nuclear weapons were not a reasonable option because their use could not be limited.

The practical response to the nuclear threat was the doctrine of mutual assured destruction, or MAD. For the United States, MAD served both as a deterrent to a Soviet nuclear attack and as a war-fighting strategy. It called for the threat of countercities nuclear warfare as a deterrent and for launching nuclear warfare if that deterrence failed. This was, in effect, a potential continuation of World War II terror bombing. In both cases, such warfare was justified in terms of the retaliatory ethic or the approach of choosing the lesser of evils, as occurs with moral relativism and situation ethics. During the 1970s and 1980s, U.S. policy shifted toward various counterforce strategies. Nevertheless, countercities warfare remained an option, and the MAD policy continued in place.

The ethical issues raised by nuclear weapons have received extensive analysis. Virtually all just war theorists condemn countercities nuclear warfare, even as a response to the prior nuclear destruction of U.S. cities.[1]

According to them, MAD retaliation violates the principles of just cause, just intent, hope of success, *ad bellum* proportionality, and discriminate means. Most just war theorists also condemn counterforce nuclear warfare as violating both the *ad bellum* and *in bello* proportionality principles and because it is thought likely to escalate into all-out genocidal war.

A notable exception among contemporary scholars is Paul Ramsey (1961, 1968). For Ramsey, nuclear warfare issues revolve around the proper interpretation of the double-effect principle, which is used in conjunction with *in bello* proportionality. The double-effect principle argues that if an action has both a good effect, in destroying enemy nuclear forces, and an evil effect, in causing extensive civilian casualties, then a moral actor must not intend the evil effect. Ramsey defines such intent as a wish or a desire. Since U.S. officials are not moral crusaders desiring enormous enemy civilian casualties, Ramsey concludes that they would not be culpable for the evil consequences of a U.S. nuclear response. Therefore, counterforce nuclear retaliation is morally acceptable. In opposition to Ramsey's position, other just war theorists argue that intent should include knowledge of the consequences of one's actions, and American officials would be held morally accountable for the deaths of millions of Soviet civilians through the use of nuclear weapons (see, e.g., Tucker 1966).

A number of elite comments reflect the intense debate over these issues. Some of our most detailed responses concern U.S. nuclear warfare policy. One is from a retired officer who was responsible for launching intercontinental ballistic missiles. His comments suggest that substantial thought is involved in developing a belief system about international conflict when nuclear issues are involved and that, indeed, nuclear weapons issues have heightened some people's moral sensibilities.

> Would I have launched those missiles? Sadly, yes. Why, because I believe that there are enough clear thinking, reasonable, honorable people in our national command authority to prevent launch of a surprise preemptive strike. On a launch order, I believe that missiles would be enroute to my home and homes of millions of Americans. . . . If I had not launched I believe that the freedom that underpins the greatness of America would be lost forever. Is that a rationalization to accept the responsibility for killing millions of people in direct opposition to Christian belief in the sanctity of human life? Of course it is, but you see I even believe that Christ would offer me salvation after a missile launch, this is my personal leap of faith.

Besides being critical of all forms of actual nuclear warfare, most just war theorists consider the declaratory deterrent strategy of MAD to be morally defensible only if one is willing to slide into the quagmire of consequentialist ethics, which accepts a lesser of evils approach. However, the lesser of evils argument generally is thought to be incompatible with deontological reasoning and with the Pauline injunction that one should not commit or threaten evil in order that good may come.

As a consequence of their rejection of virtually any way to threaten or actually use nuclear weapons, the American Catholic bishops came very close to supporting nuclear pacifism in their 1983 pastoral letter, which would have required advocacy of unilateral U.S. nuclear disarmament. Ultimately, the bishops rejected this path out of a fear of Soviet nuclear blackmail (National Conference of Catholic Bishops 1983; Castelli 1983). The dilemma that the Catholic bishops faced illustrates how institutional goals can affect the evolution of policy positions. The American bishops' final stand did not reflect the moral perfectionism of strict just war thinking but instead acknowledged a type of supreme emergency logic. However, the bishops' position was not so much a suspension of just war restrictions on the conduct of warfare as a suspension of the Pauline injunction against threatening evil that good may come. The bishops' final position rejected MAD as a declaratory policy in favor of a silent threat of disallowed evils by continuing to possess nuclear weapons. This strategy is often denigrated as *bluff deterrence*.

Like the response of most Christian churches to the doctrine of pacifism, the American Catholic bishops recognized that a nation that rejected the use of nuclear weapons unilaterally would be forced into suicidal capitulation to any nation willing to use them. If either the United States or the Soviet Union renounced the use of nuclear weapons for retaliatory purposes, it would lose its credibility as a superpower. As John Foster Dulles put it, "The ability to get to the verge without getting to the war is the necessary art. If you cannot master it, you inevitably get into war. If you try to run away from it, if you are scared to go to the brink, you are lost" (quoted in Wintle 1989, 118).

VIEWS ON NUCLEAR WAR

One of the key moral questions of the cold war was whether nuclear war or nuclear deterrence could be just. To our knowledge, no comprehensive comparative survey of this debate has been undertaken. Accordingly, we decided to probe features of this complex issue. Since our investigations were conducted sequentially, we could include in the later waves of our survey any interesting issues that were raised by the comments of earlier

Table 8.1 **Support for Nuclear Conflict Policies, by Elite Group** (in percent)

Survey Item and Principle	Members of Congress	Diplomats	Journalists	Military Officers	Priests
20. MAD deterrence	75	79	68	94	46
21. MAD retaliation	68	70	63	88	17
22. Nuclear war	74	70	62	93	38
48. Response to acquisition	—	33	29	—	7

Note: Response patterns to items 21 and 22 are reversed so that "strongly disagree" and "disagree" are taken to support the MAD position. Item 48 was not asked of members of Congress and the military. Norms are defined as positions accepted or rejected by at least 90 percent of group respondents.

respondents. One of these concerned Ramsey's justification for counterforce nuclear warfare. Consequently, we asked members of Congress whether they agree or disagree with the following statement: "The United States should not be held morally accountable for the millions of civilian Soviet casualties that might result from an American nuclear counterattack that was aimed only at Soviet military targets." Sixty percent of the surveyed members of Congress agree with the statement, which supports Ramsey's moral reasoning. Only 32 percent disagree, which is in accord with the just war view that counterforce nuclear warfare is immoral. This is interesting, because support for just war views with respect to conventional war is much greater among members of Congress than support for just war reasoning on nuclear issues (52 percent to 32 percent). This apparent reversal in position regarding nuclear warfare, which represents a minority philosophical position, suggests that a deeper examination of nuclear warfare issues is in order.

All versions of our questionnaire included an item (22) dealing with the morality of nuclear warfare. It reads, "It is better to accept defeat than participate in a nuclear war." As table 8.1 shows, despite the almost unanimous condemnation of nuclear warfare by just war scholars, U.S. elites do not generally reject nuclear warfare. All the secular elites disagree with the premise that nuclear warfare is inherently immoral, as do 38 percent of the clerics.

Item 21 probes attitudes toward MAD as a retaliation policy. It reads, "Destroying enemy cities with nuclear weapons is immoral even if our cities are attacked with nuclear weapons first." Even as a response to a similar genocidal nuclear strike, only 17 percent of the clergy support countercities nuclear warfare as moral. However, such a level of support still is striking in view of the explicit and repeated condemnations of countercities nuclear warfare by all Catholic Church authorities and Christian just war theorists. Moreover, 97 percent of the clergy answered yes to the question, "Do you feel fairly well informed about recent Catholic teachings on war and morality?" Therefore, the responses of the clergy who support MAD warfare likely reflect an explicit and well-thought-out rejection of the official position of the Catholic Church, and this was reflected in some of their comments to us.

The modal positions of the four secular elite groups support retaliatory MAD warfare, but this support reaches the level of an attitudinal norm only for the military. Among the secular elites, the lowest level of support for this nuclear war alternative — 63 percent — is provided by journalists, while 68 percent of the members of Congress, 70 percent of diplomats, and 88 percent of the military support it.

The modal secular responses on the MAD retaliation item reflect attitudes that are virtually the opposite of their views on the comparable nonnuclear items of discriminate means and just intent. The only issue that may show consistency between attitudes toward nuclear and conventional warfare is the harsh response version of the retaliatory ethic (item 29). This scenario is similar to the MAD warfare item. Earlier, we interpreted support for item 29 as approval of a harsh response against the enemy's military. We did this, in part, because most of the secular elites rejected taking revenge on enemy civilians. However, the results on the morality of MAD warfare (item 20) suggest that there is at least moderate support for the principle of returning evil with evil, which can include genocidal actions. Just war theorists also accept the notion of reprisal or negative reciprocity, but not when it is directed against innocents, as is the case with MAD retaliation.

Another issue that must be discussed in any description of nuclear warfare policies is what the United States should do when a potential enemy state — North Korea, for example — is about to develop nuclear weapons. This question was captured in one of our Iran scenarios (item 48). Of the three U.S. elite groups that were asked the question, there was substantial opposition among all respondents to taking military action against such an enemy.

MAD Deterrence

Item 20, which deals with the morality of MAD as a deterrent, reads, "It is morally acceptable to threaten the use of nuclear weapons against enemy cities as a way to prevent nuclear attacks against our cities." Agreement with this statement constitutes moral acceptance of the threat. The secular

Table 8.2 **Support for Nuclear Conflict Policies by Parish Priests and the Catholic Hierarchy**

Survey Item and Principle	Church Hierarchy (%)	Parish Priests (%)	T Value
20. MAD deterrence	43	47	1.19
21. MAD retaliation	8	22	3.69*
22. Nuclear war	38	38	.64
48. Response to acquisition	5	8	1.09

Note: Response patterns to items 21 and 22 have been reversed so that "strongly disagree" and "disagree" are taken to support the MAD position.
* P < 0.05 for a difference of means test.

elites show strong approval for MAD as a deterrent. Their support ranges from 68 percent of the editors to almost 94 percent of the military respondents, but among the five groups, only support by the military reaches the level of an attitudinal norm.

Just war theorists are divided on the deterrence issue. Some of them approve of the deterrence strategy and do so by citing the moral paradox of the MAD argument, which is a consequentialist lesser of evils approach (see, e.g., Kattenburg 1985). Making an immoral threat to use nuclear weapons in countercities warfare is moral because it is a lesser evil than suffering a nuclear attack because the threat was not made. Others follow the Pauline injunction that it is wrong to threaten evil that good may come. Among clerics, the American Catholic and United Methodist bishops have condemned MAD as a deterrent, while the French and German Catholic bishops have supported it ("French Bishops' Statement" 1983).

In particular, the diversity we found among the U.S. Catholic clerics between official church doctrine and their personal attitudes suggests the possibility that elites' organizational positions may influence their public policy positions.[2] The responses of the Catholic clergy reveal some division within their ranks on nuclear warfare issues and reflect discrepancies between cleric views and the opinions expressed in the U.S. bishops' pastoral letter (National Conference of Catholic Bishops 1983). Table 8.2 presents the average levels of support for the four MAD nuclear items by the Catholic hierarchy as compared to the parish priests. While there is some difference regarding the MAD deterrence item, there is a statistically significant difference only on MAD retaliation. While 22 percent of parish priests would accept the possibility of countercities nuclear retaliation, only 8 percent of the hierarchy expressed this view.

The one statistically significant difference between the parish priests and the church hierarchy is worthy of some note. The American bishops were very critical of MAD not only as a deterrent, but also as a declaratory strategy. The bishops accepted MAD as a deterrent only in a passive, nondeclaratory form and only as an interim ethic to be accompanied by a sincere effort to negotiate agreements calling for the bilateral verifiable reduction and eventual elimination of nuclear weapons. The American parish priests do not reflect as decidedly critical a position of MAD in its totality as the bishops. The priests' slightly higher level of support for MAD as a deterrent is closer to the more favorable attitudes expressed by the French Catholic and German Catholic hierarchies, although the latter also condemned MAD warfare as unacceptable.

In many countries, the Catholic clergy are divided by both liberal versus conservative political ideology and nationalist versus internationalist outlooks, although there is no apparent global pattern of the hierarchy versus the parish priests (Lernoux 1989). Since the Second Vatican Council in 1965, the American Catholic hierarchy has moved toward an internationalist position that is critical of hard-line policies on East-West issues, whereas the position of parish priests has not been examined extensively.

Considering the evidence from all the survey items, our findings indicate that some priests have a value orientation that is more nationalistic or anticommunist than the American hierarchy. This also was reflected in some of their comments. Since the just war doctrine has official American Catholic Church endorsement, the greater level of support for the traditional just war approach by members of the hierarchy is likely to be a function of their role as the stewards of church doctrine. It is illuminating to compare our findings on the Catholic clergy with the official positions taken by Protestant and Jewish groups on the morality of nuclear deterrence; the most comprehensive survey of official church thinking suggests that most U.S. religious groups accept the need for nuclear deterrence in the short run while urging disarmament over the long term (Love 1991).

Relating Nuclear Issues to the General Framework

The development of nuclear weapons has presented an overwhelming challenge for just war theorists as well as for reason of state proponents. Advocates of these doctrines once assumed that war could serve the moral purpose of defending the innocent or the reason of state purpose of national survival. However, the indiscriminate and destructive nature of nuclear weapons has made nuclear war both immoral and irrational to most observers. The strains that nuclear weapons issues have caused for those who evaluate warfare in a moral context are seen in recent discussions among Catholic clerics. An intense debate has occurred at the highest levels of both American and European churches, and the French and German Catholic bishops generally take a different stand from that of their American counterparts.

The contrasting value orientations of concern for universal innocent others in the strict just war belief system or the we-versus-they nationalism of the better safe than sorry belief system may account for the consistent mixed-deontological responses of the clergy on the MAD warfare item and the inconsistent responses of the secular elites. This dilemma puts those who advocate strict just war into a painful moral quandary, but it has far less effect on those who uphold the better safe than sorry doctrine, whose first interest is to safeguard in-group security. Better safe than sorry individuals are not moral crusaders, nor do they desire harm to others, but they may have fewer qualms about using nuclear weapons if that appears to be necessary.

The results on the MAD warfare items suggest a secular norm of negative reciprocity involving nuclear weapons. The idea of returning evil for evil is analogous to the international legal concept of reprisal. Broadly speaking, just war doctrine accepts the notion of reprisal against evil acts, although it insists they be directed against those responsible for the acts or their agents, the military combatants. The moral problem with MAD warfare from the standpoint of the strict just war belief system is that it reflects notions of an eye-for-an-eye thinking against the innocent rather than against the guilty. Although intended as punishment for the supreme evil of the mass slaughter of innocents, MAD constitutes a similar mass slaughter of innocents.

Has the basic attitudinal structure that we document regarding conventional war evaporated in the quagmire of new issues associated with nuclear conflict? The recent scholarly debate and the evidence presented so far might cause one to think so, but the empirically derived answer is no. Further examination of the survey data indicates that rather simple patterns regarding attitudes exist for the nuclear issues as well as for traditional ones. This is shown by the responses of better safe than sorry and strict just war advocates, as seen in table 8.3. The table presents the same evidence for the belief system categories as we presented earlier for the five elite groups. The differences here are as dramatic as they were for non-nuclear issues.

Better safe than sorry proponents overwhelmingly support both threatening to use and actually using nuclear weapons, while strict just war elites are far more reluctant to do either. Ambivalents occupy their

Table 8.3 **Support for Nuclear Conflict Policies, by Belief System** (in percent)

Survey Item and Principle	Better Safe Than Sorry	Ambivalent	Strict Just War
20. MAD deterrence	96	74	52
21. MAD retaliation	93	63	28
22. Nuclear war	94	69	37
49. Response to acquisition	63	22	10

Note: Response patterns to items 21 and 22 have been reversed so that "strongly disagree" and "disagree" are taken to support the MAD position.

customary intermediate position. The greatest difference among Americans occurs with regard to the use of military force against an enemy who is about to acquire nuclear weapons. While only 10 percent of those classified as defenders of strict just war would use force against such a state, fully 63 percent of better safe than sorry individuals would do so.

Ironically, in focusing on just war logic, the contemporary literature on nuclear issues paints a picture of moral dissension that may be exaggerated. It misrepresents the recent debate by focusing on the discussion among just war thinkers and largely excluding the opinions of those who adhere to the better safe than sorry viewpoint. It is principally the just war elites who agonize over the use of nuclear weapons. Threatening to use and actually using nuclear weapons is more consistent with the position held by better safe than sorry elites, who are particularly concerned with the possibility of suffering a supreme emergency at the hands of an evil enemy.

NINE

Attitude Formation

Egoistic theories cannot explain why people persistently follow altruistic policies. A moral sensibilities approach, on the other hand, suggests that people possess innate fundamental predispositions toward honesty, empathy, and similar virtues, and that these are not the product of explicit short-run self-interested calculation. For the truly altruistic, the effect of rational calculations is only felt in the long run, if it is felt at all. While logical reflection eventually may convince an altruist that continuing to deal with certain people on the basis of universalistic sentiments is self-defeating, the sort of evidence necessary to convince an altruist of this argument is not often easily or quickly collected.

MORAL SENSIBILITIES

Moral sensibilities are not the only source of attitudes or behavior; nor does the absence of moral sensibilities imply immoral attitudes or behavior. Examples of other sources that have little to do with core sensibilities include misperceptions, organizational influences, political pressures, lack of personal steadfastness, stress, surprise, fatigue, cultural circumstances, and so on. When judgments are estimated from our model, there is an explicit ceteris paribus assumption, which holds these other things constant as the elements of the model vary.

Two moral sensibilities, in particular, must be singled out. These are golden rule–like empathy and in-group sentiments. In foreign affairs, the golden rule means, at the very least, that a nation should take no totally unwanted action against another nation. In its traditional formulation, the golden rule argues, "Do unto others as you would have them do unto you." This conception, which serves as the ethical core for many religions, captures the sentiments of sympathy, reciprocity, and altruism. Our stress on the golden rule also accords with the conclusions of an important study of altruistic behavior. The altruists interviewed by Kristen Monroe are, in her words, "what we can best characterize as John Donne's people. They need not to send to know for whom the bell tolls. They know. And this perception of themselves as one with all mankind is such an intrinsic part of their cognitive orientation, of the way they define themselves, that they need not stop to make a conscious decision" (1990, 427).

In contrast, in-group sentiments refer to predispositions of loyalty, self-sacrifice, and elevating the interests of one's own group and hostility toward other groups. This tendency in international relations is associated with strategic, rather than altruistic, principles. It employs the language of instrumental rationality, interests, nationalism, defense, and competition. Accordingly, golden rule sentiments stand in marked tension with in-group sensibilities. The former, in foreign policy, tends toward humanitarian positions, the latter to pro-state or ethnocentric positions. This fundamental dualism is reflected in most theories of international morality (see Maxwell 1990). It also appeared prominently in our survey findings regarding group attitudes and serves as a key component of our distinction among belief systems.

A MODEL OF MORAL JUDGMENT

Our cognitive model focuses on attitudes and beliefs, as revealed by the survey data, and offers a structured framework for addressing numerous public policy paradoxes. A major purpose of this chapter is to suggest how attitude patterns can be explained using the concepts of competing moral sensibilities, the scope conditions associated with these sensibilities, perceptions of risk, and conflict belief systems. These components are related in a manner that suggests how certain moral belief systems, as derived from our empirical investigation, might arise.

Figure 9.1 offers a schematic representation of the overall model. In this model, every component performs a separate task. Each component either constitutes a decision point or represents some set of value commitments. Further, each leads to other components in a decision-tree fashion.

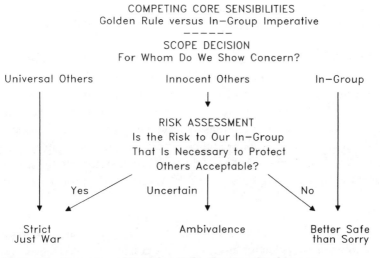

COMPETING CORE SENSIBILITIES
Golden Rule versus In-Group Imperative

SCOPE DECISION
For Whom Do We Show Concern?

Universal Others   Innocent Others   In-Group

RISK ASSESSMENT
Is the Risk to Our In-Group
That Is Necessary to Protect
Others Acceptable?

Yes   Uncertain   No

Strict   Ambivalence   Better Safe
Just War   than Sorry

Figure 9.1 **Sequence of Decision Rules for Moral Judgment**

Thus, competing moral sensibilities raise the question of how broad or restrictive one wishes to be in applying moral precepts. This, in turn, helps set out priorities and thereby eases the problem of moral conflicts. The model also suggests how some people use risk assessment as a means of temporarily managing moral dilemmas. Finally, given a knowledge of competing moral sensibilities, scope conditions for one's moral precepts, and outlook toward risk, the model estimates a person's probable belief system.

In effect, the belief system is contingent on the previous model components. Each component can be interpreted as an answer to a key question, and the resulting belief system is a product of those answers. Three questions are central to each belief system. First, is force morally acceptable to protect one's in-group? Second, given our golden rule sensibilities, for whom does one show concern? Third, is the in-group risk that one faces when protecting innocent others in foreign nations acceptable?

Competing Moral Sensibilities

Our model assumes that people are motivated by two fundamental but competing sensibilities when making policy judgments. One sensibility is an in-group morality, which demands group loyalty, team spirit, self-sacrifice, and upholding the interests of one's group over those of competing groups. In international relations, nationalism is the strongest manifestation of this sensibility. The other is based on the golden rule. It emphasizes virtues like empathy, restraint, generosity, mercy, kindness, and so on, toward others.

What empirical evidence suggests that golden rule scope decisions are a necessary component of the model? First, much has been written on this point. Perfectionist interpretations of the golden rule, sometimes referred to as the ethic of self-abnegation, teach universal love and nonviolence. More discriminating interpretations of the golden rule, such as the ethic of self-fulfillment, teach that one should discriminate between a neighbor's legitimate and illegitimate needs and that one can administer to the former while resisting the latter. These views disagree over the proper scope of golden rule responsibilities.

Second, survey evidence suggests elite scope concerns. Strains of universalistic, in-group, and innocent-others thinking are apparent in many items extracted in our factor analysis. While Americans overwhelmingly accept the golden rule principle, many of them also display strong in-group sentiments. They show a concern for innocent others in supporting just war precepts and display universalist sentiments on nuclear warfare issues. Finally, anecdotal evidence from our in-depth interviews of certain elites suggests that scope decisions, especially of the in-group and innocent-others variety, are important. This is not surprising, particularly for the military, given Americans' sensitivity since the Vietnam War toward the treatment of prisoners of war, protection of noncombatants, and rules of engagement.

Two observations should be made about these moral sensibilities. First, they both have strong survival value. Golden rule–based sentiments are necessary to promote cooperation, altruism, and standards of fairness that make a complex, ethnically diverse, and secular society possible. On the other hand, in-group sentiments give a society cohesion in war. The second observation is that golden rule-based morality and in-group morality can conflict. The former encourages compassion for others, while the latter promotes in-group loyalty and aggressiveness toward enemies.

A major value division is embodied in the key question that people face in conflict situations: Is force morally acceptable to protect my in-group? Most U.S. elites answer yes, while still feeling the pull of golden rule sensibilities. Therefore, a dilemma emerges. In such circumstances, whatever portion of this dualism is given greater attention tilts a person's belief system in a characteristic direction. This observation provides the foundation for our model.

Many elites feel crosspressured by this value conflict. We interpreted this to reflect a genuine moral dilemma rather than confusion, because there is a stable, identical, three-dimensional structure evident for all five elite groups. This identical cognitive structure suggests that all people wrestle with a universal moral dilemma. It seems improbable that all five groups should be confused and, moreover, confused in the same aggregate manner. In public opinion research, a common indicator of a fundamental value conflict is agreement with individual items that can be seen to be incompatible. Our survey patterns parallel this interpretation upon close inspection.

The extensive literature, both in the social sciences and religious studies, on the fundamental importance of the moral tension between golden rule sentiments and self-interest also convinced us of the reasonableness of our competing sensibilities conclusion. This moral tension is reflected in Jane Mansbridge's observations on the nature of pastoral responsibilities:

> Moral systems . . . usually include not only requirements of extreme moral obligation, like . . . "Love thy neighbor as thyself" . . . but also mediations of these extreme requirements, in which authoritative others, from priests to parents to peers, make clear that in fact much less is required for individuals to consider themselves moral. These authoritative, but not always mutually congruent, determinations of what is required and what is beyond the call of duty take heavily into consideration the self-interest of the moral individual, not generally requiring acts that undermine the most vital aspects of one's own and one's children's interests. (1990, 137)

Finally, the tension between self-interest and the golden rule is well established in game theory literature. In experiments that reward selfishness at the expense of the group, a significant minority of players consistently maintains an altruistic position even when offered personal rewards, anonymity, and freedom from group censure (Dawes and Thaler 1988, 194). Morality is assumed to be operating here, but self-interest can also be triggered by raising the reward to defect or by not reciprocating cooperative behavior (Isaac, McCue, and Plott 1985). In short, depending on the circumstances, most people appear to shift between self-interest and golden rule behavior.

Setting Limits on the Golden Rule

In war, the competing demands between golden rule and in-group sensibilities are especially acute. People may try to reconcile this tension by limiting the scope of their golden rule responsibilities. In essence, they are addressing the key question: For whom do we show concern? From our surveys, three broad scope decisions are identifiable: in-group priority, universalism, and concern for innocent others.

Referring to figure 9.1, the first possible path is the in-group priority, which means limiting golden rule imperatives to one's in-group. The reasoning here tends to be nonsituational, stressing duty or legality. In these circumstances, the contradictions in one's moral vision are largely eliminated, since golden rule responsibilities are coterminous with in-group loyalties. A path of universalism extends the scope of golden rule concern to everyone. This approach can take various forms, including commitment to a moral duty, virtue-centeredness, dispositional responsiveness, and so on. However, no matter what form it takes, this path rejects any particularistic cordoning off of ethical caring.

The path of concern for innocent others tries to extend the scope of golden rule responsibilities beyond one's in-group to include innocent parties in foreign states, such as enemy noncombatants. We cannot determine who qualifies as an innocent party and how far one should go in carrying out golden rule responsibilities without a close examination of the situation. Therefore, this judgment path is more complicated, because it requires entering the labyrinth of political and strategic calculations. Our evidence suggests that risk assessment is the key situational feature that guides judgments through this innocent-others pathway.

Risk Assessment

If we know that elites accept either universalist or in-group limits on golden rule sensibilities, we can estimate whether their resulting moral belief system will be better safe than sorry or strict just war. However, if elites embrace an innocent-others outlook, the situation becomes more complex. In this case, knowledge of one's competing core sensibilities and golden rule scope decisions is insufficient for identifying a likely belief system. At this point, situational calculations are crucial. Our findings indicate that the degree of risk or threat to the in-group is the major feature pondered by those who adopt a situationally oriented innocent-others view. Empirically, this is shown by the extraction of the risk sensitivity dimension.

The key question is whether to accept the risk to the in-group necessary to protect innocents. This in-group risk in our model refers to the perceived chance of military defeat and its consequences. Since war is by definition uncertain, and risk assessment is subject to many uncertainties, this further compounds one's perceptions of risk in times of conflict.

Three responses are possible concerning acceptance of risk to the in-group to protect the innocent: yes (risk-accepting), no (risk-averting), and uncertain. A risk-averting decision means that a respondent feels that the risks involved in protecting innocents are too high. The required moral constraints are believed to jeopardize unbearably the chances for victory and group safety. Accordingly, moral considerations involving others are deemphasized or ignored until our in-group safety can be secured.

In contrast, a risk-accepting stance conveys a willingness to assign priority to moral constraints. This most likely occurs when risks to in-group safety are deemed minimal, which allows one to deemphasize normal political and strategic calculations in favor of moral restrictions. Nevertheless, some elites, such as certain members of the clergy, appear willing to face significant risks to the in-group to protect innocent others.

A third modal path is one of uncertainty. We know from public opinion research that people facing a difficult decision in survey situations sometimes become fixated in a working-through stage that impedes progress toward a final principled judgment. We believe that such an interpretation applies here. This stage is marked by avoidance, procrastination, and unstable attitudes and can continue without a final resolution for a very long time.

Paths to a Belief System

The model identifies only a single path to the ambivalent outlook. One moves from a desire to protect the innocent to an inconclusive, uncertain situational risk assessment. Accordingly, one ends with an ambivalent view marked by the sentiments noted earlier.

The model indicates two judgment paths leading to a better safe than sorry belief system. First, one may assign strict priority to the in-group, leading directly to a better safe than sorry outlook. A second, more complex possibility results when one feels a commitment to innocent others and, therefore, engages in situational risk assessment. If risks to in-group safety are deemed intolerable, then a risk-averse decision also leads to a better safe than sorry conclusion.

The model also offers two paths to the strict just war outlook. First, one may hold a universalist perspective, believing that the golden rule applies to all. In this case, one would arrive in the strict just war domain. A second, more complex path moves from a commitment to innocent others to assessing the risks of a situation. If in-group risks are deemed low, then an individual moves to a strict just war position. This perspective, being highly contingent, is probably less stable than one reached by the way of the principled, universalism path.

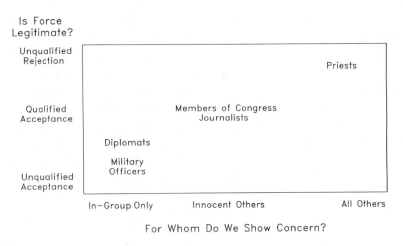

Figure 9.2 **Position of Elites Relative to Just War Constraints**

MODAL BELIEF SYSTEMS

We have seen how people are influenced by the golden rule versus in-group considerations. Differing locations in the factor space of moral possibilities indicate the diversity in elites' modal responses to their common dilemma. We began our statistical analysis by showing how the frameworks we have described are reflected in this cognitive space. Now we shall examine the belief systems that typify the thinking of U.S. elites. If we plot the mean positions of the five elite groups in the two-dimensional cognitive space of just war constraints that was introduced in figure 7.1 (above), we get some sense of their characteristic belief systems. Figure 9.2 presents the average aggregate views of each elite group in the force legitimacy and war constraints space. This figure is meant to be suggestive, since factor analysis has no natural zero point and the origin of the plot is placed for convenience of interpretation. However, elites' relative positions in the regions of various belief systems are empirically justified.

The data show that military officers and diplomats lean strongly toward in-group concerns. Military officers and (to a lesser extent) diplomats view force as legitimate to achieve national goals. The Catholic clergy clearly adhere to strict just war, while members of Congress and journalists are found in the region of mixed possibilities, but perhaps lean toward the illegitimacy of force. This means that they might be inclined toward better safe than sorry, strict just war, or ambivalence, depending on the specific risks of a situation.

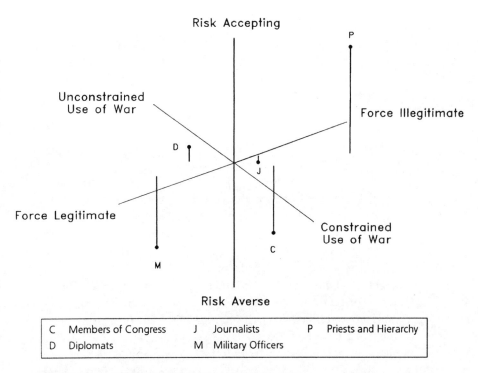

Figure 9.3 **Location of Elites in the Cognitive Space**

C	Members of Congress	J	Journalists	P	Priests and Hierarchy
D	Diplomats	M	Military Officers		

Accordingly, we must now reintroduce the risk sensitivity dimension as a step in further clarification. In figure 9.3, we see the average view of each elite group within the complete three-dimensional cognitive space. Again, the positions of military officers and clergy are most sharply distinguished relative to the risk axis, with the military showing high aggregate aversion to risk and the clergy displaying high aggregate acceptance of risk. These features are consistent with the better safe than sorry and strict just war outlooks, respectively.

The figure also shows the intermediate aggregate positions of diplomats, journalists, and members of Congress. However, foreign service officers and members of Congress sharply diverge on their response to risk. Diplomats, whose job is largely to implement U.S. policy, rather than to make it, are moderately willing to accept risk. Members of Congress, who are constitutionally charged with declaring war and who have substantial impact on many military decisions through the appropriations process, are quite risk-averse. In their aggregate response to risk, the members of Congress are closer to military officers than are the other secular elites.

Table 9.1 **Support for the Belief Systems, by Elite Group** (in percent)

Belief System	Members of Congress	Diplomats	Journalists	Military Officers	Priests
Strict just war	9	4	7	2	43
Just war / supreme emergency	3	0	1	0	0
Better safe than sorry	21	9	9	29	1
Ambivalent	68	87	84	69	56

The modal responses of U.S. elites to foreign policy risks seem to reflect their level of official responsibility. As a broad generality, the more direct responsibility of an elite group for using U.S. military force, the more risk-averse is the group. On the other hand, less responsibility is associated with greater acceptance of risk.

Members of Congress face a particularly interesting predicament. They tend to support the innocent-others constraints of the just war tradition, and this separates them from the military in the just war space. However, members of Congress are close to the military in evaluating risk, making them the most crosspressured of the five elite groups. Golden rule sensibilities draw Congress members toward universalistic policies, while their in-group sensibilities pull them in a better safe than sorry direction. Being policy practitioners, they are forced to reconcile these conflicting aims and cannot relegate them to abstract intellectual discussions. How they solve this conflict tells us something about the nature of elite reasoning.

To clarify all these possibilities and obtain a better picture of American belief structure, we examined the percentage of belief system followers in the five elite groups. This evidence is presented in table 9.1. We also have included the additional small category of crosspressured individuals who strongly support both just war constraints and better safe than sorry concerns about risk. Their position seems to reflect the supreme emergency doctrine as it is derived from the just war tradition, and they will be important for understanding congressional attitudes.

The beliefs of military officers and the Catholic clergy again are sharply distinguished in table 9.1. The military, who are the most risk-averse of all the American elites, tend toward the better safe than sorry outlook, while the priests adhere to strict just war. The intermediate positions of diplomats and journalists show up as well; they contain a higher proportion of ambivalents than the other groups.

For many members of Congress, the sharp conflict between in-group sentiments and golden rule principles, a by-product of their great aversion to risk, is solved by leaning toward better safe than sorry policies. But Congress also is the only elite group with a conspicuous number of individuals who adopt a supreme emergency doctrine as derived from just war theory. In effect, Congress as an institution adopts an elastic sort of supreme emergency logic. Unlike the military, who are quite in-group oriented, many members of Congress have significant symnpathy for universalistic principles and a measure of idealism. This is especially evident in congressional views regarding the use of force, which tends toward distaste and contrasts sharply with the military's positive view (see fig. 9.1).

However, if defending their idealistic principles entails a substantial risk to U.S. interests, many members of Congress quickly move in the direction of better safe than sorry. They see foreign interests as important and legitimate but also view the world as such a risky place that U.S. interests must take priority whenever a serious conflict erupts. In short, the congressional aversion to the use of force quickly can be overwhelmed by aversion to in-group risk. Nevertheless, in reflecting on the fundamental tension that exists between golden rule principles and in-group sentiments, some members of Congress do depart from better safe than sorry logic. They reason that whenever conflict erupts the United States should act with restraint, hence reflecting a considerable measure of idealism. Because better safe than sorry and strict just war reasoning can lead decision makers in polar opposite directions, heated foreign policy disputes are often heard in the Capitol's chambers.

Since it is significant for our discussion in the next chapter, it is important to note that U.S. elite groups differ not only in the proportions who adhere to strict just war and better safe than sorry but also in their proportion of ambivalents.[1] The evidence in table 9.1 indicates that some types of elites are more likely to adopt coherent ethical belief systems than others. Congress contains a relatively high percentage of both better safe than sorry and strict just war individuals, so when their opinions are measured in the aggregate, they tend to cancel out. Diplomats and journalists, in contrast, tend more toward ambivalence than well-structured beliefs about conflict. Consequently, their overall views appear to be about the same as those of members of Congress on a number of foreign policy issues, but such an aggregate analysis obscures deeper cleavages.

Shaping Policy Beliefs

To help understand how people arrive at their belief systems we now turn to applications of our model, which presents a set of decision rules that, when combined with the empirical findings, estimate belief system out-comes. In the process, the model suggests certain things that were not apparent from earlier analyses.

Survey responses of the Catholic clergy reveal a dominant belief system. As indicated in the decision tree of figure 9.1, we start with the dilemma of golden rule versus in-group considerations and then ask: When force is contemplated, toward whom should we show neighborly concern? In other words, should we love our neighbors as ourselves? The survey data indicate that the clergy have a strong universalist or innocent-others outlook that reflects either perfectionist or nonperfectionist views of the golden rule. Those with universal outlooks are led directly from the scope decision node to a strict just war position by way of the model's universalist path. Those with innocent-others sentiments engage in risk assessment, but since many of the clergy are willing to accept risk, they too will tend toward strict just war conclusions.

Relative to other elites, with the possible exception of the military, the model suggests that universalist clergy need not study the facts of contemporary politics in great depth to reach their conclusions about warfare. The logic of their beliefs is straightforward enough.

The military's reasoning paths, according to the model, are the mirror image of those of the clergy. Faced with the scope decision for golden rule sensibilities, the military tends toward strong in-group or, less prominently, innocent-others sentiments. Those with in-group priorities move directly from the scope decision node to a better safe than sorry position. Those with innocent-others sentiments engage in risk assessment, but since military officers are highly risk-averse by nature, they also tend toward better safe than sorry because in-group safety must not be jeopardized. Only if in-group safety is unambiguously secured do the highly risk-averse among the military embrace strict just war attitudes, and such a circumstance is not common in war.

The model also explains an interesting statistical finding mentioned earlier. While better safe than sorry thinking dominates military thought, the risk sensitivity dimension explains less variance among the military than for the other groups.[2] At first glance, this may seem odd since a better safe than sorry orientation should imply greater sensitivity to risk, not less, but the model also suggests an answer. Many military officers probably reach better safe than sorry conclusions by way of the in-group priority path. Hence, they bypass deep risk assessment altogether in a fashion similar to universalist clergy. In contrast, many nonmilitary secular elites engage in risk assessment because their scope sensibilities alone are un-likely to settle their moral questions.

The model further estimates a reasoning path for Congress members that departs from that of the other elites. Members of Congress tend to be sensitive to innocent others, but they are also risk-averse since Congress has direct responsibility for some war and other military decisions. There-fore, the model estimates that many members of Congress will move from the risk assessment node toward the better safe than sorry view, while others may travel a path that ends in the strict just war position. Still others are so crosspressured that they adopt a supreme emergency posi-tion as derived from the broader just war tradition. They believe in follow-ing just war rules unless the United States finds itself seriously imperiled from an enemy who would destroy basic American values if victorious. In such extreme situations the just war rules can be suspended.

Attitude Shifts

In assessing the elements that shape elite attitudes, the model also suggests how sharp shifts in moral outlook can occur without positing sociopsy-chological pathologies, conversion experiences, or changes in level of cog-nitive development. Groups concerned about innocent others are likely, according to the model, to engage in complex situational analysis and risk assessment. Therefore, changes in the political or military context, and thus in the perception of risk, can induce significant changes in their out-looks and cause even morally committed decision makers to make sudden shifts without much warning. An example of such a policy conversion was displayed by Senator Arthur Vandenberg, the leading proponent of Amer-ican isolationism during the 1930s. His shift away from nonmilitary solu-tions resulted from a change in the level of risk that he perceived existed in the international system. Vandenberg later commented about the Japa-nese attack on Pearl Harbor, "In my own mind, my convictions regarding international cooperation and collective security for peace took firm form on the afternoon of the Pearl Harbor attack. That day ended isolationism for any realist" (1952, 1).

Bertrand Russell's flirtation with preventive war, a considerable source of embarrassment for his followers, is an even more interesting illustration. Since World War I, Russell had been a noted antiwar crusader and conscientious objector, but when the United States acquired a monop-oly on nuclear weapons in 1945, he urged a preventive war against the Soviets before Moscow could develop a similar nuclear capacity (see Feinberg and Kasrils 1984, 11; Clark 1976, 520). This switch puzzled and annoyed his pacifist disciples, but our model suggests that Russell was acting consistently. He was not a universal pacifist but one concerned with innocent others. Russell's risk assessments had initially led him to the pacifist doctrine as the most reasonable strategy to maximize his long-run goals.

After his risk perceptions changed in 1945, he suddenly switched to a better safe than sorry view — that is, preventive war — because he concluded that the risk to the West posed by a nuclear-armed Soviet Union overrode his desire to protect all innocents from the horrors of war. After the Soviets had acquired an extensive nuclear arsenal, he shifted back to pacifism, again motivated by changes in his calculations of risk. Russell explained his final switch back to pacifism: "The main cause of my change of opinion is the shift which occurred in the balance of forces. . . . The situation now is that we cannot defeat Russia except by defeating ourselves. Those who still advocate war seem to me to be living in a false paradise" (quoted in Feinberg and Kasrils 1984, 63). In other words, by 1954 a preventive war against the Soviet Union had become too risky for Russell to embrace it.

Our model predicts that those concerned about innocent others are more likely to undergo a Russell-like switch after assessing the risks of a situation. On the other hand, elites who follow more principled virtue or temperament-based paths (e.g., universalist or in-group moralities) that do not depend on risk assessment are less likely to change their policy beliefs. Furthermore, our data suggest that elites who do not have strongly held beliefs involving the use of force are the most likely candidates for such deep-level switching. Religious leaders and military officers are less so, while some members of Congress are likely to switch quickly and radically as soon as they perceive a great risk to U.S. interests.

These observations on the complexity and contingent quality of risk assessment raise another issue. The deeper one moves into the situational interior of the model, the more likely it is that one will engage in complex and coherent thought. In particular, risk assessment implies a particular sort of complex reasoning about morality, and so we must reject Lawrence Kohlberg's view that somehow cognitive complexity offers a single privileged path to morality and John Rawls's argument that reasonable people can always hope to reach agreement on fundamental rules. Cognitive competence is not necessarily an indication of moral development, and complicated risk assessment does not always denote superior moral thought, either. Conversely, parochial or temperament-based moralities need not imply moral deficiencies. As the Russell example illustrates, high levels of cognitive competence can result in sudden moral shifts, and there is probably no single doctrinal path to moral soundness.

SUGGESTED HYPOTHESES

The model and the data analysis suggest a number of interesting hypotheses that should be made explicit. First, if a broadening or universalizing of scope sensibilities occurs, we should see a shift in all elite views toward *ad bellum* just war and golden rule outlooks. In turn, this should be reflected in more support for the strict just war position. Also, for nonmilitary elites, universalizing trends should strengthen *in bello* responsibilities. This would be especially apparent for the principle of noncombatant immunity, which most moral outlooks embrace, albeit with varying degrees of commitment.

The situation for military elites with regard to *in bello* just war constraints may be more complicated. Our model suggests that the military, unlike other U.S. elite groups, will be subject to a countertrend. As modern war decreases decision time, *in bello* just war precepts will become more difficult to follow for cognitive processing reasons. A 1988 example was the USS *Vincennes* incident, where an American missile cruiser downed an Iranian civilian airliner. But given adequate decision time, the use of precision-guided munitions and other advanced technologies may allow for greater civilian immunity and other *in bello* just war limits.

Division

The model further suggests situations of maximum moral divisiveness. In general, the most divisive sort of moral issue would be one that maximizes the inherent tension between the two core sensibilities: desire to follow the golden rule and desire to promote the comparative security of one's ingroup over competing groups. Such a maximally divisive issue would embody two features. It would be a situational context of high risk in which all groups compete fiercely but one where competitors also recognize the existence of scope sensibilities that tend toward universalizing — that is, golden rule sensibilities encompassing the enemy. These factors would tend to pull people in different directions because they are cross-pressured at the model's decision points. Civil wars often have these traits, so it is not surprising that such conflicts tend to be morally divisive.

Another divisive situation would involve conflicts in which risks are in dispute. This was true with the Vietnam War. Some Americans believed the dire predictions of the domino theory, which was based on the observation that (until recently) nations that became communist rarely reverted to capitalism and democracy. Therefore, the Vietnam challenge presented a supreme emergency to the West. If Vietnam fell, it would be followed in quick succession by Cambodia, Laos, Thailand, and so on until finally the United States would stand alone against a hostile communist world. Hence freedom itself was imperiled by the communist threat in Southeast Asia. Others saw Vietnam as a simple civil war in which the United States had no moral right to intervene; in any event, since its outcome did not affect any major U.S. security interests, no legitimate argument could be made for intervention.

Now we can understand why no consensus could be reached among Americans about the Vietnam War: People's fundamental moral sensibilities drew them in opposition directions. As the war escalated, opinions hardened and those who opposed one's own position on the war were viewed successively as wrong-headed, stupid, lacking in moral virtue, and ultimately as the physical embodiment of evil. Because many people have deeply held sensibilities about killing and murder, reasoning through the consequences of U.S. actions in Vietnam increasingly validated their beliefs and proved that those of their domestic opponents were unquestionably wrong. To conclude otherwise would require them to reject their fundamental sensibilities and abandon the principles of moral reasoning embodied in their belief systems. As the conflict progressed, ambivalence became less and less common, since the consequences of the Vietnam War were so dire from both a better safe than sorry and a strict just war perspective.

Rather than the textbook democratic ideal of public debate leading to a national consensus, the competing arguments about involvement in Vietnam increasingly drew people toward rigid, doctrinaire, and opposing positions. A period of frustration began as more and more people came to reason that any moral individual should be able to see the correct path. After all, they had been generous and patient to a fault with their domestic opponents. They had given them the benefit of the doubt and allowed them time to reconsider their errors, but their domestic opponents had failed to embrace correct policy beliefs. And so the sort of attitudes characteristic of moral crusading became more common as increasing numbers of Americans began to believe that the solution to this dilemma was to destroy their domestic foes.

Consensus

The model also suggests situations of minimal policy divisiveness. In general, these are situations were consensus exists at the decision nodes. One example is a situation in which golden rule–based sentiments are clearly restricted to one's in-group. This unquestioned in-group priority should lead quickly to a collective better safe than sorry consensus. Old Testament tribal wars are examples.

There would also be minimum moral divisiveness when people embrace a universalist outlook, which leads to a collective strict just war position. Similarly, moral divisiveness would be minimized when people share a consensus about innocent others and agree on their risk assessment decisions. The Gulf War was relatively uncontroversial because Iraq had violated just war norms by invading and then annexing a neighbor; important strategic and economic interests were at stake; the war produced few allied casualties; and it was over so quickly that there was little time for organized opposition to develop.

The model predicts that innocent-others elites are more likely to engage in complex, situational, risk-assessment calculations. Finally, it suggests which groups are more prone to switch their moral positions, namely, those who are oriented toward innocent others and engage in complex risk assessment. For such people, a changed perception of risk can lead to rapid changes in policy attitudes. Some of the fluctuations in public opinion that earlier writers called moods likely reflect this sort of instability (e.g., Allport 1937; Almond 1950). Conversely, groups that do not engage in risk assessment reasoning and instead rely on universalist or in-group priority views are much less likely to switch their policy positions.

POLITICAL IDEOLOGY

The Americans have become too liberal to fight. — Nikita Khrushchev

The conflict belief systems we have described are related to political ideology but are not identical with it. This is because people's self-reported ideologies are labels they use to succinctly summarize their general policy positions, but conflict beliefs are only one component contributing to their choice of label. At the broadest level of generalization, during the cold war many studies found that liberals tended to support cooperative internationalism, while conservatives advocated militant internationalism (see, e.g., Wittkopf and Maggiotto 1983b; Wittkopf 1986).

During the 1950s, the ideological pattern of attitudes seems to have been fairly simple, and the labels *liberal, moderate,* and *conservative* signified something of importance in both foreign and domestic politics. But the pattern that structured cold war thinking eventually unraveled. Some see this breakdown as a consequence of the domestic stresses caused by the Vietnam War (see Converse 1987; McCormick and Wittkopf 1990). Others place its acceleration in the context of the Falkland Islands War, which pitted two U.S. allies against each other. In any event, by the early 1980s fundamental changes were evident. To quote Zbigniew Brzezinski:

> Our foreign policy became increasingly the object of contestation, of sharp cleavage, and even of some reversal of traditional political commitments. The Democratic Party, the party of internationalism, became increasingly prone to the appeal of neoisolationism. And the Republican Party, the party of isolationism, became increasingly prone to the appeal of militant interventionism. And both parties increasingly found their center of gravity shifting to the extreme, thereby further polarizing our public opinion. (1984, 15–16)

A similar view of the shift from traditional labels was reflected by the thoughts of one diplomat in our study. "I'm not certain these terms mean anything anymore. When I first learned political terminology, they signified means of approach to problem solving. Now they are associated with rather rigid points of view, more or less articles of faith, or revealed truth." Of course, with the end of the cold war and the disappearance of the Soviet Union, even some of these basic organizing articles of faith largely vanished.

WHY SIMPLE BELIEF SYSTEMS LEAD TO COMPLICATED COGNITIVE STRUCTURES

Our purposes in this section are to examine the relationship of contemporary ideological labels to conflict belief systems, to propose a model of their likely relationship during the cold war, and suggest why simple ideological patterns break down as more and more policy problems enter the public arena. The average positions of the self-defined liberals, moderates, and conservatives in the cognitive space of U.S. elites are presented in figure 9.4. As the figure shows, those calling themselves political conservatives are most sensitive to the risks inherent in the international system. As a consequence, they are not as supportive of just war constraints on the use of force. Liberals are comparatively less sensitive to risk and are the most supportive of just war norms. The only surface anomaly in these

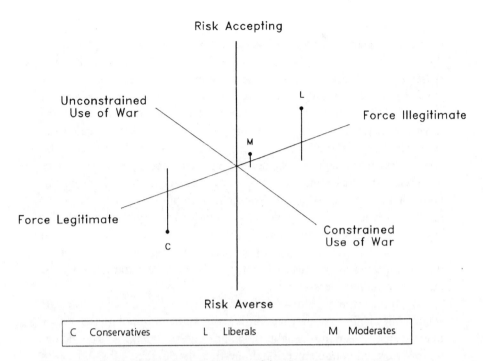

Risk Accepting

Unconstrained
Use of War

L

Force Illegitimate

M

Force Legitimate

Constrained
Use of War

C

Risk Averse

| C | Conservatives | L | Liberals | M | Moderates |

Figure 9.4 **Political Positions in the Cognitive Space**

data is that self-defined moderates do not occupy the center position but are closer to liberals than to conservatives in the elite cognitive space. A deeper examination of the sources of political labels explains why this is the case.

Commentators on the contemporary U.S. political universe often conceive it as a complex multidimensional space. So to discover a general explanation of political ideology that integrates both domestic and foreign policy attitudes it is useful to discuss an earlier, simpler period. This allows us to integrate our model of conflict beliefs with a similar analysis of domestic politics. Further, it explains why the structure of political attitudes almost inevitably inhabits a multidimensional space if they are determined by belief systems affecting different policy areas, and why ideological structure becomes unmanageably complex as the number of important issues multiplies in modern society. Eventually, the increasing inability of citizens to find viable politicians who support their salient policy concerns produces the characteristic political malaise noted by many commentators on contemporary American politics (e.g., Robinson 1976; Sigelman and Whicker 1988).

Until recently, the issue that dominated U.S. foreign policy was an overarching fear of the Soviet Union and international communism. At the extreme, some liberals did not fear the Soviet Union, and this was reflected in their advocacy of cooperative internationalism, while many conservatives saw the communist threat as a supreme emergency that threatened the survival of the United States. Domestically, predispositions toward justice norms are a fundamental building block of American belief systems (see, e.g., Kahneman, Knetsch, and Thaler 1986; Tyler 1990). The controversy that integrated the domestic policy disputes of three decades ago concerned the optimal size of government (see, e.g., Nie, Verba, and Petrocik 1976; Smith 1989). A defining feature of liberalism in the 1950s and 1960s was its advocacy of increased individual and civil rights. Liberals sought to achieve these goals through increased formal rules and government intervention. The conservatives who opposed these policies were denigrated by liberals as supporters of racial segregation, sex bias, and unfettered business activity.

An application of golden rule logic provides a description of domestic social policy belief systems that parallels our explanation of foreign policy belief systems. Seen in this light, the major question that intellectual conservatives faced in implementing domestic policy in the 1950s and 1960s was whether greater rights could be guaranteed to others without unacceptable risk to one's in-group.[3] Such conservatives did not necessarily want to "keep others down" as a crusading goal, but could see no way to provide others with rights equal to their own without unacceptably compromising their own group's interests. They saw increased government intervention and the civil rights movement as sources of crime, social disruption, and a potentially unacceptable loss of wealth for their political constituencies. Similarly, people who oppose environmental regulations today argue that new rules and increased government bureaucracy would cause unacceptable losses to their communities.

In this light, we also can apply a golden rule formulation to domestic decision making during the cold war. During the 1950s and 1960s, if one envisioned unacceptable consequences to one's in-group, one would have adopted a conservative social position. But if one foresaw that the potential costs of enlarging the scope of golden rule concerns toward others would be acceptable, then one would have advocated a more interventionist and larger national government.

A person who believed that the golden rule applied to both international and domestic situations would have been a liberal in the 1950s and 1960s. One who believed that the golden rule was not practical in either

Table 9.2 **Ideological Structure During the Cold War**

Perception of Soviet Threat	Optimal Size of Government	
	Large	Small
USSR is basically defensive and therefore not a serious threat.	Dominant liberal position	Little adopted isolationist position
Communism poses a supreme emergency since the USSR is expansionist.	Minority liberal position	Dominant conservative position

situation would have been a conservative. But one who saw important differences in risk between the two domains would be pulled in opposite directions. These attitudes can be examined in table 9.2. People who were not crosspressured held the dominant liberal and conservative positions. However, some believed that the golden rule could be applied domestically but that the Soviet Union and international communism constituted a supreme emergency. This was a minority liberal position during much of the cold war.

By themselves, the responses of these three political groupings mean that the ideological positions of Americans cannot be adequately captured in a one-dimensional space. While the minority liberal position might be shoved into the moderate category for classification purposes, that became impossible toward the end of the cold war with the advent of neoisolationism, and the fourth possibility shown in table 9.2 became a viable alternative. This group wanted a small government domestically but no longer saw the Soviet Union as a major threat. Neoisolationism was never popular with conservatives during the cold war, but with the demise of the Soviet Union as a superpower its banner was adopted by such conservatives as Patrick Buchanan and his America First campaign.

This typology implies that during the cold war and toward the end of our period of data collection people identifying themselves as conservatives should have been relatively unified in their beliefs because they did not have a plausible neoisolationist position. Those who thought of themselves as liberals, however, would have been more divergent or ambivalent in their views, because their domestic liberalism could take them in a different direction from that of their foreign policy beliefs. The conflict is embodied in the comments of a senior diplomat, stationed in Latin America, who participated in our study. Although he identified himself as a liberal, he evoked better safe than sorry reasoning when discussing the

Table 9.3 **Support for the Belief Systems, by Political Ideology** (in percent)

	Strict Just War	Ambivalent	Better Safe Than Sorry
Liberal	23	17	5
Moderate	66	59	40
Conservative	11	24	55

Table 9.4 **Political Ideology, by Belief System** (in percent)

Belief System	Liberal	Moderate	Conservative
Strict just war	15	14	8
Ambivalent	82	77	46
Better safe than sorry	3	9	45

situation in Nicaragua and set forth a contemporary version of the domino theory.

> I think that what you are really trying to get at is not whether our country tries to live by the principles which are so much a part of its civic culture. The whole issue of Nicaragua has nothing to do with Nicaragua in and of itself. Nicaragua's threat is the potential threat to destabilize Mexico and to foment insurrection and instability in Panama. That is why Nicaragua is a foreign policy problem.

The dissent that our ideological model indicates should have existed among liberals during the cold war, but not among conservatives, is suggested by figure 9.4, which places liberals and moderates more closely together. This pattern is confirmed by tables 9.3 and 9.4. There is a relatively similar distribution of ideological labels among strict just war and ambivalent elites, but this is not the case for better safe than sorry elites. Over half of the better safe than sorry elites identify themselves as conservatives. While there is a lower percentage of supporters of strict just war among conservatives than among liberals and moderates, the proportion of ambivalents is much higher for liberals and moderates than for conservatives.

TEN

The Importance of Moral Sensibilities

The convictions that leaders have formed before reaching high office are the intellectual capital they will consume as long as they continue in office.
—Henry Kissinger

In chapter 9 we saw that professions and political ideologies are significantly related to attitudes toward international conflict. In this chapter, we offer some evidence about the relative importance of moral sensibilities in forming such attitudes. Since the international system is a complex environment laden with many contingent possibilities, it is unreasonable to think that knowing people's moral sensibilities will allow total prediction of their attitudes. Nevertheless, basic moral sensibilities do cause people to lean in a characteristic direction, and such feelings may dominate other influences.

Scholars often use two broad theories to explain why people adopt the sorts of belief systems that we have described. The most commonly cited is called the learning curve or professionalization hypothesis. Attitude coherence increases with long-term reflection on important issues. Among professionals, like all the elites in our study, this thoughtful reflection concerns the issues involved in their life's work. The problems they encounter cause some of them to search for proper "professional" rules of behavior to deal with the potential recurrence of troublesome situations. This theory predicts that elites in similar circumstances should adopt similar types of norms and explains why an individual's career is a good predictor of certain attitudes.

Alternatively, the sources of people's beliefs about public policy may not lie in their career situations but in their fundamental sensibilities toward the golden rule and the in-group. Specific attitudes result from application of these sensibilities to real-world situations. The moral sensibilities hypothesis also explains why common people sometimes hold as strongly felt beliefs about public policy as do well-educated, seasoned professionals.

THE LEARNING CURVE EXPLANATION

In both Eastern and Western cultures, religious leaders and philosophers have argued for thousands of years that a higher level of consciousness can be achieved through reflection on moral problems. Seen in this light, political ideologies are well-thought-out maximizing strategies for achieving particular goals. The essence of this learning curve model was used by Augustine, Thomas Aquinas, and the other medieval theologians who developed just war doctrine as a logical consequence of the desire to protect innocent parties. The philosopher-theologian Alan Donagan puts the argument this way in interpreting the system of common morality developed by Thomas Aquinas:

> The first common principles are self-evident . . . to human reason, and the (relevant secondary) precepts . . . can be known from them straight off with a little thought. . . . As for the more specific precepts of morality, although they can be inferred from the precepts . . . by diligent inquiry, . . . only the wise are capable of carrying out such inquiries. Ordinary folk will therefore receive the more specific precepts by instruction. (1977, 60)

This Catholic interpretation suggests that societies should have a moral elite responsible for determining correct behavior and instructing even the highest political leaders on the moral responsibilities of government. Why? While everyone can understand the rudiments of proper ethical reasoning, only after long years of study is the moral elite competent to interpret its intricacies. Max Weber offered a parallel interpretation of bureaucracies and described the authoritative pronouncements of their stratification systems as similar to how people understand the principles of mathematics. Only a small proportion of the elite who are mathematicians know how calculation is generated, while everyone else must apply the rules they disseminate, based on an almost blind faith that their interpretation is correct (see Hummel 1977, 85–86).

A corollary of such a model is found in the socialization aspects of norms. With the desire for a professional career comes a stake in maintaining and enhancing one's profession and an incentive to develop professional norms of conduct. The reason that specific types of norms develop in particular organizational settings is that the level of rewards for their members can be increased by adopting certain strategies in repeatedly played non-zero-sum games. In these games, implicit cooperative agreements develop in order to increase the rewards of the entire organization or a more restricted in-group of the organization's elite. Some gaming strategies are superior to others in yielding greater returns. As soon as these strategies are discovered, they are copied by high-ranking members and are transmitted by formal or informal instruction to their newly admitted junior colleagues. This is the way organizational norms of conduct are thought to evolve.

The nature of the situation facing members of many organizations can be made clearer by examining the extreme possibilities available to people pursuing self-interest. At one end of a continuum are those who have no long-run interest in the goals of their profession, and, consequently, have no incentive to maximize anything but short-run self-interest, narrowly defined. Social choice theory explains such behavior quite well. Only monetary incentives or peer pressures can induce these people to move into agreement with group norms, and these will be violated as soon as "economic man" thinks it is advantageous.[1]

At the other extreme of the continuum are individuals with a long-run commitment to an institution. Wanting to make it their life's work, they are interested in maintaining professional norms, because the preservation of an orderly structure of expected and proper behavior makes their day-to-day dealings easier and less time-consuming and also increases the overall rewards of organizational membership. While it may be that only the top elite of an organization can divine the intricacies of such proper conduct, the rules they implement will be those that maximize important organizational goals. The more institutional cohesion in an organization and the more relevance certain beliefs have to its organizational purpose, the more coherent should be the attitudes of its members toward their dominant belief system.

In the case of international conflicts, strict just war and better safe than sorry beliefs play prominent roles. The following comments reflect the preeminence of such beliefs as they are fostered by military academies.

> Service academies . . . and other institutions . . . not only give technical
> trainings, but also teach loyalty to these institutions and the type of persons

who are their faculty or alumni. Where these institutions are aligned with the government . . . the curriculum that best serves its alumni not only teaches technical skills, but also loyalty to the type of person who is a fellow graduate. . . . The elite graduate is unselfish in serving his country; nevertheless, due to the biases in his values, the interests of the elite end up being served, as well perhaps as the interest of the country. (Akerlof 1983, 54–55)

THE MORAL SENSIBILITIES EXPLANATION

At the other extreme of possible explanations for the adoption of beliefs, the building blocks of belief systems might be based largely on moral sensibilities that are deeply ingrained rather than learned or deduced by logical reflection. Three suggestive pieces of evidence support this explanation. First, we have seen that certain types of elites are drawn toward better safe than sorry and strict just war logic because of their deeply held beliefs. Second, most people seem to think that their own moral beliefs are the only true beliefs, and they are incapable of seriously contemplating alternative moral systems.[2] Third, intellectual shifts involving changes in basic values are rare, and even in such an extreme case as that of Bertrand Russell, it is not necessary to posit a shift in fundamental sensibilities to explain sharp shifts in public policy positions.

Substantial evidence in the literature supports the moral sensibilities thesis, as well. For example, the political attitudes of college students do not appear to be much affected by their classes or their professors' opinions. In particular, military cadets do not experience much change in basic attitudes after entering the academy.[3] Since value changes seem to be only marginal after one leaves high school, it appears that most of those who enroll in service academies have self-selected a life's role that suits their fundamental sensibilities. Accordingly, academies and seminaries do not so much change basic opinions as reinforce preexisting tendencies, help to clarify them, and perhaps drive out a few people who have poorly chosen a career.

EVIDENCE FOR U.S. ELITES

The essence of our research so far has been to determine the structure of elite beliefs about international conflict, and most of our survey items centered on this issue. Nevertheless, we also included a variety of demographic and psychological items in our surveys. These are described briefly in chapter 4. Using them, we can present some evidence on the compara tive importance of the learning curve versus the fundamental sensibilities explanation for conflict beliefs. Between these extremes, a mixed possibilities explanation allows for the importance of both fundamental sensibilities and rational reflection in adult life.

As a first step, we divided elites into two groups. One consists of ambivalents and the other of both strict just war and better safe than sorry types — that is, those with strong coherent belief systems.[4] While there are substantial differences in the number of supporters of these belief systems among the groups, there is also much variation within each elite group regarding the coherence of individual beliefs.[5] As seen in our previous analyses, group membership is a very good predictor of whether morally committed elites adopt better safe than sorry or strict just war as a belief system. And while group membership is not as good a predictor of whether a person will be ambivalent or will adopt one of the two consistent belief systems, it is still a highly significant statistical predictor of moral commitment at the 0.0001 level. Elite membership, by itself, allows us to correctly predict what 56 percent of individuals will adopt as a coherent belief system.[6] This is our statistical baseline for comparison, and it leaves a great deal of room for other variables to predict elite commitment. In fact, given the emphasis in theological literature on the importance of religion in moral development, in philosophical literature on the importance of intellectual reflection, and in economics and social choice literatures on the benefits of searching for maximizing strategies, it would be surprising if we did not find a number of other strong predictors of the coherence of elite attitudes.

Demographic Characteristics

In the learning curve model, any influence increasing the chance of one's reflecting on conflict problems should increase the coherence of one's attitudes, leading to an increased likelihood of adopting either a better safe than sorry or strict just war belief system rather than ambivalence. A wide variety of demographic characteristics are associated with general foreign policy beliefs (see Holsti and Rosenau 1988). A possible explanation for these correlations is that most demographic variables act as surrogates for certain types of specialized knowledge whose possession increases attitude coherence. Military officers, for example, have more coherent views than newspaper editors on matters of conflict, perhaps because the military are more acquainted with the day-to-day difficulties of managing a war.

Despite this assessment, we initially found that standard demographic characteristics are not very useful in explaining which military officers adopt the strict just war or better safe than sorry belief system (see Brunk, Secrest, and Tamashiro 1990). To test more fully the tentative conclusion that the modal attitudes of elite groups can be predicted but that attitudes of individual members are much harder to predict, we included a wide variety of additional demographic inquiries in our later questionnaires. The following items were suggested by the literature as possible explanatory factors: whether a parent had a military career, race, gender, religious denomination, father's education as a surrogate for social class, and state of birth as an indicator of political culture. Finally, we asked about hometown size as a measure of the likelihood of repeated personal contacts during one's youth, which some believe is a source of altruism. Nevertheless, when an elite's career choice is controlled, none of these variables is a statistically significant predictor of whether an individual will remain ambivalent.

Reflections on War

Five types of variables were included in our surveys as measures of the chance of reflecting on the moral issues involved in war. According to a learning curve explanation, the more time one has had to reflect on such matters and the greater the importance of these issues to one's institutional position in society, the greater the likelihood that one will adopt a coherent belief system. The collective impact of these variables provides an estimate of the effect of a learning curve model of cognitive development for our subjects.

The first variable is age. The longer one lives, the longer one has to contemplate the moral implications of public policy and the more coherent one's views should be about professionally important policy issues.[7] The second potential explanatory variable that flows from the learning curve explanation is a person's education. As Oli Holsti and James Rosenau put it, "Perhaps the most persisting generalization about public opinion is that there is a strong positive relationship between education and internationalism" (1988, 283). With increased education comes a greater ability to frame important issues cognitively and the more technical knowledge one has about them.

The third factor is rank. The higher one's rank in an organization, the more likely that one has faced critical issues involving the welfare of others.[8] Rank also is a measure of certain technical capacities, and elites in important positions may be called upon to defend their organization's policies to outsiders. A fourth potentially important factor is interest in politics. An increased level of political attention should bring increased reflection on America's world role.

The fifth factor that might cause reflection on the problems associated with international conflict is an interest in religious matters. Many American anticommunist movements are tied to religious fundamentalism. During the 1950s, this was embodied in Fred Schwarz's Christian Anticommunist Crusade, while later it was manifested in the televangelism of such TV preachers as Pat Robertson and Jerry Falwell. Nevertheless, the degree of influence attributable to religion in forming political and ethical attitudes among Americans is in dispute. While theologians give religion much credit in ethical development, numerous empirical studies show that popular religiosity is not very helpful in causing people to become more virtuous.

In our initial analysis of military officers, we were unable to explain much variation in the adoption of conflict beliefs (Brunk, Secrest, and Tamashiro 1990, 100–03). Consequently, in later waves of the study we experimented with differences in how our questions were asked. These differences were particularly great for variables relating to interest in politics and religion. The exact format of the survey items is not the same for each elite group, and sometimes several items are used to try to tap the same attribute.[9] In the end, we chose our items so as to maximize explained variance. We did this to emphasize that as individual variables and as a class of variables they are not very good predictors of what an individual will adopt as a belief system.

In fact, none of the commonly suggested explanatory variables that measure the chance for reflection on the moral issues surrounding conflict performed well in predicting who will adopt a committed belief system. As noted earlier, the only elite group with any statistically significant differences in attitudes about conflict regarding a person's rank is the clergy. This is likely because the U.S. hierarchy has been called upon to publicly defend the church's position on nuclear deterrence. But these differences for the clergy are not important enough to bring the organization rank variable to the level of statistical significance. In fact, using all the variables that measure the possibility for reflection on warfare matters in one large statistical equation does not significantly increase the level of prediction above that explained by elite profession.

Overall, what does our empirical analysis tell us so far? First, if we know that an individual has adopted one of the major belief systems about international conflict, and if we know that individual's profession, it is often possible to predict which framework was adopted. Second, further knowledge of individual characteristics measuring whether an individual is apt to reflect on morality and on warfare issues explains nothing more of importance. Neither age, nor education, nor rank can be significantly related to whether one will adopt systematic beliefs about conflict after we control for elite profession.[10] No individual characteristics other than profession are associated with conflict belief systems. This suggests that fundamental sensibilities are very important, indeed.

PREDICTING SPECIFIC ATTITUDES FROM GENERAL PREDISPOSITIONS

Until the development of a hierarchical approach to studying attitudes, it proved difficult to demonstrate that there was much systematic structure in positions about foreign policy. At best, attitudes toward particular policy problems could be very weakly predicted by statistical models. But, as shown in chapter 7, one can explain a reasonable amount of the difference in elites' support for better safe than sorry and strict just war rationales for using military force in specific instances by referring to fundamental moral sensibilities. It is often possible to predict the specific policy positions of committed elites, while the ambivalents who fall between the two belief systems of better safe than sorry and strict just war have more unstable and highly situationally specific ways of reasoning.

The rest of this chapter examines the overall proportion of variability in the adoption of specific policy positions that can be explained by our cognitive framework. In doing so, we must keep in mind that the attitudes of ambivalents are highly unstable and more difficult to predict. We use regression to compare the results of a moral sensibilities model to one that also takes into account political ideology and profession. If a moral sensibilities explanation is reasonable, we should be able to predict the likely positions of elites on specific decisions about war, given their location in the three-dimensional space of cognitive possibilities.

The scenarios we examine concern Nicaragua and Iran. Our first step is to construct a measure of support for action against Nicaragua by summing the number of times an individual supported using U.S. military force in the scenarios previously described (items 40 to 45). This produces a seven-point scale ranging from answering that none of the scenarios is sufficient to justify military action to believing that all the scenarios are sufficient cause for intervention. A second scale, based on the Iran scenarios, measured when U.S. elites would support abandoning moral con-

Table 10.1   **Effect of Cognitive Dimensions and Other Variables on Support for U.S. Action**

	Risk Aversion	Force Legitimacy	War Constraints	Political Conservatism	Profession	R^2
Cognitive Dimensions						
Iran scenarios	.50	−.19	−.13	—	—	.32
Nicaragua scenarios	.32	−.18	−.18	—	—	.23
Cognitive Dimensions plus Political Conservatism and Profession						
Iran scenarios	.56	−.24	−.15	.03	−.14	.33
Nicaragua scenarios	.37	−.32	−.19	.13	−.16	.25

Note: Table presents standardized regression coefficients. The minimum number of cases per equation is 1,201. All coefficients are significant ($P < .05$, two-tailed) except for conservatism (0.03) in the second Iran question.

straints in dealing with an enemy (items 46 to 51). Both scales have substantial variability. While it is easy to predict the modal positions of those who advocate the strict just war and better safe than sorry positions on these specific matters, including the ambivalents would lower the level of explained variance.

Having discovered that a rather exhaustive list of demographic characteristics is not strongly related to elite beliefs, we can dismiss them quickly in order to simplify the regression. In this analysis, we use as predictors the three dimensions that constitute the cognitive space, self-defined ideology, and elite profession. The equations for the Iran and Nicaragua conflict scenarios are presented in table 10.1. Here our baseline model employs only the three cognitive dimensions of aversion to risk, legitimacy of force, and constraints on war. It explains 32 percent of the variance in support for the Iran scenarios involving the use of military force and 23 percent of the variance in support for the Nicaragua scenarios involving suspending moral constraints. These are the amounts of variation in specific policy positions for all American elites that can be explained by knowing an individual's fundamental predispositions. Of course, it is higher when only better safe than sorry and strict just war elites are considered and the ambivalents are excluded.

We then added political ideology and profession as predictors.[11] While we have seen that ideology is a statistically significant predictor of the highly politicized Nicaragua options, ideology was not a significant predictor regarding the Iran alternatives, which had been given little media attention at the time of our surveys. Furthermore, political ideology and profession add only minimally to the overall level of explained variance, and their coefficients are low, being only one-third or less the magnitude of risk aversion. This indicates that ideology and profession are not nearly as influential in structuring this area of public policy attitudes as are the fundamental moral sensibilities we have identified.

To summarize these findings, all the additional influences that we have considered as predictors of specific policy attitudes contribute only 2 percent more explained variance to the statistical equations than is provided by fundamental moral sensibilities. Our analysis shows that the three cognitive dimensions we identify are the strongest predictors of elite attitudes on specific warfare matters and that risk sensitivity, in particular, is important for determining foreign policy attitudes. These fundamental sensibilities dominate all other factors suggested in the literature.

While profession and political ideology are often significantly correlated to policy attitudes, their effects in shaping them are much less important than are fundamental sensibilities. In matters of international conflict, fundamental sensibilities seem to have a preeminent impact. The same may be true in many domestic policy areas, as well, but social scientists have not yet identified with any precision the fundamental sensibilities at work in those realms.

Given this evidence, it appears that much of the apparent difference noted by past researchers between the attitudes of military veterans and the general public, church members and nonmembers, conservatives and liberals, and so on, about international conflict is spurious. The real cause of many policy attitudes apparently lies in people's fundamental moral sensibilities. These sensibilities also direct them toward particular types of careers and particular political positions. For those who are strongly affected by such sentiments, their basic predispositions likely are well established by the time they assume their institutional roles in society. Secondary influences, such as profession and political ideology, are not nearly as powerful in shaping foreign policy attitudes as are fundamental sensibilities about the importance of the golden rule and calculations of risk.

Still, further qualifications are in order. Foreign policy views do not come about through a totally unthinking process, nor are they highly deterministic for all people. Just being a general, a journalist, a senator, a diplomat, or a bishop does not mean that an individual has adopted a coherent framework toward the evaluation of international affairs. In fact, few of the elites in our study display highly coherent views, and the opinions of ambivalents are more difficult to predict than those who advocate strict just war and better safe than sorry views. While role in society is strongly related to belief systems about conflict, nothing more of importance can be said about which individuals will hold such beliefs. Furthermore, since the international realm is highly complex, a knowledge of one's belief system does not allow complete prediction of one's policy views. There are too many intermediate steps involved in such calculations to allow anything approaching total prediction.

ELEVEN

Further Insights

Our research has uncovered several broad results regarding public policy. First, all U.S. elites seem to be aware of the demands of morality in international politics. Very few, if any, are willing to ignore moral considerations completely in the service of greater technical efficiency or political expediency, but this does not mean that international moral norms always dominate a responsible nation's policy—far from it. Why, then, do elites sometimes formulate and support public policies that clearly violate their moral preferences? In what sense can such people be described as morally aware?

Our study reveals that two basic moral sensibilities are central to people's thinking: golden rule concerns and in-group loyalty. Golden rule sentiments universalize moral concerns. In-group loyalty restricts moral concerns. The golden rule embraces all those in one's moral community. In-group loyalty excludes outsiders as beyond the protection of moral respect, fairness, and generosity. At times, golden rule and in-group loyalties are policy consistent, but in war these sensibilities are often in tension and point in different directions. It is this context that provides the most interesting theoretical circumstances.

When morality and political practicality clash, people's attitudes about international conflict fall along a spectrum characterized by three modal possibilities. The strict just war position extends moral protection to all. The better safe than sorry view embraces expediency. Ambivalence wavers among various degrees of expediency and moral restraint, depending on particular circumstances and the degree of risk. Among American elites, the clergy tend toward the strict just war position, and military officers tilt in the better safe than sorry direction. Journalists and foreign service officers are found between these two extremes, while members of Congress are particularly crosspressured.

In general, relatively few Americans embrace the strict just war position in its pure form. Most secular elites are unwilling to reject nuclear warfare as a matter of policy, and even among the clergy, a significant minority do not accept the strict just war position as it pertains to some aspects of nuclear war. For many people, situational risk seems to account for much of the inconsistency in their attitudes toward war. Risk inhibits golden rule sensibilities. The greater the risk to one's group from extending golden rule protections to innocent others, the less likely many people will embrace a risk-taking policy.

This generalization seems to apply in the domestic as well as the international realm, and it explains a number of paradoxes in social policy. Why did San Francisco, for example, with its long tradition of social liberalism, implement a plan to systematically harass the city's homeless population during the economic downturn of the 1990s in the hope that they would tire of such treatment and leave the area? Were not such actions a violation of the historic golden rule sensitivities of that metropolis? In a similar vein, why did Governor Pete Wilson try to deny social benefits to the children of California's illegal immigrants at a time of economic hardship exactly when the benefits were needed the most? These children had no control over their situations and might be considered the economic equivalent of civilian noncombatants.

Such dramatic shifts in domestic policy seem to be equally explainable using the general framework of our model. As the direct costs and externalities of extending to others social benefits that people want to have for themselves multiplied, many Californians reasoned they could no longer extend golden rule protections to others. Ironically, continuing to give others traditional social benefits during an economic recession may be seen as unacceptably increasing the risk to one's in-group, particularly if providing social benefits to the homeless could increase the city's criminal element, as some San Franciscans believed. The numerous stresses of an economic downturn also likely cause some people to redefine their relevant in-group and to restrict its membership. This observation explains, as well, the unexpected finding that during hard times some recent immigrants are among the most vocal proponents of prohibiting further immigration into their adopted country.

Nevertheless, our empirical findings do not support the idea that situational factors explain all policy judgments, since risk considerations do not dominate everyone's decision calculus. For a special minority, such as certain members of the clergy, settled ways of moral thinking exist that seem very far removed from situational risk. This suggests caution in reaching all-purpose conclusions about judgments not tied to situational concerns and, conversely, caution in reaching conclusions about situational influences on moral judgment without reference to a particular group.

THEORETICAL ISSUES

Our work has particularly interesting implications for foreign policy theorizing. The traditional Hobbesian view of international relations as an international anarchy ungoverned by social contracts is not supported by our evidence. None of the groups we surveyed believes that U.S. war policy is exempt from moral scrutiny because of the irrelevance or futility of such thinking. The closest thing to a Hobbesian view among American elites is the better safe than sorry position, which still allows for conditional moral restraint. On the other hand, our research does not support a melioristic view of international politics, either. Under certain conditions, very harsh policies can be sanctioned by the better safe than sorry outlook.

Of particular theoretical interest is the school of thought in international relations that embraces the cosmopolitan assumption that people have powerful sympathies for other members of the human species (see, e.g., Beitz 1979; Shue 1980). Our research suggests that this assumption in unqualified form does not hold for most U.S. elites with respect to war. This is because in-group sentiments and aversion to risk are strong inhibitors of golden rule sensibilities among many Americans. Such an observation is relevant to another group of scholars, as well. The world order school argues that nation-states are a major obstacle to peace and justice. This school holds that political decision makers are attracted to muddling-through and safety-first policies as a means of preserving national power. Accordingly, many world order proponents are skeptical of political elites and bureaucratic institutions like the United Nations. These theorists prefer to emphasize popular movements and grass-roots initiatives (e.g., Falk, Kim, and Mendlowitz 1982). Our research tends to support part of the world order diagnosis, in that many U.S. elites are risk-averse and proponents of the better safe than sorry position.

What specific situations sharpen the tendency to place people outside the protection of morality and justice? The growing body of research in social psychology on moral exclusionism is useful here. Focusing on both individual and situational factors, it concludes that extreme conflict lessens moral concern for others (Bar-Tal 1990; Deutsch 1990; Opotow 1990). This accords with our finding that despite the supposed ubiquity of ideological crusades in American history, few contemporary elites are moral crusaders. Apparently, ideological crusades are largely the product of continued frustration with extended and unsuccessful conflicts rather than intellectual responses to policy issues. If one's side is victorious, then the enemy's threat subsides, and crusading attitudes largely evaporate with its passing. But if neither group is permanently defeated, the frustration of conflict continues, hardening attitudes and institutionalizing a moral crusading fervor. In the contemporary world, Northern Ireland and Yugoslavia are two examples of this process. Given the images of international politics that flourish during wartime that stress national interest, competitiveness, and superiority, military conflict is likely to promote moral exclusion. The closer a conflict approaches a zero-sum profile, the stronger these in-group maximizing attitudes become.

Such findings from the social psychology literature are consistent with the dominant preoccupations with threat among many of the elites in our study whose careers spanned World War II and the cold war. Typical circumstances that promote moral exclusion include unstable political regimes, culturally sanctioned violence, authoritarian institutions, and, of course, war itself (Staub 1989). At the individual level of awareness, the key factors found to promote moral exclusion include feeling unconnected to outsiders, having little cooperative contact with potential victims, ambiguous moral norms, lack of moral reciprocity by an enemy, and moral uncertainty (Deutsch 1973; McElroy 1992).

Nevertheless, against these formidable situational and individual-level forces, some people are able to maintain an altruistic outlook that approaches the heroic. These people, as exemplified by the selfless rescuers of Jews in Nazi Europe, ignore both risk and cost calculations (Monroe 1991). Instead, they are motivated by a powerful and deep-seated humanitarian sentiment that supersedes narrow group loyalties. These are John Donne's people, who do not need to ask for whom the bell tolls. The most basic sensibility defining their cognitive structure tells them for whom it tolls. They are almost the mirror image of those described by the self-interest paradigm of economics. Few ever attain such a high level of altruism, and for many people in times of political adversity, group loyalty translates into indifference or hostility to those who are not members of one's in-group (Rosenberg 1965).

How, then, can one be politically realistic and at the same time hold out the possibility that people can be encouraged to expand their concern for others? After all, realism in international politics is associated with strategic, not altruistic, principles. Realism speaks the language of rationality, interests, competition, and power. Yet despite these irrefutable truths, there are a number of ways that foreign policy realists might embrace unselfish, golden rule policies without undergoing a complete moral or religious transformation.

Realists, considered solely as agents of their governments, hold that it is rational for states to pursue their self-interest and that to do otherwise is risky or imprudent (Oppenheim 1991). Indeed, as seen in earlier chapters, risk concerns are central to the thinking of all U.S. elites, not just the realists. Given this desire to avoid risks, people can construct policies consistent with the golden rule. Foreign aid and arms control agreements are two examples. Of course, such policies would be defended by realists in terms of self-interest or rationality, not morality. Nevertheless, these policies, no matter how they are justified, would have a benevolent quality.

Further, game theory shows that given enough mutual trust between states, rationality can lead to cooperation that leaves everyone better off. This is the happy circumstance where collective rationality and the golden rule coincide (Rapoport 1982). Indeed, it is argued that moral norms in international politics play an important and practical function for nations. They are used to signal one's good intentions and can markedly increase a state's influence (McElroy 1992). Again, such cases reinforce the possibility of contingent compassion by realists. Saintliness is not necessary to produce moral policies — the recognition of benevolent self-interest is often enough.

What of those harsh zero-sum or near zero-sum conflicts where trust and the possibilities of compromise are minimal? What of war? First, risk concerns frequently lead realists to avoid military intervention and war, except as a last resort. Modern warfare, being extremely costly and destructive, is quite likely to be contrary to a state's national interest. Accordingly, for the political realist, there is no need to invoke the immorality of war; questioning its rationality is often sufficient (Kennan 1985; Weinberger 1990).

However, this does not settle the issue regarding the potential tension between political realism and morality. At times, waging war is compatible with the national interest, and then the realist's instrumental rationality, on the one hand, and principles of morality, on the other, can tilt in opposite directions. Strategic opportunities may be both rational and immoral — for example, the surprise attack. Rationality is not always moral, and morality is not always rational. Even so, ethical possibilities are not entirely precluded by strategic rationality.

Game theory research shows that when exit costs are low, it is rational to break off a conflict rather than seek victory. This strategy, technically called *prudent morality,* is compatible with both realism and morality (Vanberg and Congleton 1992). Even when exit costs are prohibitive and combat ensues, possibilities for limited cooperation are not extinguished. Given reciprocity between combatants, voluntary military constraints, such as not targeting each other's food sources, prisoner-of-war conventions, and biological-chemical war prohibitions can be rationally established and defended (Axelrod 1984).

Of course, we should not exaggerate the potential compatibility between realistic prudence and rationality, on the one hand, and morality, on the other. As our research shows, antagoinists can combine aversion to risk and rational appraisal of risk in a way that leads to greater violence and more immoral behavior, not less. Risk analysis can lead to better safe than sorry methods as well as strict just war constraints. Indeed, in elite thinking, the former is often more likely.

If one demands the immediate primacy of universalistic attitudes and concerns, then our study provides a gloomy perspective. However, if one adopts a gradualist outlook and asks whether people can be led to care about the well-being of some outsiders, perhaps in the next generation, then we can be more optimistic. The evidence suggests that elite in-group concerns can be expanded, especially if people recognize that their ends are often complementary rather than mutually exclusive. Our research shows, for example, that U.S. elites see the prevention of nuclear war in this light. Accordingly, promoting concern for innocent others and the risk-accepting outlook can move policies toward the strict just war position without requiring that one adopt universalized golden rule sentiments. The policing of international drug trafficking and peacekeeping activities serve as illustrations.

Other research also suggests that moral concerns and a sense of fairness can be expanded, given favorable circumstances. If this is to be achieved, people must be made more aware of the moral issues implicit in many public policy decisions. Framing foreign relations problems in impersonal terms will likely produce an amoral, technical answer. Describing refugees in terms of logistics is apt to elicit a very different response from descriptions counched in humanitarian or human rights terms. Moreover, decision makers are apt to be preoccupied with political and bureaucratic routines that discourage moral sensitivity. However, further discussion of such specific measures might have an impact on this amoral bias by heightening elite moral awareness and undermining a sense of disengagement (Roloff and Miller 1980; Stephen and Stephen 1984; Kelman and Hamilton 1989).

Second, at the level of individual motivations, unselfish behavior such as empathy, strong commitments to duty or principle, and an intense universalistic humanitarianism, can be elicited in many ways (Mansbridge 1990, 133–34; Monroe 1991). These motivations frequently are intermingled, but individuals vary in their sensitivity to these different motivating forces. Pure altruists, who have a deep humanitarian commitment, appear to ignore both costs and risks and do not need empathic feelings to perform heroic acts of kindness, but such people are few. In contrast, rational actors, who probably represent a large proportion of government elites, require empathic ties to trigger their moral sensitivities. Furthermore, assessing risk and potential reciprocity are also vital motivating ingredients. If the risks are perceived as too great or if cooperation is not reciprocated, then feelings of sympathy and moral principle are rapidly extinguished.

Finally, situational influences appear to be powerful motivators of moral inclusion for most people. Examples of such influences are cooperative intergroup efforts to achieve joint goals (Cook 1984) or situational pressures such as moral norms, role requirements, peer pressures, and third party sanctions (Snyder 1982; Keohane 1984; Staub 1989; McElroy 1992). The United States' renunciation of biochemical weapons production in 1989 and the Panama Canal Treaties of 1978 are two prominent examples of policies that were strongly motivated by such situational pressures (McElroy 1992).

CONJECTURES AND SPECULATIONS

If people can be brought to expand their sensibilities toward others, what changes and problems might we expect? Our research suggests that expanding sensibilities about conflict attitudes would shift all people, in varying degrees, toward the just war position with respect to *ad bellum* proportionality decisions. Also, for nonmilitary elites, universalizing trends should strengthen *in bello* sensibilities. This would be especially true for the noncombatant immunity principle. The trend, should it unfold, would strengthen the sense of a global moral community and, consequently, circumscribe the harsher features of realist thinking.

Basically, political realism argues that in a world devoid of a sense of community, where we are all on our own, states have no choice but to look to their national interests. This is the only rational and prudent option. As George Kennan puts it, these interests are the "unavoidable necessities of a national existence and therefore not subject to classification as either 'good' or 'bad'" (1985, 206). Such an outlook is associated with strategic, rather than altruistic, principles and with war rather than peace. Nevertheless, as a sense of moral inclusion expands, one would expect a growing inclination toward moral scrutiny and skepticism toward war policy and a corresponding progressive weakening of realist sentiments.

One possible outcome of this moral inclusion would be to limit the freedom of governments to engage in war while expanding their responsibilities with respect to how war is conducted. At least four pathways for this moralizing of war policy can be identified: the consciences of individual decision makers; domestic public opinion and political pressures; concern for a nation's international reputation, to which governments will be increasingly subjected; and international networks of government and nongovernment organizations such as the European Community and Amnesty International. The growth of global democratization and communications will continue to increase the impact of all these pathways (Fukuyama 1992).

Interestingly, expanding people's sense of moral concern about war raises complex problems. First, as with other elites, *in bello* demands will likely shift more military officers from exclusive in-group thinking toward a concern for innocent others and assessment of risk. This, in turn, will demand more information and cognitive processing time. Unfortunately, modern war tends to decrease decision time. Consequently, applying *in bello* just war precepts may become harder for cognitive processing reasons (Fotion 1990), and this pressure could strengthen a better safe than sorry instinct. Such was the case in the 1988 USS *Vincennes* incident, when the commander of a U.S. cruiser operating in the Persian Gulf was time-pressured into launching his missiles against an Iranian civilian airliner that was mistaken for a hostile fighter. However, if decision makers are given adequate time, advancements in weapons technology could possibly strengthen the immunity of noncombatants and other *in bello* constraints on the use of force.

A second uncertainty regarding *in bello* just war precepts and the military involves the problem of accountability and manipulation. Even when officers move from the better safe than sorry view to other moral positions, they still retain battlefield responsibility. Of necessity, they will have the task of calculating immediate risks and consequences. This burden is complex and difficult enough in peacetime. In war, it may become overwhelming. Accordingly, leaders feel a powerful tendency to shift the foundations of their moral judgments from the realm of ordinary sensibilities to the routinized and operational intelligence of technicians. This, in turn, risks encouraging the sort of insensitivity that developed during the Vietnam War. Another possibility is that the military will try to manipulate media reporting to reduce moral criticism of their war policies. This has been done successfully since Vietnam by restricting access of reporters to the war zone and restricting their numbers by using media pools.

Furthermore, approaching *in bello* responsibilities by way of risk management can actually increase the military's vulnerability to blackmail. An enemy can ratchet up the military risks to pressure an opponent into violating moral scruples and embracing a better safe than sorry position. During the fighting in the Balkans, it appears that United Nations forces in Sarajevo were secretly shelled by the Bosnians, the very group the peacekeepers were trying to protect. The Bosnians hoped that the Serbs would be blamed, which would force the United Nations to abandon its peacekeeping mission and fight with the Bosnians against the Serbs.

Some believe that Saddam Hussein used hostages and civilians to shield his army before the Gulf War in hopes of provoking allied attacks against Iraqi civilians, which he could use for propaganda purposes. This did not work, but an earlier blackmail effort by the Iranians did. In the Iran-contra affair Tehran demanded that the Reagan administration take criminal action in supporting an arms deal to avoid the threat of an even greater evil against U.S. hostages. Under such pressure, a person like Oliver North might reasonably conclude that lying to Congress and violating U.S. laws were preferable to the death of American hostages. Therefore, the problem of an opponent strategically manipulating operational risks may prevent the military from moving significantly beyond its current *in bello* commitments.

A third question, involving moral responsibility to one's in-group, is particularly prominent in the retrospective debate about the use of the atomic bomb on Japan. What are the limits to the sacrifices we must ask of people to assure the morality of our policies? How much risk and cost should we impose on our community to help outsiders? How much military risk should we accept so that the enemy's noncombatants may escape suffering? How do we calculate the trade-off between quickly and ruthlessly ending a war, and hence the suffering it causes, and waging a war with restraint and thereby prolonging the risks to our side?

A fourth, related issue involves the question of moral limits. Assuming that a government accepts moral responsibilities in war, where do these responsibilities end? Limitless moral obligations are paralyzing, so guidelines are needed. Yet such guidelines in war are unclear. While we may accept the responsibility of trying to avoid targeting noncombatants, if we extend our moral view, we may also wish to avoid targeting the social and economic support systems, such as water supplies and electrical grids, on which noncombatants depend. This question, in fact, arose during the Gulf War, where the allied air campaign tried to avoid inflicting direct civilian casualties but caused massive indirect suffering in Iraq by disrupting the country's social and economic infrastructure (Arkin, Durrant, and Cherni 1991). All U.S. elites feel that American war conduct should be subject to moral scrutiny, but, not surprisingly, they are unable to agree on moral limits.

These matters of communal costs and trade-offs are especially acute in zero-sum conflicts, where all gains by outsiders entail losses for the in-group. Furthermore, the more decision makers try to extend moral responsibilities in war, the more numerous become the resource claims and costs imposed on the in-group, and hence, the more painful will be the trade-offs. If one's resource base is very large or if one's technological edge is very great — as in the Gulf War — then the trade-offs will be bearable. But if one's resources are not substantially greater than the claims made on them by outsiders, then better safe than sorry policies will be difficult to resist. Hence, powerful wealthy nations may be more willing to restrict their actions in the name of advancing international morality than will smaller states. The weak have a smaller resource base and cannot as easily afford to accept risk. Foreign policy mistakes are unlikely to jeopardize the existence of great powers like the United States, but the missteps of small countries can lead to their swift extinction. Not surprisingly, this harsh reality imposes severe limits on the golden rule inclinations of small, beleaguered states.

In general, it is the nature of morality that no matter how powerful the arguments advanced on its behalf, they can always be contested. By placing our study within the context of other relevant social science research and speculation, we wish to demonstrate that, within the realm of realpolitik and the morally contestable, it is possible to expand the boundaries of one's moral community to encompass nonmembers while remaining realistic about the challenges involved. The collective image of U.S. elites that we have painted is one of inhibited moralists. They must thread their way between decency and self-preservation in a world where good and evil often seem inextricably bound together. In this world, political reality provides strong incentives for contemplating moral issues. That our survival often is at stake in war, strangely enough, invites us to make moral sense of our lives. Existence without risk would deprive our choices of this moral content. The significance of our actions concerning war consists precisely in the potential for great loss. Without such risk, our attentiveness might slacken, for risk is an important device in discovering what is moral. So, paradoxically, it is useful that we must confront stern realities in the public policy arena from time to time. It is in such circumstances that we can more fully develop our reasoning powers and grow morally.

NOTES

Chapter 1. Ethical Values and Public Policy

1. An important exception to this generalization is that both the Gallup and Harris organizations did pose questions about the morality of the Vietnam War, but their inquiries were not detailed enough to be very useful (Brunk and Wilson 1991, 163–64).

2. Scholars in other disciplines also inquire into the nature of moral attitudes but generally use quite restricted data bases, and their results are highly interpretive. A good example is Lawrence Kohlberg (1980, 1981), who proposes a general theory of moral development and argues, in part, that the political ideology of liberalism represents the highest level of cognitive thought.

3. This lack of consensus is reflected in most contemporary high school textbooks, which go to great lengths to avoid discussing controversial issues and consequently fail to inform readers about many important aspects of American history.

4. Others are no less enthusiastic. Dennis Mueller writes that "the only assumption necessary to a descriptive and predictive science of human behavior is egoism" (1986, 14).

5. Even when the voting behavior literature considered the potentially moral factor of citizen duty, it served as as a patch. Those who vote were assumed to place a high value on duty, while those who did not must have a low duty coefficient. This is hardly a great revelation. The failure of the rational paradigm in voting led to a major defensive effort to try to save it. In the mid-1970s, the *American Political Science Review* devoted eight articles to various patches, and numerous other papers appeared in such journals as *Public Choice*.

6. Our work progressed over almost a decade. In this book, we have retained most of the terminology used in our developmental papers but have made a few changes to better represent our evolving understanding of the normative concepts derived from our statistical analysis.

Chapter 2. Traditional Frameworks

1. *Egoism* is also the term the economist F. Y. Edgeworth (1881) used in describing economic behavior as fundamentally motivated by self-interest. Interestingly, though,

he thought that the two categories of human activity that are the most amenable to an economic calculus are contracts and war.

2. Amartya Sen (1978) was one of the first social choice theorists who attacked the assumption that pure self-interest was the only motivation that needed to be considered in modeling human behavior. He argues that people have sympathy for others and hold important commitments to general principles, two of the key ingredients of the just war school of international conflict.

3. Among international politics theorists, Arnold Wolfers examines the self-abnegation approach and argues that nations occasionally pursue policies that "place a higher value on such ends as international solidarity, lawfulness, rectitude, or peace than they place even on national security and self-preservation" (1962, 93).

4. See, e.g., Tullock (1979). This is essentially what Jane Mansbridge describes as the proper goal of normative democratic theory (1990, 22).

5. For representative treatments of the golden rule and analogous principles, see Wolfers (1949), Ramsey (1951), Thomas (1955), Baier (1958), Bainton (1960), Gordis (1964), Rawls (1971), Donagan (1977), Gewirth (1978, 1982, 128–42), and Green (1988).

6. On the supreme emergency, see Oppenheim (1955), Tucker (1966), Walzer (1977), and Johnson (1984).

7. On legalism, see Weber (1946), von Kleffens (1960), Walzer (1977), Cohen (1989), Kelman and Hamilton (1989), and Lackey (1989).

8. On the moral crusade and holy war doctrines, see Khaddari (1955), Bainton (1960), Johnson (1975, 1981), Erdmann (1977), Craigie (1978), Hartigan (1982), and Morgenthau and Thompson (1985).

9. On pacifism, see Bainton (1960), Mayer (1966), Miller (1966), Brock (1970), Gandhi (1972), and Lackey (1989).

10. See Lackey (1989, 13–16). Nevertheless, Gandhi's advocacy of nonviolence also can be seen as a strategy for maximizing desired political ends (see Klitgaard 1971; Chatterjee 1974).

11. On nuclear pacifism, see Tucker (1966), Ramsey (1968), Walzer (1977), Castelli (1983), Kattenburg (1985), Johnson (1984), Lackey (1984, 1989), Finnis, Boyne, and Grisez (1987), Cohen (1989), and Sichol (1990).

12. For treatments of reason of state logic, see Machiavelli (1979a, 1979b), Niebuhr (1932), Morgenthau (1946), Meinecke (1957), Organski (1968), Thompson and Myers (1977), Sterling (1974), Walzer (1977), Lackey (1984), Morgenthau and Thompson (1985), and Smith (1986).

13. For treatments of the principles underlying the retaliatory ethic, see U.S. Department of the Army (1956), Taylor (1970), Mavrodes (1975), Walzer (1977), Kurtz (1988), and Cohen (1989).

14. On fatalism, see Burns (1960), Krickus (1965), and Frankena (1973, 73–78).

15. For treatments of fatalism, see Brandt (1972), Frankena (1973, 1976), Walzer (1977), Boyce and Jensen (1978), and Lackey (1984).

16. The only people who would not need to justify this contradiction are those who opt for the likely suicidal self-abnegation ethic.

17. This position was particularly evident among some of our respondents who objected to any survey of the morality of U.S. war plans because, by definition, whatever the United States does is moral.

Chapter 3. Investigating Belief Systems

1. For various perspectives, see Weber (1946), Price and Bell (1970), Asher (1973), Kirkpatrick and Regens (1977), Weingast (1979), and Fiore, Brunk, and Meyer (1992).

2. See Miller (1967), Montagna (1968), Mosher (1982), Sorensen and Sorensen (1974), Hodges and Durant (1989), and Fiori, Brunk, and Meyer (1992).

3. William Riker (1986) discusses heuristics for demonstrating the consequences of the voters' paradox to undermine one's political opponents or disliked public policies.

4. Examples of this stream of thought include Piaget (1932), Bandura (1977), Kohlberg (1981), Boyce and Jensen (1978), and Pennington (1986).

5. See Monroe (1991) for a review of the hypotheses that flow from the different research traditions that attempt to explain the origins of altruistic behavior.

6. Our dual-causation arrows between reality beliefs and normative beliefs are intended to show that people's attitudes stem from a combination of these two sets of influences. Naturally, there are many causes of attitudes and behavior other than rational thought. We have indicated these by the other-causes arrow.

7. The closest equivalent to figure 3.1 in the study of international relations is employed by Jon Hurwitz and Mark Peffley (1987), who use a core values framework to explain American foreign policy attitudes.

8. Of equal interest to our research, while these studies find that people's attitudes become more coherent as they gain substantive information, this does not mean that consensus is automatically reached. Far from it. In such areas as environmental policy, it seems instead that people's attitudes become hardened in support of polar opposite policy positions as their knowledge increases. Consequently, the traditional democratic argument that if only our citizens were better informed we could hope to reach a national consensus on important policy issues is highly questionable.

Chapter 4. Research Design

1. Likewise, Thomas Kuhn (1962) argues that physicists and chemists often use models in their teaching. These are similar simple abstractions that serve the same function as proverbs in teaching moral discourse. Also see Nisbett and Ross (1980).

2. In measuring support for these frameworks, we occasionally adopted the strategy of asking questions that contain two necessary precepts. An affirmative answer requires that a respondent agree with all the embedded precepts (Sabatier and Hunter 1989). Sometimes our items also imply two ends of a scale that sets the context for the answer. Take the statement, "Moral principles are absolute and do not depend on the situation." If an individual answers in the context of moral perfectionism versus nonperfectionism, then this is not a double-barreled item. If U.S. elites do not use that approach, there will be no systematic pattern to responses indicating the use of perfectionism versus nonperfectionism as an organizing principle.

3. This means that responses to some items need to be reversed in the analysis to be correctly interpreted. These items are noted in table 4.1.

4. For general reviews of the factors that have been hypothesized to affect military attitudes, see Bachman, Sigelman, and Diamond (1987) and Brunk, Secrest, and Tamashiro (1990). See Monroe (1991) for a similar list of factors thought to affect altruistic behavior.

5. While information on hometown size was collected for four elite groups, we did not inquire about this characteristic of members of Congress because, taken together with a few other simple questions, it identified most of them, and we wanted to preserve their anonymity.

Chapter 5. American Endorsement of Normative Criteria

1. Individuals also could respond that they were "uncertain" regarding the issue posed by a particular survey item.

2. Because of differences in the number of respondents from the five groups, data about the military officers and diplomats contribute the most to the construction of table 5.1. The data in later tables are broken down by elite group to control for possible attitude differences.

3. On the moral arguments regarding Central America prominent during the late 1980s, see Johnson (1988), Kornbluh (1987, 169–212), Lacey (1986), Miles (1986), Secrest (1986), and Walker (1987).

4. The Nixon administration earlier had taken an even more extreme position with regard to the freely elected government of Chile. Although President Salvador Allende had gained power through democratic means, Henry Kissinger justified American covert actions against the Chilean government by saying, "I don't see why we have to let a country go Marxist just because its people are irresponsible" (quoted in Hunt 1987, 184).

Chapter 6. Fundamental Structure

1. Of course, it is possible that some individuals are more inclined to use situational logic, but their proportion must be roughly equal among all the elite groups. If that was not the case, then we would find aggregate differences in the level of sophistication among the groups.

2. Correct predictions can be made, as well, for many items having factor weights that are less than 0.40, but as the coefficients decrease in value, random error begins to overwhelm systematic variation, and a detailed interpretation of the importance of items is no longer of much value.

3. This dimension has similarities to Hurwitz and Peffley's (1987) core value of morality of warfare.

4. The just war items whose correlations are less than 0.40 deal with the prosecution of a war in terms of the probability of success and proportionality principles. See Secrest, Brunk and Tamashiro (1991a, 1991b), where we discuss such differential support for just war principles.

5. Since these loadings are the average correlations between a factor and the component principles of a traditional school, the range of potential values is from −1.00 to +1.00.

Chapter 7. Characteristic Principles

1. As a group, military officers are strong supporters of better safe than sorry, but risk aversion is not as important in distinguishing among their attitudes as it is for other elites because most military officers are very prudent.

2. Another statistical way to define the better safe than sorry belief system is to include the five supplementary items in a factor analysis with the original items, but then we can only examine the responses of elites in the last three waves of the survey who answered all thirty-nine items. Such results provide even more support to our interpretation, as the magnitudes for the two strongest items are greater than 0.70.

3. One reason contemporary politicians are held in such low public regard is that so many of them seem to have inherently ambivalent personalities. As a network commentator noted about one of Bill Clinton's dramatic and unexpected shifts, the president could not resist the common urge of politicians to try to please an audience, and when speaking before a dinner of millionaires indicated that he felt their pain from the tax increase he had forced through Congress. Another example of this tendency was George Bush's plea that he wanted to become the education president, the environmental president, and the president of the treasured cause of just about every other special interest whose supporters he addressed during his first presidential campaign. But despite his statement, "Read my lips: No new taxes," which seemed so sincere and strongly held at the time, Bush had no difficulty in ignoring these promises after becoming president.

4. Our work in this section suggests another interesting hypothesis. Many writers note that the United States is suffering from a political malaise. There is general disaffection with politicians, which is reinforced by social choice models that view them in the worst possible moral light. But our evidence suggests that, at least in foreign affairs, many politicians do not have particularly bad motives. In fact, a majority may be trying to pursue some conception of the general good. The public relations problem facing politicians is that their contemporaries are held in such low regard that it is difficult for an honorable politician to rise above this perception. What distinguishes statesmen from others in such a climate may not be so much the true nobility of their motives as their success in demonstrating that they are not ambivalent.

5. Since we wished to make the better safe than sorry and strict just war groups of approximately equal size, we defined a strong supporter of better safe than sorry as one who responded in the affirmative to five or more of the seven items most strongly associated with the risk dimension. For strict just war, the criterion was support for at least six of the seven standard criteria for a just war.

6. Unless we discuss them explicitly, in our subsequent analyses these eleven individuals are be classified with the better safe than sorry supporters.

Chapter 8. Nuclear Deterrence

1. On nuclear weapons issues, see Tucker (1966), Ramsey (1968), Walzer (1977), Johnson (1984), National Conference of Catholic Bishops (1983), Kattenburg (1985), Wohlstetter (1985), United Methodist Council of Bishops (1986), Lackey (1989), Bullert (1989), Cohen (1989), and Sichol (1990).

2. We examined this possibility in detail for all the elite groups, but it seems to be the case only for Catholic clerics.

Chapter 9. Attitude Formation

1. In this discussion, it is important to remember that the statistical determination of what set of item responses properly constitutes an ambivalent view is not carved in

stone. We determined the proportion of ambivalents by setting the number of strict just war and better safe than sorry elites to be approximately equal; the others were categorized as ambivalent. Using a slightly different definition will change the proportion of ambivalents somewhat but will not change the basic interpretation of any data.

2. Such a statistical anomaly occasionally can be seen in studies of attitude constraint, since the variation among groups may be substantially different from the variation within groups. Public opinion studies often employ such statistics as the average gamma of all paired combinations of survey responses to indicate the extent of ideological structuring of a group's attitudes. Such a methodology is appropriate for a one-dimensional concept, but since attitudes toward international conflict are multidimensional, our methodology is based on factor analysis, and the degree of structuring of elite attitudes is measured using the level of explained variance.

3. Consequently, the multidimensional space we describe changes over time as the issues of major political importance shift.

Chapter 10. The Importance of Moral Sensibilities

1. As in our examples of the ambivalence of some contemporary politicians on important public policy matters, such people may be similarly ambivalent regarding professional norms. While they usually observe them, they do so only for self-serving reasons. Having no deep commitment to such rules, they disregard them as soon as doing so is seen to further their careers.

2. Many of our elite subjects expressed such feelings in their open-ended responses to our inquiries.

3. Those who eventually are commissioned as officers tend to be only marginally more politically conservative and a little less committed to the world as a reference group (see, e.g., Priest, Fullerton, and Bridges 1982; Bachman, Sigelman, and Diamond 1987).

4. In this part of our study we used discriminate function analysis. Such a methodology is appropriate when one examines a dichotomous variable, in this case, whether an individual has or has not adopted a belief system.

5. Thus, we need to establish a baseline for subsequent comparison. A statistical model using only group membership as a predictor tells us how much variability in commitment to conflict belief systems is explained by profession. Other measures of individual attributes thought to be associated with the learning of norms can then be added to the analysis. The added variability explained by an expanded statistical equation over the baseline equation provides an estimate of the explanatory power of the learning curve versus the moral sensibilities model. However, we do claim that this is a definitive test of relative importance because our independent variables are imperfect measures of the total probability of reflection on the moral issues of conflict and because some of them have restricted variance — for example, everyone in this study is an elite and our data were collected after they had began their careers. Nevertheless, if the results are clear and relatively straightforward, they will provide further insight into how people come to structure their beliefs.

6. For those unfamiliar with discriminate analysis, a caveat is in order. The technique always correctly classifies a substantial portion of cases. Suppose you want to predict whether a coin will land "heads" or "tails." If you always guess "heads," you

have correctly predicted half the events. This is why it is important to establish a baseline of comparison for later analysis. The baseline here is the 56 percent of individuals who can be correctly classified as ambivalents or morally committed elites, using only group membership as a predictor.

7. While most people would argue that age increases the chances for reflection and adoption of coherent belief systems, there is an interesting variant of this claim in the literature on legislative behavior. Ideological arguments are thought to be preferred by many politicians, but freshmen, who must follow their constituents' preferences more closely to win reelection, cannot adopt ideological positions so successfully (Davis and Porter, 1989). But as time passes, these politicians gain the advantages of incumbency, become less worried about their reelection chances, and consequently have the freedom to become more ideological.

Another possible way to explain attitudes by using age is to hypothesize a cohort effect. Some international relations theorists suggest that the Munich generation, which witnessed the consequences of appeasement to Hitler, opposed the policy preferences of the Vietnam generation, which saw the consequences of a wrong-minded attempt to unjustly apply the supposed lessons of Munich (see, e.g., Converse 1987; Jennings 1987). To test this thesis, we split elites into four groups on the basis of when they came of age relative to U.S. involvement in World War II, Korea, and Vietnam (see Holsti and Rosenau 1988, 284–85). However, this approach does not yield significantly better predictions than simple chronological age.

8. In the case of the military, we directly inquired about this issue by asking if an officer had been involved in combat.

9. In particular, and because of confidentiality restrictions, we did not ask as detailed a set of inquiries of members of Congress and, in order to preserve cases for analysis, in some instances substituted the mean value for individuals who did not respond to a specific item.

10. However, if group membership is not taken into consideration, education and various other demographic variables are significantly related to one's beliefs. This means these relationships are spurious and caused by differing average levels of the independent variables among the elite groups. Often such demographic characteristics are weakly related to attitudes in other policy areas, but the variables achieving statistical significance tend to differ among studies. Our finding suggests that most of these weak correlations will disappear, as well, as soon as the belief systems structuring moral attitudes in other policy areas have been successfully identified.

11. Ideology is measured as a conservatism scale. The baseline profession is the clergy; the other four groups are not significantly different from one another when the three cognitive dimensions are included in the equations.

BIBLIOGRAPHY

Abrahamsson, Bengt. 1972. *Military Professionalism and Political Power*. Beverly Hills, Calif.: Sage.

Acton, Philip. 1991. "The Just War Tradition and the Moral Character of Nuclear Deterrence." *Political Studies* 39: 5–18.

Akerlof, George A. 1983. "Loyalty Filters." *American Political Science Review* 73: 54–63.

Allison, Graham. 1971. *Essence of Decision*. Boston: Little, Brown.

Allport, F. H. 1937. "Toward a Science of Public Opinion." *Public Opinion Quarterly* 1: 7–23.

Almond, Gabriel A. 1950. *The American People and Foreign Policy*. New York: Praeger.

Arkin, William M., Damian Durrant, and Marrianne Cherni. 1991. *On Impact: Modern Warfare and the Environment*. Washington, D.C.: Greenpeace.

Asher, Herbert B. 1973. "The Learning of Legislative Norms." *American Journal of Political Science* 67: 500–12.

Asher, Herbert B., and Herbert F. Weisberg. 1978. "Voting Change in Congress." *American Political Science Review* 22: 391–425.

Axelrod, Robert M. 1984. *The Evolution of Cooperation*. New York: Basic Books.

Axelrod, Robert M., and Robert O. Keohane. 1985. "Achieving Cooperation under Anarchy." *World Politics* 38: 226–54.

Bachman, Jerald G., John D. Blair, and David R. Segal. 1977. *The All-Volunteer Force*. Ann Arbor: University of Michigan Press.

Bachman, Jerald G., Lee Sigelman, and Greg Diamond. 1987. "Self-Selection, Socialization, and Distinctive Military Values." *Armed Forces and Society* 13: 169–87.

Baier, Kurt. 1958. *The Moral Point of View*. Ithaca: Cornell University Press.

Bainton, Roland H. 1960. *Christian Attitudes toward War and Peace*. New York: Abingdon.

Balswick, Jack O. 1970. "Theology and Political Attitudes among Clergymen." *Sociological Quarterly* 11: 397–405.

Bandura, Albert. 1977. *Social Learning Theory*. Englewood Cliffs, N.J.: Prentice-Hall.

Banfield, Edward C., and James Q. Wilson. 1964. "Public-Regardingness as a Value Premise in Voting." *American Political Science Review* 58: 876–87.

Bardes, Barbara, and Richard W. Oldendick. 1978. "Beyond Internationalism." *Social Science Quarterly* 59: 496–508.

Bar-Tal, Daniel. 1990. "Causes and Consequences of Delegitimization." *Journal of Social Issues* 46: 65–81.

Bayer, Richard C. 1990. "Empirical Application of Justice Theories." *International Social Science Journal* 43: 565–76.

Beitz, Charles. 1979. *Political Theory and International Relations.* Princeton: Princeton University Press.

Blair, J. D. 1975. *Civil-Military Belief Systems: Attitudes toward the Military among Military Men and Civilians.* Ph.D. diss., University of Michigan, Ann Arbor.

Blight, James. 1990. *The Shattered Crystal Ball.* Savage, Md.: Rowman and Littlefield.

Bond, Doug, and Jong-Chul Park. 1991. "An Empirical Test of Rawl's Theory of Justice." *Simulation and Gaming* 22: 443–62.

Boyce, William D., and Larry C. Jensen. 1978. *Moral Reasoning.* Lincoln: University of Nebraska Press.

Brandt, Richard. 1972. "Utilitarianism and the Rules of War." *Philosophy and Public Affairs* 1: 145–65.

Brock, Peter. 1970. *Twentieth Century Pacifism.* New York: Van Nostrand Reinhold.

Brunk, Gregory G. 1989. "The Role of Statistical Heuristics in Public Policy Analysis." *Cato Journal* 9: 165–89.

Brunk, Gregory G., John Adams, and Subha Ramesh. 1988. "Contagion-Based Voting in Birmingham, Alabama," *Political Geography Quarterly* 7: 39–47.

Brunk, Gregory G., Donald E. Secrest, and Howard Tamashiro. 1990. "Military Views of Morality and War." *International Studies Quarterly* 34: 83–109.

Brunk, Gregory G., and Laura A. Wilson. 1991. "Interest Groups and Criminal Behavior." *Journal of Research in Crime and Delinquency* 28: 157–73.

Brzezinski, Zbigniew. 1984. "The Three Requirements for a Bipartisan Foreign Policy." In *The Washington Quarterly White Paper.* Washington, D.C.: Center for Strategic and International Studies, Georgetown University.

Buchanan, James M., and Gordon Tullock. 1962. *The Calculus of Consent.* Ann Arbor: University of Michigan Press.

Bullert, Gary. 1989. "The Catholic Bishop's Policy on Strategic Defense." *Journal of Social, Political, and Economic Studies* 14: 283–98.

Burns, Edward McNall. 1960. *Ideas in Conflict: The Political Theories of the Contemporary World.* New York: Norton.

Burr, Nelson R. 1961. *A Critical Bibliography of Religion in America.* Princeton: Princeton University Press.

Campbell, D. T. 1975. "On the Conflict between Biological and Social Evolution and Between Psychology and Moral Tradition." *American Psychologist* 30: 1103–26.

Caspery, W. R. 1968. "United States Public Opinion during the Onset of the Cold War." *Peace Research Society Papers* 9: 25–46.

Castelli, Jim. 1983. *The Bishops and the Bomb.* Garden City: Image Books.

Cayer, N. Joseph. 1986. *Public Personnel Administration in the United States.* New York: St. Martin's.

Cayer, N. Joseph, and Louis F. Weschler. 1988. *Public Administration: Social Change and Adaptive Management.* New York: St. Martin's.

Chamberlin, Roy B., and Herman Feldman. 1950. *The Dartmouth Bible*. Boston: Houghton Mifflin.

Champion, Dean J. 1975. *The Sociology of Organization*. New York: McGraw Hill.

Chatterjee, Bishwa B. 1974. "Search for an Appropriate Game Model for Gandhian Satyagraha." *Journal of Peace Research* 11: 21–30.

Childress, James. 1980. "Just War Criteria." In *War or Peace?* ed. Thomas Shannon. Minneapolis: Augsburg.

Chittick, William O., and Keith R. Billingsley. 1989. "The Structure of Elite Foreign Policy Beliefs." *Western Political Quarterly* 42: 202–24.

Clark, Ronald. 1976. *The Life of Bertrand Russell*. New York: Alfred Knopf.

Cockerham, Clark E. 1983. "The Radical Gospel and Christian Prudence." In *The Ethical Dimensions of Political Life*, ed. Francis Canavan. Durham: Duke University Press.

Cockerham, William C. 1978. "Attitudes Toward Combat Among U.S. Army Paratroopers." *Journal of Political and Military Sociology* 6: 1–15.

Cockerham, William C., and Lawrence E. Cohen. 1980. "Obedience to Orders." *Social Forces* 58: 1272–88.

Cockerham, William C., and Lawrence E. Cohen. 1981. "Volunteering for Foreign Combat Missions." *Pacific Sociological Review* 24: 329–54.

Cohen, Sheldon M. 1989. *Arms and Judgment*. Boulder: Westview.

Conover, Pamuel J., and Stanley Feldman. 1984. "How People Organize the Political World." *American Journal of Political Science* 29: 95–126.

Converse, Philip E. 1964. "The Nature of Belief Systems in Mass Publics." In *Ideology and Discontent*, ed. David E. Apter. New York: Free Press.

——. 1987. "On the Enduring Impact of the Vietnam War on American Public Opinion." In *After the Storm*. Taipei, Taiwan: Academic Sinica.

Converse, Philip E., and Greg B. Markus. 1979. "Plus ça change. . . . The New CPS Election Study Panel." *American Political Science Review* 73: 32–49.

Cook, S. W. 1984. "Cooperative Interaction in Multiethnic Contexts." In *Groups in Contact*, ed. N. Miller and M. Brewer. Orlando, Fla.: Academic.

Craigie, Peter. 1978. *The Problem of War in the Old Testament*. Grand Rapids, Mich.: W. B. Eerdmans.

Crocker, Jennifer, Dalene B. Hannah, and Renee Weber. 1983. "Person Memory and Causal Attributions." *Journal of Personality and Social Psychology* 44: 55–66.

Davie, Maurice R. 1968. *The Evolution of War*. Port Washington, N.Y.: Kennicat.

Davis, Michael L., and Philip K. Porter. 1989. "A Test for Pure or Apparent Ideology in Congressional Voting." *Public Choice* 60: 101–11.

Dawes, Robyn M., Alphons J. C. van de Kraft, and John M. Orbell. 1988. "Not Me or Thee but We." *Acta Psychologica* 68: 83–97.

Dawes, Robyn M., and H. Thaler. 1988. "Cooperation." *Journal of Economic Perspectives* 2: 187–96.

Decosse, David E., ed. 1992. *But Was It Just?* New York: Doubleday.

Deutsch, Karl W., and R. L. Merritt. 1965. "Effects of Events on National and International Images." In *International Behavior*, ed. H. C. Kelman. New York: Holt, Rinehart and Winston.

Deutsch, Morton. 1973. *The Resolution of Conflict*. New Haven: Yale University Press.

———. 1990. "Psychological Roots of Moral Exclusion." *Journal of Social Issues* 46: 21–25.

Donagan, Alan. 1977. *The Theory of Morality*. Chicago: University of Chicago Press.

Downs, Anthony. 1957. *An Economic Theory of Democracy*. New York: Harper.

Dyson, Freeman. 1984. *Weapons and Hope*. New York: Harper and Row.

Edgeworth, F. Y. 1881. *Mathematical Psychics*. London: C. K. Paul.

Eldridge, Albert F. 1979. *Images of Conflict*. New York: St. Martin's.

Elliston, F., J. Keenan, P. Lockhart, and J. V. Schaick. 1985. *Whistle-Blowing: Managing Dissent in the Workplace*. New York: Praeger.

Erdmann, Carl. 1977. *The Origin and Idea of Crusade*. Princeton: Princeton University Press.

Falk, Richard, Samuel Kim, and Saul Mendlowitz. 1982. *Toward a Just World Order*. Vol. 1. Boulder: Westview.

Fallows, James. 1979. "The Passionless Presidency." *Atlantic Monthly* 243, no. 5 (May): 33–58.

Faulkner, S. 1973. "War Crimes." *Guild Practitioner* 31: 131–44.

Feinberg, Barry, and Ronald Kasrils, eds. 1984. *Betrand Russell's America*. Vol. 2, *1945–1970*. London: Allen and Unwin.

Finley, David J., Ole R. Holsti, and Richard R. Fagan. 1967. *Enemies in Politics*. Chicago: Rand McNally.

Finnis, John, Joseph M. Boyne Jr., and Germain Grisez. 1987. *Nuclear Deterrence, Morality and Realism*. Oxford: Clarendon.

Fiore, William, Gregory G. Brunk, and C. Kenneth Meyer. 1992. "Norms of Professional Behavior in Highly Specialized Organizations." *Administration and Society* 24: 81–99.

Fiorina, Morris. 1986. "Information and Rationality in Elections." Occasional Paper 86–4. Center for Political Studies of Harvard University, Cambridge.

Fiske, Susan T., and Shelley E. Taylor. 1984. *Social Legislation*. Reading, Pa.: Addison-Wesley.

Fleishman, John A. 1988. "Attitude Organization in the General Public." *Social Forces* 67: 159–84.

Fletcher, Joseph F. 1966. *Situation Ethics: The New Morality*. Philadelphia: Westminster.

Fotion, Nicholas. 1990. *Military Ethics*. Stanford, Calif.: Hoover.

Frankena, William K. 1973. *Ethics*. Englewood Cliffs: Prentice-Hall.

———. 1976. "Love and Principle in Christian Ethics." In *Perspectives on Morality*, ed. K. E. Goodpaster. Notre Dame: University of Notre Dame Press.

"The French Bishops' Statement." 1983. *Origins* 13: 441–60.

Fukuyama, Francis. 1992. *The End of History and the Last Man*. New York: Free Press.

Gaddis, John Lewis. 1987. *The Long Peace*. New York: Oxford University Press.

Gandhi, Mahatma. 1972. *Non-Violent Resistance in War and Peace*. New York: Garland.

Gewirth, Alan. 1978. *Reason and Morality*. Chicago: University of Chicago Press.

———. 1982. *Human Rights*. Chicago: University of Chicago Press.

Glazer, Amihai, and Bernard Grofman. 1989. "Why Representatives Are Ideologists Though Voters Are Not." *Public Choice* 61: 29–39.

Gordis, Robert. 1964. *Religion and International Responsibility*. New York: Council on Religion and International Affairs.

Gordon, J. W. 1986. "Principled Organizational Dissent: A Theoretical Essay." *Research in Organizational Behavior* 8: 1–52.

Green, R. M. 1988. *Religion and Moral Reason: A New Method for Comparative Study*. New York: Oxford University Press.

Hamilton, Richard F. 1968. "A Research Note on the Mass Support for 'Tough' Military Initiatives." *American Sociological Review* 33: 439–45.

Hare, Richard Merogn. 1981. *Applications of Moral Philosophy*. New York: Oxford University Press.

Hartigan, Richard S. 1982. *The Forgotten Victim*. Boulder: Westview.

Henken, Louis, Richard C. Pugh, Oscar Schackter, and Hans Smit. 1987. *International Law: Cases and Materials*. St. Paul, Minn.: West.

Herrmann, David. 1985. "American Perceptions of Soviet Foreign Policy." *Political Psychology* 6: 375–411.

Hodges, Donald G., and Robert F. Durant. 1989. "The Professional State Revisited." *Public Administration Review* 19: 474–85.

Holsti, Ole R. 1962. "The Belief System and National Images." *Journal of Conflict Resolution* 6: 244–52.

Holsti, Ole R., and James N. Rosenau. 1986. "Consensus Lost, Consensus Regained." *International Studies Quarterly* 30: 375–409.

Holsti, Ole R., and James N. Rosenau. 1988. "The Domestic and Foreign Policy Beliefs of American Leaders." *Journal of Conflict Resolution* 32: 248–94.

Holsti, Ole R., and James N. Rosenau. 1990. "The Structure of Foreign Policy Attitudes among American Leaders." *Journal of Politics* 52: 94–125.

Hoose, Bernard. 1987. *Proportionalism*. Washington, D.C.: Georgetown University Press.

Hummel, Ralph P. 1977. *The Bureaucratic Experience*. New York: St. Martin's.

Hunt, Michael H. 1987. *Ideology and U.S. Foreign Policy*. New Haven: Yale University Press.

Hurwitz, Jon, and Mark Peffley. 1986. "The Means and Ends of Foreign Policy as Determinants of Presidential Support." *American Journal of Political Science* 31: 236–58.

Hurwitz, Jon, and Mark Peffley. 1987. "How Are Foreign Policy Attitudes Structured?" *American Political Science Review* 81: 1099–20.

Hurwitz, Jon, and Mark Peffley. 1990. "Public Images of the Soviet Union." *Journal of Politics* 52: 3–28.

Isaac, Robert, Kenneth McCue, and Charles Plott. 1985. "Public Goods." *Journal of Public Economics* 26: 51–74.

Jefferson, Thomas. 1848. *The Writings of Thomas Jefferson*. Vol. 9. New York: Putnam.

Jencks, Christopher. 1979. "The Social Basis of Unselfishness." In *On the Making of Americans*, ed. Herbert J. Gans, Nathan Glaser, Joseph Gusfield, and Christopher Jencks. Philadelphia: University of Pennsylvania Press.

Jennings, M. Kent 1987. "Residue of a Movement." *American Political Science Review* 81: 367–82.

Jervis, Robert. 1976. *Perception and Misperception in International Politics*. Princeton: Princeton University Press.

———. 1989. *The Meaning of the Nuclear Revolution*. Ithaca: Cornell University Press.

Johnson, James T. 1975. *Ideology, Reason, and the Limitation of War*. Princeton: Princeton University Press.

———. 1981. *Just War Tradition and the Restraint of War*. Princeton: Princeton University Press.

———. 1984. *Can Modern War Be Just?* New Haven: Yale University Press.

Johnson, James T., and George Weigel. 1991. *Just War and the Gulf War*. Washington, D.C.: Ethics and Public Policy Center.

Johnson, Robert H. 1988. "Misguided Morality." *Political Science Quarterly* 103: 509–29.

Jos, Philip H., Mark E. Tomkins, and Steven W. Hays. 1989. "In Praise of Difficult People." *Public Administration Review* 49: 552–61.

Kahneman, Daniel, Jack L. Knetsch, and Richard Thaler. 1986. "Fairness as a Constraint on Profit Seeking: Entitlements in the Market." *American Economic Review* 76: 728–41.

Kant, Immanuel. 1969. *Foundations of the Metaphysics of Morals* [1785]. Indianapolis: Bobbs Merrill.

Kanwisher, Nancy. 1989. "Cognitive Heuristics and American Security Policy." *Journal of Conflict Resolution* 33: 652–75.

Karnow, Stanley. 1983. *Vietnam: A History*. New York: Viking.

Karsten, Peter. 1978. *Law, Soldiers, and Combat*. Westport, Conn.: Greenwood.

Kattenburg, Paul M. 1985. "MAD Is the Moral Position." In *The Nuclear Reader*, ed. Charles W. Kegley and Eugene R. Wittkopf. New York: St. Martin's.

Keegan, John. 1976. *The Face of Battle*. New York: Viking.

Kegley, Charles W. 1986. "Assumptions and Dilemmas in the Study of Americans' Foreign Policy Beliefs." *International Studies Quarterly* 30: 447–71.

Kegley, Charles W., and Eugene R. Wittkopf. 1987. *American Foreign Policy*. New York: St. Martin's.

Kegley, Charles W., and Eugene R. Wittkopf, eds. 1985. *The Nuclear Reader*. New York: St. Martin's Press.

Kelman, Herbert C., ed. 1965. *International Behavior*. New York: Holt, Rinehart and Winston.

Kelman, Herbert C., and L. H. Lawrence. 1972. "Assignment of Responsibility in the Case of Lt. Calley." *Journal of Social Issues* 28: 177–212.

Kelman, Herbert C., and V. L. Hamilton. 1989. *Crimes of Obedience*. New Haven: Yale University Press.

Kennan, George F. 1951. *American Diplomacy*. Chicago: University of Chicago Press.

———. 1985. "Morality and Foreign Policy." *Foreign Affairs* 64: 205–18.

Keohane, Robert. 1984. *After Hegemony*. Princeton: Princeton University Press.

———. 1990. "Empathy and International Regimes." In *Beyond Self-Interest*, ed. Jane J. Mansbridge. Chicago: University of Chicago Press.

Key, V. O. 1949. *Southern Politics*. New York: Knopf.

Khaddari, Majid. 1955. *The Law of War and Peace in Islam*. Baltimore: Johns Hopkins University Press.

Kinder, Donald R. 1983. "Diversity and Complexity in American Public Opinion." In

Political Science: The State of the Discipline, ed. Ada Finifter. Washington, D.C.: American Political Science Association.

Kinnard, Douglas. 1985. *The War Managers.* Wayne, N.J.: Avery.

Kirkpatrick, Samuel A., and James L. Regens. 1977. "Military Experience and Foreign Policy Belief Systems." *Journal of Military Sociology* 6: 29–47.

Klare, Michael T., and Peter Kornbluh. 1987. "The New Interventionism." In *Low Intensity Warfare,* ed. Michael T. Klare and Peter Kornbluh. New York: Pantheon.

Klitgaard, Robert E. 1971. "Gandhi's Non-Violence as a Tactic." *Journal of Peace Research* 9: 143–54.

Kohlberg, Lawrence. 1980. "The Future of Liberalism as the Dominant Ideology of the West." In *Moral Development and Politics,* ed. Richard W. Wilson and Gordon J. Schochet. New York: Praeger.

———. 1981. *Essays on Moral Development.* San Francisco: Harper and Row.

Kornbluh, Peter. 1987. *Nicaragua: The Price of Intervention.* Washington, D.C.: Institute for Policy Studies.

Krauthammer, Charles. 1985. *Cutting Edges.* New York: Random House.

———. 1986. "Morality and the Reagan Doctrine." *New Republic,* Sept. 8, 1986.

Kreml, William P., and Charles W. Kegley. 1990. "Must the Quest Be Elusive? Restoring Ethics to Theory Building in International Relations." *Alternatives* 15: 155–76.

Krickus, Richard J. 1965. "On the Morality of Chemical/Biological War." *Journal of Conflict Resolution* 9: 200–10.

Kuhn, Thomas S. 1962. *The Structure of Scientific Revolutions.* Chicago: University of Chicago Press.

Kuklinski, James H., David S. Metlay, and W. D. Kay. 1982. "Citizen Knowledge and Choice on the Complex Issue of Nuclear Energy." *American Journal of Political Science* 26: 615–42.

Kurtz, Lester R. 1988. *The Nuclear Cage.* Englewood Cliffs: Prentice-Hall.

Lacey, Hugh. 1986. "United States Intervention in Central America in the Light of the Principles of the Just War." *Journal of Social Philosophy* 17, no. 2: 3–19.

Lackey, Douglas P. 1984. *Moral Principles and Nuclear Weapons.* Totowa, N.J.: Rowman and Allanheld.

———. 1989. *The Ethics of War and Peace.* Englewood Cliffs, N.J..: Prentice-Hall.

La Civilta Cattolica. 1992. "Modern War and the Christian Conscience." In *But Was It Just?* ed. David E. DeCosse. New York: Doubleday.

Lane, Robert E. 1962. *Political Ideology.* New York: Free Press.

Larson, Deborah Welch. 1985. *Origins of Containment.* Princeton: Princeton University Press.

Lau, Richard, Thad Brown, and David O. Sears. 1978. "Self-Interest and Civilians' Attitudes toward the Vietnam War." *Public Opinion Quarterly* 42: 464–83.

Lernoux, Penny. 1989. *People of God: The Struggle for World Catholicism.* New York: Viking.

Levy, David. 1981. "Toward a Neoaristotelean Theory of Politics." *Public Choice* 42: 39–54.

Lewis, R. A. 1975. "A Contemporary Religious Enigma: Churches and War." *Journal of Political and Military Sociology* 3: 57–70.

Love, Janice. 1991. "From Pacifism to Apocalyptic Visions." In *After the Cold War,* ed. Charles W. Kegley and K. Schwab. Boulder: Westview.

Luttbeg, Norman R. 1968. "The Structure of Beliefs Among Leaders and the Public." *Public Opinion Quarterly* 32: 398–409.

Machiavelli, Niccolò. 1979a. *The Discourses* [1531]. New York: Penguin.

——. 1979b. *The Prince* [1516]. New York: Penguin.

Maclear, Michael. 1981. *Vietnam: The Ten Thousand Day War*. New York: St. Martin's.

Mandelbaum, Michael A., and William Schneider. 1979. "The New Internationalisms." In *Eagle Entangled*, ed. Kenneth A. Oye, Donald S. Rothchild, and Robert J. Lieber. New York: Longman.

Mansbridge, Jane J., ed. 1990. *Beyond Self-Interest*. Chicago: University of Chicago Press.

Mapel, David R. 1990. "Prudence and the Plurality of Value in International Ethics." *Journal of Politics* 52: 433–56.

Mavrodes, George I. 1975. "Conventions and the Morality of War." *Philosophy and Public Affairs* 4: 117–31.

Maxwell, Mary. 1990. *Morality Among Nations*. Albany: State University of New York Press.

Mayer, Peter. 1966. *The Pacifist Conscience*. New York: Holt, Rinehart and Winston.

McCormick, James M., and Eugene R. Wittkopf. 1990. "Bipartisanship, Partisanship, and Ideology in Congressional-Executive Foreign Policy Relations, 1947–1988." *Journal of Politics* 52: 1077–1100.

McElroy, Robert. 1992. *Morality and American Foreign Policy*. Princeton: Princeton University Press.

Meinecke, Friedrich. 1957. *Machiavellism: The Doctrine of Raison d'Etat and Its Place in Modern History*. New Haven: Yale University Press.

Merton, Robert K. 1956. *Social Theory and Social Structure*. New York: Free Press.

Miles, Sarah. 1986. "The Real War: Low-Intensity Conflict in Central America." *Report on the Americas* 20, no. 2: 18–48.

Milgram, Stanley. 1974. *Obedience to Orders*. New York: Harper and Row.

Miller, George A. 1967. "Professionals in Bureaucracies." *American Sociological Review* 32: 755–68.

Miller, Richard B. 1991. *Interpretations of Conflict: Ethics, Pacifism, and the Just-War Tradition*. Chicago: University of Chicago Press.

Miller, William. 1966. *Nonviolence*. New York: Schocken.

Monroe, Kristen Renwick. 1991. "John Donne's People." *Journal of Politics* 53: 394–433.

Montagna, Paul D. 1968. "Professionalism and Bureaucratization in Large Professional Organizations." *American Journal of Sociology* 74: 138–45.

Morgenthau, Hans J. 1946. *Scientific Man vs. Power Politics*. Chicago: University of Chicago Press.

——. 1967. *Politics Among Nations*, 3d ed. New York: Knopf.

Morgenthau, Hans J., and Kenneth W. Thompson. 1985. *Politics Among Nations*, 6th ed. New York: Knopf.

Mosher, Frederick. 1982. *Democracy and the Public Service*. New York: Oxford University Press.

Moskos, Charles C. 1978. "The Enlisted Ranks in the All-Volunteer Army." In *The All-Volunteer Force and American Society*, ed. John B. Kelley. Charlottesville: University of Virginia Press.

Mueller, Dennis. 1986. "Rational Egoism versus Adaptive Egoism as Fundamental Postulates for a Descriptive Theory of Human Behavior." *Public Choice* 51: 3–23.

National Conference of Catholic Bishops Ad Hoc Committee on Peace and Disarmament. 1983. *The Challenge of Peace*. Washington, D.C.: National Conference of Catholic Bishops.

Nie, Norman H., Sidney Verba, and John R. Petrocik. 1976. *The Changing American Voter*. Cambridge: Cambridge University Press.

Niebuhr, Reinhold. 1932. *Moral Man and Immoral Society*. New York: Charles Scribner's Sons.

Nisbett, Richard E., and Lee Ross. 1980. *Human Inference*. Englewood Cliffs, N.J.: Prentice-Hall.

Nye, Joseph, Jr. 1986. *Nuclear Ethics*. New York: Free Press.

O'Brien, William V. 1981. *The Conduct of Just and Limited War*. New York: Praeger.

Opotow, Susan. 1990. "Moral Exclusion and Injustice." *Journal of Social Issues* 46: 1–20.

Oppenheim, Felix E. 1991. *The Place of Morality in Foreign Policy*. Lexington, Mass.: Lexington Books.

Oppenheim, Lassa. 1955. *International Law*. New York: Longmans, Green.

Organski, A. F. K. 1968. *World Politics*. New York: Knopf.

Peffley, Mark, and Jon Hurwitz. 1985. "A Hierarchical Model of Attitude Constraint." *American Journal of Political Science* 29: 871–90.

Pennington, Donald C. 1986. *Essential Social Psychology*. London: Edward Arnold.

Perry, David L. 1993. "Ethical Issues in Espionage Methods." In *Ethics and Public Administration*, ed. George Frederickson. New York: St. Martin's.

Piaget, Jean. 1932. *The Moral Judgment of the Child*. London: Kegan Paul.

Price, Charles M., and Charles G. Bell. 1970. "The Rules of the Game." *Journal of Politics* 32: 839–55.

Priest, R., T. Fullerton, and C. Bridges. 1982. "Personality and Value Changes in West Point Cadets." *Armed Forces and Society* 8: 629–42.

Ramsey, Paul. 1951. *Basic Christian Ethics*. New York: Charles Scribner's Sons.

———. 1961. *War and the Christian Conscience*. Durham: Duke University Press.

———. 1968. *The Just War*. New York: Charles Scribner's Sons.

Rapoport, Anatol. 1968. "Concluding Remarks." In *On War*. Baltimore: Penguin.

———. 1982. "Prisoner's Dilemma: Recollections and Observations." In *Rational Man and Irrational Society*, ed. Brian Barry and Russell Hardin. Beverly Hills, Calif.: Sage.

Rapoport, Anatol, and A. M. Chammah. 1965. *Prisoner's Dilemma*. Ann Arbor: University of Michigan Press.

Rawls, John. 1971. *A Theory of Justice*. Cambridge: Harvard University Press.

Reagan, Ronald. 1984. "U.S. Interests in Central America." In *Realism, Strength, Negotiation*. Washington, D.C.: U.S. Department of State, Bureau of Public Affairs.

Reynolds, David R., and Fred Shelly. 1985. "Procedural Justice and Local Democracy." *Political Geography Quarterly* 4: 267–88.

Ricoeur, Paul. 1990. "On John Rawls' 'A Theory of Justice.'" *International Social Science Journal* 42: 553–64.

Riker, William H. 1986. *The Art of Political Manipulation*. New Haven: Yale University Press.

Robinson, Michael J. 1976. "Public Affairs Television and the Growth of Political Malaise." *American Political Science Review* 70: 409–32.

Roemer, John E. 1985. "Rationalizing Revolutionary Ideology." *Econometrica* 53: 85–108.

Roloff, M., and G. Miller. 1980. *Persuasion*. Beverly Hills, Calif.: Sage.

Rosenau, James N. 1961. *Public Opinion and Foreign Policy*. New York: Random House.

Rosenberg, Milton. 1965. "Images in Relation to the Policy Process." In *International Behavior*, ed. Herbert Kelman. New York: Holt, Rinehart and Winston.

Sabatier, Paul, and Susan Hunter. 1989. "The Incorporation of Causal Perceptions into Models of Elite Belief Systems." *Western Political Quarterly* 42: 229–61.

Schaffer, Ronald. 1985. *Wings of Judgment*. New York: Oxford University Press.

Secrest, Donald E. 1986. "American Military Intervention in Grenada." *Midwest Quarterly* 27, no. 2: 230–51.

Secrest, Donald E., Gregory G. Brunk, and Howard Tamashiro. 1991a. "Empirical Investigation of Normative Discourse on War." *Journal of Peace Research* 28: 393–406.

Secrest, Donald E., Gregory G. Brunk, and Howard Tamashiro. 1991b. "Moral Justifications for Resort to War with Nicaragua." *Western Political Quarterly* 44: 541–59.

Sen, Amartya K. 1974. "Choice, Orderings and Morality." In *Practical Reason*, ed. S. Korner. Oxford: Clarendon.

———. 1978. "Rational Fools." In *Scientific Models and Men*, ed. H. Harris. London: Oxford University Press.

Shapiro, Robert Y., and Benjamin I. Page. 1988. "Foreign Policy and the Rational Public." *Journal of Conflict Resolution* 32: 211–47.

Shue, Henry. 1980. *Basic Rights: Subsistence, Influence and U.S. Foreign Policy*. Princeton: Princeton University Press.

Shultz, George. 1986. "Nicaragua and the Future of Central America." *Current Policy* 803 (March).

Sichol, Marcia W. 1990. *The Making of a Nuclear Peace*. Washington, D.C.: Georgetown University Press.

Sigelman, Lee, and Marcia Lynn Whicker. 1988. "The Growth of Government, the Ineffectiveness of Voting, and the Pervasive Political Malaise." *Social Science Quarterly* 69: 299–310.

Simon, Rita. 1974. *Public Opinion in America*. Chicago: Rand McNally.

Singer, J. David. 1986. "Normative Constraints on Hostility Between States." *Journal of Peace Research* 23: 209–12.

Singer, Marcus G. 1967. "The Golden Rule." In *The Encyclopedia of Philosophy*, ed. Paul Edwards. Vol. 3. New York: Macmillan.

Skorupski, John. 1978. "The Meaning of Another Culture's Beliefs." In *Action and Interpretation*, ed. Christopher Hookway and Philip Pettit. Cambridge: Cambridge University Press.

Smith, Eric R. A. N. 1989. *The Unchanging American Voter*. Berkeley: University of California Press.

Smith, Michael. 1986. *Realist Thought from Weber to Kissinger*. Baton Rouge: Louisiana State University Press.

Sniderman, Paul M., and Philip E. Tetlock. 1986. "Interrelationship of Political Ideology and Public Opinion." In *Political Psychology*, ed. Margaret E. Hermann. San Francisco: Jossey-Bass.

Snyder, M. 1982. "When Believing Means Doing." In *Consistency in Social Behavior: The Ontario Symposium*, ed. M. Zanna, E. Higgins, and C. Herman, Vol. 2. Hillsdale, N.J.: Erlbaum.

Sorensen, James E., and Thomas L. Sorensen. 1974. "The Conflict of Professionals in Bureaucratic Organizations." *Administrative Science Quarterly* 19: 98–106.

Stark, Oded. 1985. "On Private Charity and Altruism." *Public Choice* 46: 325–32.

Staub, Erwin. 1989. *The Roots of Evil*. New York: Cambridge University Press.

Stephan, W., and C. Stephen. 1984. "The Role of Ignorance in Intergroup Relations." In *Groups in Contact*, ed. N. Miller and M. Brewer. Orlando, Fla..: Academic Press.

Sterling, R. 1974. *Macropolitics*. New York: Knopf.

Stout, Jeffrey. 1990. "Justice and Resort to War." In *Cross, Crescent and Sword*, ed. James Turner Johnson and John Kelsay. Westport, Conn.: Greenwood.

Swomley, John M. 1970. *American Empire*. New York: Macmillan.

Tamashiro, Howard. 1984. "Algorithms, Heuristics and Artificial Intelligence Modeling of Strategic Statecraft." In *Foreign Policy Decision Making*, ed. Donald Sylvan and Steve Chan. New York: Praeger.

Tamashiro, Howard, and Gregory G. Brunk. 1985. "Expert Based Systems as Elite Foreign Policy Advisors." In *Proceedings of the I.E.E.E. Symposium on Expert Systems in Government*. Silver Spring, Md.: Institute of Electrical and Electronics Engineers Press.

Tamashiro, Howard, Donald E. Secrest, and Gregory G. Brunk. 1989. "The Underlying Structure of Ethical Beliefs Toward War." *Journal of Peace Research* 26: 139–52.

Tamashiro, Howard, Donald E. Secrest, and Gregory G. Brunk. 1993. "Ethical Attitudes of Members of Congress and American Military Officers Toward War." In *Ethics and Public Administration*, ed. George Frederickson. New York: St. Martin's.

Tarski, Alfred. 1944. "The Semantic Conception of Truth and the Foundations of Semantics." *Philosophy and Phenomenological Research* 4: 341–75.

Taylor, Paul W. 1961. *Normative Discourse*. Englewood Cliffs, N.J.: Prentice-Hall.

———. 1967. *Problems of Moral Philosophy*. Belmont, Calif.: Dickenson.

Taylor, Telford. 1970. *Nuremberg and Vietnam*. Chicago: Quadrangle.

Thomas, George F. 1955. *Christian Ethics and Moral Philosophy*. New York: Charles Scribner's Sons.

Thompson, Kenneth W. 1983. "Ethics and Foreign Policy." In *The Ethical Dimension of Political Life*, ed. Francis Canavan. Durham: Duke University Press.

Thompson, Kenneth W., and Robert J. Myers. 1977. *Truth and Tragedy*. Washington, D.C.: New Republic Books.

Tolstoy, Leo. 1942. *War and Peace* [1889]. New York: Simon and Shuster.

Trivers, Robert. 1971. "Evolution of Reciprocal Altruism." *Quarterly Review of Biology* 46: 35–57.

———. 1985. *Social Evolution*. Menlo Park, Calif.: Benjamin Cummings.

Truman, David. 1951. *The Governmental Process*. New York: Knopf.

Truman, Harry S. 1980. *Off the Record*. Ed. R. H. Ferrell. New York: Harper and Row.

Tucker, Robert W. 1966. *The Just War*. Baltimore: Johns Hopkins University Press.

Tullock, Gordon. 1979. "Public Choice in Practice." In *Collective Decision Making*, ed. Clifford S. Russell. Baltimore, Johns Hopkins University Press.

Tyler, Tom R. 1990. "Justice, Self-Interest and Legitimacy of Legal and Political Authority." In *Beyond Self-Interest*, ed. Jane J. Mansbridge. Chicago: University of Chicago Press.

United Methodist Council of Bishops. 1986. *In Defense of Creation*. Nashville: Graded Press.

U.S. Department of the Army. 1956. *Field Manual 27–10: The Law of Land Warfare*. Washington, D.C.: Government Printing Office.

Vanberg, Viktor, and Roger Congleton. 1992. "Rationality, Morality and Exit." *American Political Science Review* 86: 418–31.

Vandenberg, Arthur H., Jr., ed. 1952. *The Private Papers of Senator Vandenberg*. Boston: Houghton Mifflin.

Von Glahn, Gerhard. 1981. *Law Among Nations*. New York: Macmillan.

Von Kleffens, Eelco. 1960. "The Place of Law in International Relations." In *The Theory and Practice of International Relations*, ed. David McLellan, William Olson, and Fred Sondermann. Englewood Cliffs, N.J.: Prentice-Hall.

Wakin, Malham W., ed. 1986. *War, Morality, and the Military Profession*. Boulder: Westview.

Walker, Stephan G. 1983. "The Motivational Foundations of Belief Systems." *International Studies Quarterly* 27: 179–201.

Walker, Thomas W. 1987. *Reagan Versus the Sandinistas: The Undeclared War on Nicaragua*. Boulder: Westview.

Walzer, Michael. 1977. *Just and Unjust Wars*. New York: Basic Books.

———. 1992. "Justice and Injustice in the Gulf War." In *But Was It Just?* ed. David E. DeCosse. New York: Doubleday.

Wasserstrom, Richard. 1970. *War and Morality*. Belmont, Calif.: Wadsworth.

Weber, Max. 1946. *From Max Weber*. Ed. H. Gerth and C. W. Mills. New York: Oxford University Press.

Weigel, George. 1992. "From Last Resort to Endgame: Morality, the Gulf War, and the Peace Process." In *But Was It Just?* ed. David E. DeCosse. New York: Doubleday.

Weinberger, Caspar. 1990. *Fighting for Peace*. New York: Warner.

Weingast, Barry R. 1979. "A Rational Choice Perspective on Congressional Norms." *American Journal of Political Science* 23: 245–62.

Wilson, George C. 1985. "Reagan Will Hear Conflicting Advice about Retaliation for Terrorism." *Washington Post*, June 23, 1985.

Wilson, Richard W., and Gordon J. Schochet. 1980. *Moral Development and Politics*. New York: Praeger.

Wintle, Justin. 1989. *The Dictionary of War Quotations*. New York: Free Press.

Wittgenstein, Ludwig. 1961. *Tractatus Logico-Philosophicus* (1921). Ed. O. F. Pears and B. F. McGuinness. London: Routledge and Kegan Paul.

Wittkopf, Eugene R. 1987. "Elites and Masses: Another Look at Attitudes Toward America's World Role." *International Studies Quarterly* 31: 131–59.

Wittkopf, Eugene R., and Michael A. Maggiotto. 1983a. "The Two Faces of Internationalism" *Social Science Quarterly* 64: 288–304.

Wittkopf, Eugene R., and Michael A. Maggiotto. 1983b. "Elites and Masses: A Comparative Analysis of Attitudes toward America's World Role." *Journal of Politics* 45: 303–34.

Wittkopf, Eugene R., and Michael A. Maggiotto. 1986. "On the Foreign Policy Beliefs of the American People." *International Studies Quarterly* 30: 425–44.

Wittkopf, Eugene R., and James M. McCormick. 1990. "The Cold War Consensus: Did It Exist?" *Polity* 22: 627–43.

Wohlstetter, Albert. 1983. "Bishops, Statesmen, and Other Strategists on the Bombing of Innocents." *Commentary* 75, no. 6: 15–35.

Wolfers, Arnold. 1949. "Statesmanship and Moral Choice." *World Politics* 2: 179–95.

———. 1962. *Discord and Collaboration*. Baltimore: Johns Hopkins University Press.

Yodor, John. 1984. *When War Is Unjust*. Minneapolis: Augsburg.

INDEX

Abolitionism, 9, 34
Afghanistan, 97
Ali, Muhammad, 135
Allende, Salvador, 210
Allison, Graham, 65
Almond, Gabriel, 8, 48, 179
Altruism, 51, 100, 199, 202, 209; and game theory, 23, 81; and moral sensibilities, 163–67; and risk, 74; and social choice, 3, 11; and sociobiology, 55, 57; and youth experiences, 190
Ambivalent belief system, 140–46, 169–70; and elite beliefs, 170–73, 189–96; and nuclear war, 161–62; and personality, 211; and political ideology, 184; and prolonged conflict, 178; and war scenarios, 147–49
America First Campaign, 183
Animosity, 143
Anticommunism, 160, 191
Antilegalism, 52, 87
Aquinas, Thomas, 32, 35–36, 53, 68, 71, 79, 186
Arms control agreements, 200
Atomic bomb, 39–40, 89, 154; Soviet acquisition of, 135; use of against Japan, 27, 40, 204
Atrocities, 86
Attitude coherence, 10, 55, 70, 173, 185, 212
Attitude shifts, 16–17, 73, 175–77, 179
Attitude sophistication, 111
Augustine, Aurelius, 32, 35–36, 53–54, 186
Axelrod, Robert, 12, 39–40, 55, 67, 71

Bacon, Francis, 96
Balance of power, 95
Banishment, 34
Belief systems, 1, 59; and attitude change, 16–17, 175–77; and attitude complexity, 180–84, 195; and attitude constraint, 10, 55, 70, 173, 185, 212; and attitude formation, 163–74; and cold war, 180–84; and consistency of reasoning, 68; definition of, 18, 48; and difficulty in understanding other's, 6–7; and domestic policy, 182–84, 213; and game theory, 55; and group goals, 68, 139, 185–95; hierarchical approach to studying, 9–10, 79; and interpersonal utility, 55; learning curve explanation of, 185–91, 213; manageable number of, 59, 69; of the mass public, 51; and moral sensibilities, 57–58, 185–95; and norms, 49–50; and organizations, 51–52; and political ideology, 179–80; and problems in studying, 55, 59–69; and professionalism, 51–55, 185–95; and proverbs, 15; and real world belief systems about warfare, 127–51; and risk, 126, 132; and Vietnam War, 178
Bentham, Jeremy, 11, 41
Better safe than sorry belief system, 131–40; and Congress, 173–75; and elite beliefs, 168–75; and moral sensibilities, 185–95; and nuclear war, 161–62; and other belief systems, 140–46; and policy consensus, 179; and political ideology, 184; and Russell, 175–77; and strategic